INNOVATION AND NEW PRODUCT MARKETING

INNOVATION AND NEW PRODUCT MARKETING

DAVID F. MIDGLEY

CROOM HELM   LONDON

658.5
M629i

Printed in Great Britain
by Redwood Burn Ltd, Trowbridge and Esher

80-2530

CONTENTS

PREFACE

This book is concerned with the diffusion of innovations, and more specifically with the management of new product introductions. While there appear to be many excellent texts on new product management, and some on the diffusion of innovations, it is regrettable that, to the author's knowledge, there are none which attempt to integrate both these facets of the whole in a systematic manner. In many ways this deficiency is surprising. How is it possible to *manage* new products effectively without an understanding of the basic phenomenon — the diffusion of innovations? A knowledge of numerous highly specialised management techniques is of little use without a detailed model of the market behaviour involved in the diffusion of a new product. Just as a thorough knowledge of the theories of the diffusion of innovations is of little use to the practising manager without the necessary tools to effect a successful new product launch.

In the book an attempt has been made to overcome this deficiency and integrate what is known about the spread of new products with the practical methods available to the manager. To achieve this objective it proved necessary to formulate what may be considered a new theory of innovative behaviour, or at least a new way of looking at the phenomenon. This allows the development of a system for new product management, and one I would hope is an advance over current practices. Indeed this total market behaviour oriented view suggests that much of what is currently done in industry is misguided, if not detrimental to the survival of the organisations concerned.

I would not claim to have achieved a complete synthesis. There is much that remains to be done both at a conceptual and practical level. What I hope to have achieved is a start in the right direction.

That this topic is worthy of such attention should be apparent to every practising manager and every marketing student. Most product decisions are either new product decisions themselves or the direct consequence of previous new product decisions. The fact of the matter is that to date the majority of these decisions have been poor, quite simply because those making them have lacked even an elementary understanding of the market processes involved.

This text is, therefore, for anyone interested in the management of new product introductions be they students, researchers or managers.

Throughout I have attempted to keep to the main theme and to avoid digressing into highly specialised areas. For those interested in reading further, numerous references are provided. I have also avoided the use of mathematics at anything more than an elementary and symbolic level. While a knowledge of calculus might be a help to the reader in Chapter 5 it is not a necessity. The remainder of the book presumes no such skills.

In the course of preparing the book I have received a great deal of assistance from many sources, and in particular I would like to acknowledge Professors James M. Carman, Roger Layton, Everett M. Rogers, and Gordon S.C. Wills. I would also like to thank Carol Partridge for typing the manuscript, and finally my wife, Gail, for her help both literary and supportive.

Sydney, June 1976   David F. Midgley

1 INNOVATION AND MARKETING

1.1 The Necessity of Innovation

That the life of any commercial product is finite is inescapable. The horizons of individual consumers are constantly broadened by new ideas, inventions and experiences, and their buying preferences show a marked progression. A product which was once 'new' soon becomes 'established', and a brief period of stability is inevitably followed by decline and extinction. Consumers may have become bored with the product, or a subsequent idea may have rendered it obsolete. This concept of the limited life cycle is well known, and will be discussed in greater detail in subsequent chapters. The opening point being emphasised here is that with a finite life the sales of any one product eventually become unprofitable, requiring it to be replaced in the company's product range, and thus initiating the cycle again with another, newer product. The obvious consequence of this situation is the constant search for new products, an activity which most, if not all, companies engage in. However the very nature of the consumer processes which lead to this life cycle also make the development of new products perhaps the most hazardous area of management. It still remains difficult to specify the likely performance of a particular new product ahead of some measurement of consumer response. Indeed quite often it is not feasible to assess the product until it has been placed in a substantial number of retail outlets, and purchased by a sizeable number of consumers. Furthermore, as this book will, in part, attempt to show, most managers are unaware of what is known about consumer behaviour in this area, a fact which makes it impossible for them to make reliable predictions until the product reaches the mass market. By then, of course, it may be too late.[1]

Launching a new product therefore involves a great risk to the company and management concerned. While the actual magnitude of the resources and effort committed to the project will vary tremendously from company to company, and industry to industry, when viewed in terms of the possible damage to the organisation's profitability, or even its chances of survival, the dangers will be considerable.[2] On the one hand no company, whatever its size or market, can afford not to launch new products reasonably frequently; on the other hand, neither can it afford to have too many of these which fail to meet their set objectives.

The emphasis of this book is on reducing the dangers associated with new product management. For while it is not possible to guarantee success, it is possible to lay down guidelines and procedures which will make success more likely, and which will substantially reduce the risks involved in marketing innovation.

In discussing new product marketing many authors commence by citing studies on the number of new products which 'fail', quoting such statistics as 5 out of 10 new products never reach the launch stage, or 92 out of 100 new products fail to survive for more than one year on the market.[3] The precise definition of a 'new' product, or of 'failure' will be the subject of subsequent discussion, but the main thrust of such contentions would not be disputed. What will be said is that while this overall, and depressing, picture may well be true, there can be little doubt that some companies are substantially more successful with their new products than others.[4] This does not mean these organisations have any secret recipe for success, or a special fund of good luck. Rather, it can and will be argued that these organisations approach the task with some insights into consumer processes, and with a 'scientific' attitude toward finding solutions to their marketing problems. Whatever may be contended elsewhere, 'hunches' and 'inspirations' do not create successful products on a reliable and regular basis. A 'flash of genius' may well create the idea for an innovation, but for this idea to be turned into a market success requires painstaking and critical research, and an objective means of assessment. In other words a scientific approach to the problem.

Indeed in many ways the development of a new product mirrors the construction of a scientific theory quite closely. In both cases the starting point is existing knowledge (existing methods and products) from which a problem is defined (of satisfying a set of consumer needs).[5] A set of hypotheses (new product ideas) is then postulated as theoretically solving the problem (satisfying the needs). This set is then tested by a process of observation, measurement and experiment. By repeatedly modifying and refining these hypotheses a viable solution is found (the new product).[6] The role of creativity is primarily in identifying the problem and conceptualising a new product to solve it, the remainder of the process being a form of self-correcting procedure which leads to the goal of a potentially viable new product. The final 'test' is to place the product on the market, and thus confirm the theory that it satisfies the assumed consumer needs. This book will concentrate on the procedure, leaving the discussion of the origin and nature of creativity to more qualified authors.[7] Neither will the problem of developing organisational structures which encourage creativity be touched on in any great depth.[8]

Nor will much space be given to discussing broader aspects of corporate strategy such as company objectives, or diversification. Here the company's objectives are taken as given, and the new product ideas, or more correctly marketing problem areas, as existing. From such a starting point the techniques and methods for turning those ideas into a viable product proposition are explored. The reasons for taking this particular emphasis are as follows.

First, it is obviously necessary to define in some way the area to be covered by the book. Topics relating to organisational behaviour and corporate planning are well covered elsewhere, and their inclusion here would add little of value, and might well run the risk of diluting the message of the text. Second, the problems of defining corporate strategy, and of identifying new product areas, are less troublesome than those of assessing which ideas will produce a successful addition to the company's product range. Any developed set of corporate objectives will stress the need for new products, and will indicate the areas in which effort should be directed. From such an indication it is normally an easy task to generate numerous new product ideas.[9] The difficulty comes in selecting which product concepts are viable, and hence the emphasis on the methodological aspects of new product marketing. However merely to view these aspects as a set of independent techniques to apply in an intuitive manner would indeed be a sterile and dangerous conclusion. For the third, and most important, reason for the suggested emphasis is that we effectively know a substantial amount about the process of innovation and the behaviour of consumers, whether individually or in groups. This knowledge does not yet allow new product ideas to be fed into a computer programme, the output of which is a guaranteed market leader, but the existing research does sharply delineate the 'boundaries of the possible'.[10] Further, the present theoretical structure enables the various techniques to be applied in an ordered manner, with definite and realistic goals in mind. Potentially it is feasible to design a framework or overall methodology for new product development, and this text represents one attempt at achieving such an aim.

Unfortunately, apart from a few poorly understood concepts, the vast bulk of this extant knowledge remains unknown to practising managers. Most of the blame for this situation must lie with academics in general, for few attempts have been made to integrate the results of previous studies, or to develop applications to management problems.[11]

It will be argued here, and hopefully demonstrated in subsequent chapters, that by developing the above framework, and thereby integrating the relevant aspects of existing studies, it is possible to reduce the risks of new product introduction by an order of magnitude. It should certainly be possible to reduce the number of new product failures to a more acceptable level than exists at present. Such an achievement would be of obvious benefit to the companies concerned, but it would also be of immense benefit to consumers and society as a whole. A new product which is unsuccessful represents something the consumer did not need, did not like, and therefore rejected — although possibly having already wasted time and money in discovering the product's deficiencies. A failure of this kind, quite apart from causing dissatisfaction amongst the consuming public, also represents a considerable waste both of corporate resources, and of society's limited stock of material assets. A more efficient and reliable method of assessing the viability of new products would therefore be of benefit to all.[12]

1.2 The Management of Innovation

In many ways the various management problems relating to new product introduction are aspects of the same overall problem, that of assessing the likely final impact on the market. While it is obviously useful to delineate various stages in the development process, and thus facilitate discussion and analysis, the ultimate objective of this process must always be kept in mind. In essence the starting point is an idea or product concept, or more normally several such concepts, which are postulated as meeting some consumer needs, and at a profit to the organisation concerned.[13] The very nature of such initial concepts is to be imprecise, and it is therefore necessary to refine and develop them considerably. The way this development is achieved is by applying a series of 'tests', which not only enable increasingly more realistic predictions of likely acceptance to be made, but also highlight the concept's present deficiencies and thereby assist in its modification. These 'tests' can be general, such as 'does product concept X capitalise on the known strengths of the company', or particular, such as 'in a laboratory situation do 25 per cent of the sample consumers rate prototype Y highly on scale Z'. However, and in parallel with 'the scientific method', the direction is always from the general to the particular. In the initial phases of product development it is not possible, or desirable, to ask specific questions or set specific performance criteria. Only when the product concept has become well-defined, and it is feasible to produce some form of prototype, can consumer reactions be gauged.[14] Hence tests in these earlier stages are more normally those where product concepts are rated by management on various desired attributes, without reference to empirical research as such, these attributes being derived from corporate objectives.

Therefore, whatever its nature or place in the development process, each test will set a standard which the product concept must reach at that stage of its development, or no further effort will be expended on it. The key problem is really that of determining the optimum point at which to reject a concept, in other words to ascertain which product concepts will not fulfil corporate objectives. On the one hand, management runs the risk of 'killing off' a viable proposition too early, and on the other of wasting resources on unprofitable ideas. The problem then is one of rejection, and most of the techniques to be described later are screening procedures which subject the product concept to objective measures. With each successive measurement the minimum performance requirement for the final product becomes clearer, and the subsequent tests more rigorous and specific. Naturally the fact that rejection levels are established does not necessarily mean that a rejected product concept is completely abandoned. It may be possible to reformulate and modify the concept so that it passes the barrier and proceeds to the next test. In this situation the exact path that will be followed will depend on the costs and benefits of modification, as opposed to other alternatives. However, regardless of the route which any particular product has taken in its development it is vitally necessary that it should pass every assigned test, and in accordance with objective criteria laid down previously. All too often managers become committed to one product idea at the expense of others, and 'bend the rules' when the favoured idea fails a test — a certain recipe for disaster.

The above also illustrates one of the major differences between consumer and industrial markets. Many consumer products can remain as ideas, or low cost prototypes, for a considerable length of time, the principal costs being those of the associated market research. All of which is not true of industrial products where it may be necessary to invest large amounts in the development of a prototype, or in fundamental research into the field chosen. Marketing activity will thus form only a small part of the total, and expenditure on re-evaluation and modification will be relatively minimal. However, more important in such situations is to spend these relatively small amounts on market research early on in the development, and not become committed to unprofitable large-scale ventures. A major modification to a prototype brand of detergent is not nearly the same as a redesign of a prototype aircraft.

While the duration and cost of each phase of the development programme may thus differ widely from industry to industry, what it is hoped to illustrate here is that the essential structure of the evaluative framework will be similar. Furthermore it will be suggested that the value of extant academic knowledge is in indicating the nature of this framework, that is in inter-relating the various methods for assessment and testing. It will be argued that this can be achieved by utilising the core of understanding which now exists in relation to innovative behaviour. Viewed in the light of this knowledge management problems become more tractable, and the techniques begin to slot into place. The subsidiary management problems which will also be treated are those of translating this theoretical framework into practical management systems.

1.3 Innovation in a Broader Context

In developing a managerially useful understanding of new product adoption it is fruitful to look at the subject in a broader context than merely that of marketing. For one thing the subject area of innovation has been studied widely, and in many disciplines other than marketing or economics. It therefore seems prudent to extract the relevant results and concepts from as wide a field as possible.

A second and more pressing reason is that there appear to be basic similarities between the innovation processes that are observed in different societies, and which are the result of very different types of innovation. Not only does this provide some support for the current theoretical explanations of the adoption process, but it also allows the construction of an evaluative framework of considerable generality and flexibility.

Lastly it would appear that within the academic marketing tradition undue emphasis has been placed on certain aspects of the process, to the exclusion of other equally important facets of the overall picture. This will become more apparent in Part II, but it is undoubtedly one reason for the poor development of practical techniques as opposed to theoretical measures.

In discussing innovation, more correctly termed the *diffusion or communication of innovation,* as a subject area in its own right then the extent and nature of the related research findings quickly become evident. There are numerous contributions, and from many disciplines or 'research traditions' as Rogers and Shoemaker term them.[15] These authors list seven such 'major' research traditions and cite some 850 empirical publications from within these, together with some 230 studies from 'minor' traditions.[16] The major traditions are given as anthropology, early sociology, rural sociology, education, medical sociology, communication and marketing.[17] Of these, perhaps rural sociology has the most developed literature on the topic, whilst marketing is one of the newer and faster growing of the traditions. Out of the above 1,080 odd studies the authors quote 64 as being from the marketing area.[18] Whilst the latter are more obviously relevant to this treatise the advantage of the wider view is that many findings are replicated across traditions. Rogers and Shoemaker provide 107 empirical generalisations culled from the total pool of knowledge but with many having direct relevance to new product marketing.[19] Obviously care is needed in interpreting any particular generalisation in the context of a specific new product, but the fact that the generalisation may have been found to hold from India to America, and from farming techniques to push-button telephones, lends great credence to it. If such findings had arisen solely from the relatively few marketing studies then there would be substantially less credibility for them, and consequently for the arguments advanced in the following chapters.

There are good grounds for viewing all innovations that are actual (physical) objects as a form of new product introduction, since they involve economic transactions between an innovating organisation and a group of consumers. However, authors such as Rogers and Shoemaker are not primarily concerned with a commercial viewpoint, but more with the social processes involved and with the consequences resulting from these processes. Indeed, their commendable emphasis is on the problems of encouraging 'desirable' change in underdeveloped societies, that is of instilling progressive attitudes into members of the society, rather than the problems of developing the innovation. Rogers and Shoemaker take the innovation as existing in its final form, and proceed from this point to analyse its adoption, and its success or failure. In terms of achieving desired social change this is in some ways a curious attitude; surely in some situations it would be more profitable to design an innovation to meet needs and achieve the requisite change simultaneously. Scientific development of the 'product' would produce dividends in the above field, just as it would in new product marketing. However while there are undoubted similarities and links between the two fields of endeavour this text is orientated toward the commercial viewpoint. The problems of marketing innovation in underdeveloped societies will not be ignored, but the main emphasis is on developed societies, and sophisticated new products, as perceived by the managers of Western commercial organisations.

Therefore while the broader context, and emerging generalisations, will be fully utilised, these will be interpreted in the context of marketing relatively sophisticated new products. The subsequent chapters concentrate on the more relevant traditions, namely marketing, communication and psychology, whilst the development of evaluation techniques draws heavily on management studies as a whole.

1.4 The Potential Contribution to New Product Marketing

Allusions have already been made to the usefulness of such knowledge for the new product manager, but at this point it is possible to indicate some more concrete examples.

First and foremost, what is now known about the diffusion of innovations, and hence of new products, is that it is a certain type of dynamic process, and one which will, almost invariably, behave in a certain manner. This alone makes it possible to formulate more realistic plans.

Second, the empirical generalisations about innovative behaviour suggest certain relationships between dependent variables such as 'innovativeness' and independent measures such as age, social class, etc. To some extent therefore it is possible to predict the exact characteristics of the adopting population at any point during the process. More importantly, it is becoming possible to segment out the key consumers — those who influence the future course of the innovation — and thus direct market research and promotional activities.[20]

Finally, the extant knowledge contains considerable information on the likely role and possible influence of various communication channels (both those under the direct control of the innovating organisation and those independent of this control). It is also possible to suggest the basic requirements a product must have in order to stand any chance of success.

1.5 Summary

The first chapter has served mainly to introduce the ideas to be developed later. The discussion commenced from the finite life of all products, and from this to the need for constant replacement of the old products by the new. The considerable management problems of new product development have been mentioned and in particular the as yet undefined concept of 'risk' introduced. It has been pointed out that while most new products 'fail' this need not be the case, and that means exist by which the associated risks can be substantially reduced. Further it has been suggested that the optimum way to develop a new product is very closely akin to the scientific method. This is a suggestion which will be elaborated later, but basically what is desired is to establish rejection criteria which discriminate against new products which will not fulfil corporate objectives. The emphasis of this work is on establishing these criteria, and not in isolation from each other. That is, rather within an overall framework for assessing new products, a framework which is grounded in all that is known about innovation in general, and new product marketing in particular.

Lastly the various philosophical and ethical problems of new product marketing have been raised. While a cogent analysis of such topics is obviously beyond the scope of this more general text, it is hoped to suggest some of the lines along which solutions may be sought in the future.

1.6 The Purpose, Structure and Scope of the Book

The main purpose of this book is to expound a better methodology for evaluating and developing new products. In order to attempt this, it is first necessary to review current literature and research, and to extract the conclusions and generalisations which are relevant to new product marketing. Once this prerequisite has been achieved, then it becomes possible to assign a role to the various product assessment and testing techniques which will be discussed later. It also becomes possible to suggest both better techniques and more effective management systems.

The structure of the book has been broadly laid out in the preceding discussion. Part II is concerned with distilling the relevant strands from academic research and knowledge, whilst Part III is devoted to constructing the 'framework' for the development of new products.

Part II therefore examines the dynamics of the adoption process. Chapter 3 is concerned with the characteristics of innovativeness in society, and Chapter 4 with the nature of the communication flows amongst members of this society. Chapter 5 represents an attempt to integrate all that is known within a general mathematical theory of innovative behaviour.

Part II opens with a more detailed exposition on the need for new products, the existence of the product life cycle, and the relation of the latter to the adoption process. In Chapter 7, the practical difficulties of translating the 'framework' into organisational structures are examined, and possible solutions are advanced. This chapter also deals with the emerging conflict between new product introduction and the shortage of resources, and with the various philosophical and ethical problems with which managers will be faced in the future. The concept of 'perceived intrinsic value' is developed in some detail. Chapters 8 and 9 are the ones most directly concerned with the framework, and explore the problems of selection, testing and prediction in considerable depth.

This framework or integrated set of new product procedures, is thought to be applicable to all consumer products, and most industrial products as well. Regrettably there is little published work on industrial innovations as yet, but what there is suggests that, as long as the social processes of innovation are present, then these markets operate much as their consumer counterparts (see Webster, 1970; Hayward, 1972; Peters and Venkatesan, 1973; and Czepiel, 1974). That is, markets where there are, say, more than twenty customers and where the buying executives of these companies are linked by an informal communications network. Thus, when the term 'consumer' is used in the text, the associated comments will normally apply to industrial goods as well.

The basic ideas presented here could also be extended to service industries, and even social issues, but the author has not attempted this.

Notes

1. With appropriate modifications these comments apply to industrial goods as well.
2. In terms of absolute resources the differences between launching a new computer or a new brand of detergent might appear substantial. However, relative to the size of company involved the degrees of risk are not too dissimilar.
3. See Pessemier (1966), Kotler (1971) or Robertson (1971) as examples. Most quote Booz, Allen and Hamilton (1965) as a source of basic statistics.
4. To support this line of argument it is only really necessary to ask the question of whether companies such as IBM, Du Pont, Procter and Gamble, etc., would still be major forces if 9 out of 10 of their past new products had failed.
5. Very few innovations, with the possible exception of the wheel, have arisen outside of existing knowledge and practice. It is normally impossible to envisage an innovation except in terms of the knowledge and ideas existing at that point in time.
6. This will be recognised as the hypothetico-deductive method. For a detailed discussion see Bunge (1967), and for an exposition in terms of consumer behaviour Zaltman *et al.* (1973).

7. Gruber *et al.* (1963), Parnes and Harding (1962), Stein and Heinze (1965), Taylor (1964) and de Bono (1967).
8. See Becker and Whisler (1967) and Knight (1967) for some discussion on this topic. Both are also reproduced in Hayhurst, Midgley and Wills (1973).
9. Indeed some techniques to be discussed in Chapter 8 are designed to deal with the problem of too many ideas.
10. That managers invariably do not understand what is possible in this area has been demonstrated on numerous occasions. To take one example Bass (1968) forecast, by use of a simple innovation model, the peak sales of colour television in the USA as 7 million sets in 1968 (a prediction which was subsequently proved accurate). At the time the forecast was made industry sources were estimating a peak of 8 million units in 1967. Actual sales in 1967 were closer to the Bass model's forecast of 5.8 million!
11. With the exception of Robertson (1971).
12. By implication, I am equating viability (in corporate terms) with intrinsic worth to society as a whole. This is a concept which will be further developed in Chapter 7.
13. By 'impact' is therefore implied the resultant revenue to the firm. It is obviously easier to satisfy individual consumer needs without such a profit constraint. The science of marketing is concerned with identifying groups of consumers with similar needs, and reaching a mutually agreeable compromise between these aggregated needs and the current economics of production.
14. Of course a 'prototype' need not necessarily be a physical product, it could be a verbal or visual representation.
15. A research tradition being 'a series of investigations on a similar topic in which successive studies are influenced by preceding inquiries'. Rogers and Shoemaker (1971), p.45.
16. Empirical in that the authors of such publications report their own research findings.
17. The 'minor' traditions are agricultural economics, geography, general economics, speech, general sociology and psychology. Rogers and Shoemaker (1971), p.69.
18. Rogers and Shoemaker (1971), p.51.
19. Rogers and Shoemaker (1971), pp.347-85. Any work in the area of innovation must necessarily lean heavily on the work of Rogers and his co-authors, if for no other reason than that he has collected and synthesised the work of most others in the field. In the general discussion in this Chapter it therefore seems pointless to look any further than the excellent text cited.
20. Within certain limitations, as will be discussed in Chapters 3 and 4.

2 THE DIFFUSION OF INNOVATIONS

2.1 The Origins and Evolution of the Subject

It would appear to have been the sociologist Tarde (1903), who first suggested that the adoption of new ideas followed an S-shaped cumulative distribution over time. Tarde also indicated a rationale for this process, principally in terms of the behaviour of 'opinion leaders' being imitated by the rest of the population.[1] However the number of studies in this tradition, early sociology, remained small and the real impetus to diffusion research did not come until the 1940s and 1950s, and was then due to the rural sociologists. Mostly academics, these research workers were concerned with the adoption of agricultural techniques by farmers, and at first concentrated solely on the USA. Subsequently the emphasis has changed to include the encouragement of better farming methods throughout the developing world, and more recently to other topics such as family planning and health services.

The classic study in the area was that of Ryan and Gross (1943), relating to the adoption of hybrid seed corn by two Iowa farming communities. This was an interview study based on recall by the respondents, and established several findings since replicated in other studies, and indeed in areas other than rural sociology. The main results were that the adoption of the innovation followed a bell-shaped distribution over time, and that it was possible to categorise earlier and later adopters and thus discern differences in their social characteristics (age, social status, etc.). Furthermore, the farmers first heard about the hybrid seed corn from salesmen, but were primarily persuaded to try it by their neighbours. Again such a result will appear in many other areas.

This study forms a milestone not only for research in the rural sociology tradition but for diffusion research as a whole. It perhaps marks the beginning of concerted scientific investigation of the diffusion of innovations. Unfortunately it is also true that this study, and its successors in the field of rural sociology, had an undue and detrimental effect on other traditions. Rogers and Shoemaker (1971) point out that far too many of the subsequent studies have utilised the same research methodology without regard to the subject being investigated:

Much of the total body of diffusion research, especially such matters as the innovation-decision studied, the reliance upon recall data from personal interviews, and the individual variables correlated with innovativeness, bears the indelible stamp of its intellectual ancestry in rural sociology. And this academic inheritance is frequently inappropriate for the varied settings in which diffusion research is conducted today.[2]

In particular Rogers and Shoemaker point out that the marketing tradition has leant heavily on rural sociology, and as will be argued later in this text the methods appropriated have severe drawbacks. The most damaging criticism of these methods is that, as will be shown shortly, the adoption process is essentially dynamic and yet the above measures are static both in conception and execution. To make an illustration, and there are many, an early study in the marketing tradition, that of Bell (1963), has considerable similarity with that of Ryan and Gross as far as the methodology is concerned. Bell too was intent on categorising the population, at a point in time, and discerning the social characteristics of different groups. As will be seen this begs several important questions.

Thus while the dynamic nature of innovation will become increasingly clear in the following pages, the evolution of diffusion *research* is becoming apparent at this point. Most studies are static and seek to relate individual characteristics to arbitrary classifications. Indeed nearly all the traditions rely on the survey interview methodology, and surveys administered at one point in time. Only 132 of the 1,084 studies cited by Rogers and Shoemaker make any attempt at studying the process over time.[3] These criticisms will be returned to in Chapters 4 and 5, where some attempt will be made to review the current theoretical status of diffusion studies. Suffice it to say here that this ancestry and evolution has in some ways hampered the development of theories of the process, and that because of this it is only recently that it has been possible to discuss a general schema with any degree of confidence. Prior to 1970 this schema was in the main descriptive, and its related concepts and hypotheses unconfirmed. More recently it has become possible to view certain aspects of it as supported by the evidence. Of course the fact that such a more desirable situation has occurred at all is also due to the rural sociologists, for they were primarily responsible for stimulating interest in the topic in other academic disciplines. Whatever the deficiencies of their approach, or perhaps more correctly its application by their imitators, their contribution must be recognised. Since the late 1950s diffusion research has increased explosively, and continually broadened to encompass more varied phenomena. Rogers and Shoemaker indicate that the number of publications on the subject has tripled in eight years.[4]

Before turning to discuss the above general schema, and since the individual research traditions will not be discussed in any great detail — except as they contribute to knowledge as a whole — it is perhaps worthwhile to comment on how a study of each might be of benefit to managers in particular new product situations.

Rural sociology has already been outlined, and is of obvious relevance to the manufacturer of agricultural appliances, fertilisers, etc. Such a person could do worse than study some of the references cited in Rogers and Shoemaker.

Medical sociology is concerned mainly with the adoption of new drugs or techniques by doctors, a topic of immediate concern to pharmaceutical firms. This tradition contains another classic study, that of Coleman, Katz and Menzel (1957), on the spread of a new drug amongst 228 doctors in Illinois. This study is important because of its use of the sociometric method, and because time of adoption was measured objectively from prescription records.[5,6] The study is also discussed in Coleman (1964).

The communication tradition concentrates primarily on mass media and interpersonal channels of communication, and as these affect human behaviour. Workers in this tradition seek to study the diffusion of news, rumours, technological or scientific ideas, etc. As such they do not deal mainly with one type of innovation, such as a new drug or a new farming technique, but rather with the process of innovation. Therefore the findings in this area are not of particular importance to one type of new product alone, but of general relevance to new product marketing as a whole. As new product introduction involves both mass media and interpersonal channels of communication this tradition will be returned to in Chapter 4.

Of the remaining traditions, anthropology and early sociology only have relevance for their influence on the early development of the subject. They are of no conceivable use for a specific marketing problem. The education tradition, concerned with the spread of new teaching techniques, might possibly be of significance to a publisher wishing to assess future trends in this market. However, this tradition, in common with education research as a whole, has been characterised by lack of scientific rigour and little has been contributed to overall knowledge.[7]

This concludes the analysis of the origins and evolution of diffusion research and the description of its various academic backgrounds. From now on the sum total of extant knowledge will be used in the context of new product marketing, and centred around the relevant traditions of marketing, communication and psychology. The major and minor traditions listed have contributed to a general schema and a variety of empirical generalisations. While much remains to be achieved by way of developing this schema into a powerful theory (as will be discussed in Chapter 5), the current structure is sufficiently supported to form the basis for the arguments advanced in this text. The framework for new product development outlined in Chapter 1 will be formed around the general schema for the diffusion of innovations, and draw heavily on the numerous confirmed hypotheses which relate to this schema.

2.2 The General Schema

This schema can be separated into two components, which will be termed here cognitive processes and social processes. Cognitive processes are those internal to the individual, in effect the mental states a person goes through in considering the adoption of a new idea or product. Social processes are the aggregation of these individual cognitive processes within a communication network, and studies in this area are primarily concerned with the inter-relation of individuals amongst themselves, and with the innovating organisation. In terms of the development of the subject the social processes were the first to be examined, but here the cognitive processes will be discussed first as it seems more logical to proceed from individual to mass behaviour.

It will become apparent that considerably less is known about these internal mental processes than is known about social processes. However it is fortunate that this state of affairs is not of major significance for new product marketing, where the social effects are more important. Furthermore the diffusion of innovations is really about the social effects, and the internal individual processes are in some ways an added theoretical gloss. The 'theory' as it currently stands could equally well function with the consumer being treated as a 'black box', rather than the 'translucid box' which will be described shortly. However as Bunge (1967) has cogently argued, the latter treatment is always preferable, which is why space will be devoted to a brief outline of the models for individual cognitive processes.[8] Hopefully this outline will also clarify any contradictions previously raised, and in particular show why it is possible to have confidence in the overall schema while one component remains largely unexplored.

Cognitive Processes

Rogers and Shoemaker group individual cognitive processes together under the heading 'the innovation-decision process', this being defined as 'the mental process through which an individual passes from first knowledge of an innovation to a decision to adopt or reject, and to confirmation of this decision'.[9] The original model for this process (Rogers, 1962) was as follows:

1. Awareness stage. The individual learns of the existence of the new idea but lacks information about it.
2. Interest stage. The individual develops an interest in the innovation and seeks information about it.
3. Evaluation stage. The individual makes mental application of the new idea to his present and anticipated future situation and decides whether or not to try it.
4. Trial stage. The individual actually applies the new idea on a small scale in order to determine its utility in his own situation.
5. Adoption stage. The individual uses the new idea continuously on a full scale.

The influence of the rural sociologists on this model can clearly be seen, particularly with regard to the last three stages, and this conceptualisation has been criticised on many counts. In terms of new product marketing two broad deficiencies can be discerned, corresponding to durable and non-durable products. For the former it could be asked whether it is possible for a consumer to 'try' the products, and for the latter whether consumers really use such a detailed and extensive process in regard to products such as detergents or toothpastes. If it is therefore necessary to make considerable modifications for each type of innovation the usefulness of the above becomes doubtful. Indeed Rogers has subsequently modified this model to take account of the fact that people may reject an innovation, and that they may engage in dissonance reducing activity after adoption.[10] The new model is thought to be 'consistent with the learning process, theories of attitude change, and general ideas about decision making'.[11] A particular debt to the work of Hovland (1953) was acknowledged. This new model for the innovation-decision process is as follows:

1. Knowledge. The individual is exposed to the innovation's existence and gains some understanding of how it functions.
2. Persuasion. The individual forms a favourable or unfavourable

attitude toward the innovation.
3. Decision. The individual engages in activities which lead to a choice to adopt or reject the innovation.
4. Confirmation. The individual seeks reinforcement for the innovation-decision he has made, but he may reverse his previous decision if exposed to conflicting messages about the innovation.[11]

This second model would appear intrinsically more satisfying; it should be remembered, however, that it is an abstraction, as we know little about these mental states. As might be expected research on this topic has foundered on the problem of measurement, and all that it appears possible to state at this point in time is that there are stages in an individual's innovation-decision process. As to whether these are the same as the above or whether they follow in such a sequence remains open to doubt.

Why, then, is it possible to discuss the macro-level processes if the micro-level processes remain indeterminate? One rationale is that the social processes are mainly concerned with the social behaviour of individuals rather than their internal mental processes. We investigate topics such as interpersonal communication and persuasion, and measure the effects of such factors by the changes in behaviour produced. To oversimplify the argument grossly, we seek to connect an input (communication), with a change of behaviour (adoption). In this case all that it is really necessary to know is when the individual adopted the innovation, the mental processes being largely irrelevant. This, of course, is the black box approach and essentially only works for aggregated systems. If we were to seek to relate an individual communication to an individual adoption we would probably be unsuccessful (especially in the predictive sense).[12] At this level individual behaviour remains inherently random and unpredictable. Only by aggregating large numbers of individuals does the phenomenon become more observable, and therefore more predictable, large-scale phenomena being easier to measure and conceptualise than behaviour on an individual level. Thus by its emphasis on observable behaviour (communication, adoption, etc.) the theoretical structure for the social processes can legitimately treat the consumer as a black box and function adequately without a detailed knowledge of cognitive processes.

However while such an approach would be sound, the 'translucid box' approach does have some considerable value. First, by postulating stages such as, and in particular, 'knowledge', it is possible to study their aggregate manifestation in system terms. As an illustration the individual model indicates that there would be a relationship between knowledge of, and adoption of, an innovation. By studying the growth of total knowledge (of the innovation) in a social system and the corresponding aggregate adoption, this relationship has been clarified. By postulating 'persuasion' the individual model suggests the role of communication in forming attitudes after knowledge of the innovation but before adoption, and so on. Thus however rudimentary the cognitive processes model is, it does suggest certain things about the social processes and therefore gives added insights into the diffusion of innovation. Second, it is obvious that the area of cognitive processes will be increasingly important in the future, and provide the source material for further sophistication of the whole schema. The social processes are now understood to some extent, and further development is likely to come from individual level hypotheses which suggest new facets of social behaviour.

Therefore while we could ignore one component of the schema, in the long term this would be a sterile approach.

Social Processes

By 'social' is meant the particular social system under study, and by 'processes' the various patterns of social behaviour which are assumed to operate within this social system. Behaviour which produces observable phenomena such as the adopter distribution. Obviously 'system' can be interpreted as anything from a village to a country, but here the emphasis is on systems which comprise consumer markets. The 'processes' are predominantly similar across various social systems; indeed if they were not there would be little point in diffusion research as a whole. The only major difference would appear to be the rate of adoption, which primarily depends on the amount of interpersonal communication in the specific society. This will be explored shortly, but it is first necessary to introduce the main points of the schema.

Rogers and Shoemaker give the crucial elements in the diffusion of innovations as '(1) the innovation (2) which is communicated through certain channels (3) over time (4) among members of a social system'.[13] They stress the similarity between this and more general communication models, mentioning the debt due to Berlo (1960). Perhaps a debt should also be acknowledged to Shannon and Weaver (1949), the originators of many communication concepts, since they were among the first to put forward the source, message, channel, receiver and effects model (S-M-C-R-E). Shannon and Weaver defined communication as 'all of the procedures by which one mind may affect another', and this is the essence of the diffusion of innovations.[14] In the outline to be given Shannon and Weaver's 'procedures' are in fact the 'social processes', while the overall schema is a communications model, but one which is solely concerned with new ideas rather than all ideas. Thus the social processes are facets of the whole, and all centre around the passing of information between individuals by verbal interpersonal communications. Information passed between the innovating organisation and individuals normally proceeds via mass media channels, or via change agents (salesmen in our context). A special case will subsequently be made for treating this type of information as separate, and external to the social system.

The fact that these different facets are separated out is mostly to make conceptualisation and research more manageable. In the end the various processes must be integrated to reform the whole.

At this point it is worthwhile discussing each of these elements in turn, and in the context of new product marketing. An 'innovation' is 'an idea, practice, or object perceived as new by an individual'.[15] As Rogers and Shoemaker rightly point out it is the individual's perception which matters, not whether the idea is objectively new or not. New product managers, and new product marketing texts, often become enmeshed in the problem of whether the idea is really new or a reinterpretation of something old, completely ignoring the fact that the consumer does not have this 'total' knowledge or viewpoint. If it is 'new' to the consumer (and this is something which ought to be easy to test) then it is a *new* product.

'Communication channels' are 'the processes by which messages are transmitted from source to receiver', an idea very akin to Shannon and Weaver's 'procedures'.[16] The only real point to be made here is that there are interpersonal channels and mass media channels.

'Over time' refers to the fact that the diffusion process is a dynamic one, and that it is the time dimension which is perhaps the most important in the whole process, and as such is the dimension which is normally overlooked. The deficiency of current research methods is that they tend to be static rather than dynamic.

The 'system' being defined in 'among members of a social system' is 'a collectivity of units which are functionally differentiated and engaged in joint problem solving with respect to a common goal'.[17] In the context of this treatise, the system will normally be composed of 'all households', 'all housewives', or, for industrial marketing, 'all machine-tool purchasers', etc.

The first social process to be analysed is the relation between knowledge and adoption, termed by Rogers and Shoemaker 'the diffusion effect'.[18] Again this is a logical starting point rather than in the historical sequence of diffusion research, since the effect has only been expounded comparatively recently. It is defined as 'the cumulatively increasing degree of influence upon an individual to adopt or reject an innovation, resulting from the increasing rate of knowledge and adoption or rejection of the innovation in the social system'.

The cognitive process model already outlined includes some basic assumptions about the relationship between knowledge and adoption at the individual level. By aggregating these individual events then the social processes, cumulative *knowledge over time,* and cumulative *adoption over time,* can be represented in the manner of Figure 2.1.

Fig. 2.1: Two Social Processes

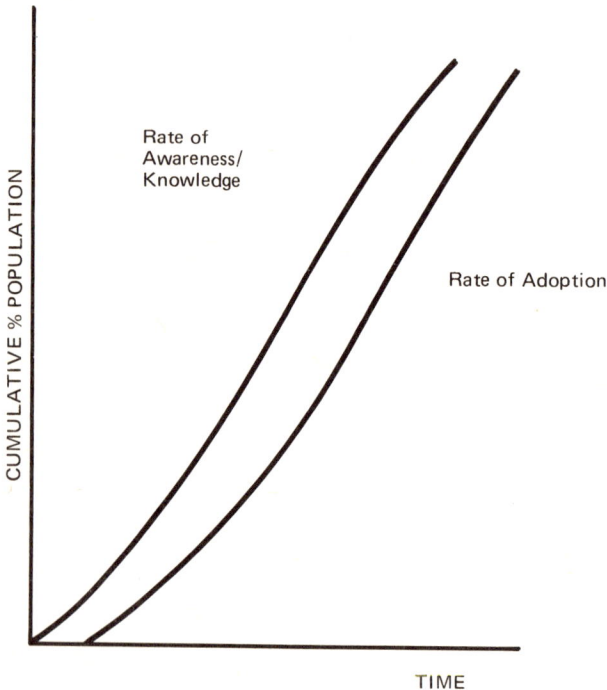

Source: Adapted from Rogers and Shoemaker (1971), p.130, and used by permission of the Free Press.

In this figure it can be seen that knowledge of the innovation spreads ahead of, and at a faster rate than, adoption of this innovation. This is a result which has been replicated in many fields, and which is, of course, eminently plausible. It can therefore be inferred that as the level of knowledge in the social system increases, then the corresponding influence on individuals to adopt also increases. This relationship has recently been demonstrated by Gaikwad (1971) and is illustrated by Figure 2.2. Here the social process *knowledge against adoption* is plotted, and it can be seen that the figure implies a threshold of knowledge below which little adoption occurs (20 per cent). Once this point is passed, added knowledge produces increasing returns in terms of adoption.

Fig. 2.2: The Diffusion Effect

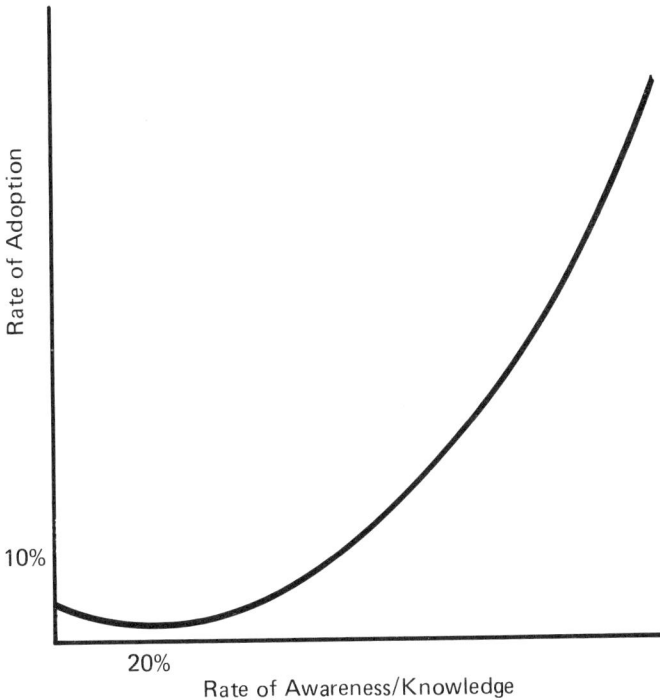

Source: Adapted from Rogers and Shoemaker (1971), p.162, and used by permission of the Free Press.

Rogers and Shoemaker state that 'until an individual has a certain minimum level of information and influence from his system's environment, he is unlikely to adopt. But once this threshold is passed adoption of the idea is further increased by each additional input of knowledge and influence to the system's communication environment'. They add: 'Furthermore the threshold seems to occur at about the point where the opinion leaders begin to favour the innovation', opinion leaders being those more involved in interpersonal communication with their social contacts.[19]

Therefore the links between the micro-level cognitive processes, individual knowledge and individual adoption, and the above social processes, which might be termed aggregate knowledge and aggregate adoption, become clearer.

Individual knowledge is aggregate knowledge as transmitted by the various channels to individuals, and as the aggregate increases individuals are persuaded (stage 2 in the cognitive process) to take up an attitude toward the innovation, an attitude which will determine adoption. For the moment the possibility of rejection is ignored, and therefore each resulting adoption adds to the aggregate adoption, and by doing so increases aggregate knowledge, which in turn produces further adoption. The social process knowledge-adoption is therefore a positive feedback system, and the 'feedback' is transmitted via interpersonal channels to individuals as yet to adopt.

Thus this first social process is partly responsible for the well-known adopter distribution (also termed the adoption curve), which in many ways was the origin of the whole subject. This was the phenomenon which Tarde suggested, and the empirical occurrence of such curves is the basis of much work in the area. Figures 2.3 and 2.4 show the adopter distribution in its frequency and its cumulative form. Both show the same phenomenon but the S-shaped cumulative curve is perhaps the better known, and is used as the rationale for many mathematical models of the process. The frequency curve is shown as the bell-shaped normal curve, but the consensus of past research appears to be that the curve approximates to the normal curve rather than actually being a normal distribution.[20]

Hence we have finally arrived at the phenomenon which first attracted people to the area, the adoption of innovations as described over the time dimension. However it is more logical to discuss this now than to have done so earlier, because the adopter distribution is the result of the inter-related operation of various social processes, and in particular the one described above. It is also true that adoption is not the end of the process; as has already been illustrated there is a complex feedback relationship by which adoption affects subsequent adoption,

Fig. 2.3: Adopter Distribution (Frequency)

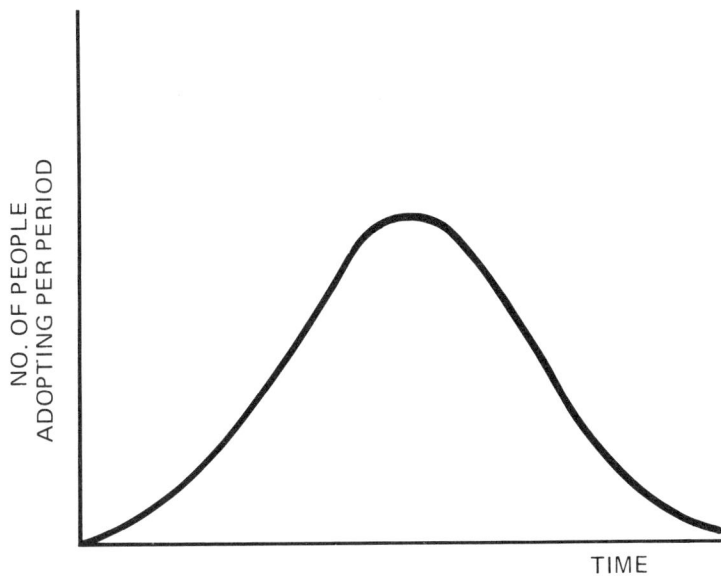

Fig. 2.4: Adopter Distribution (Cumulative)

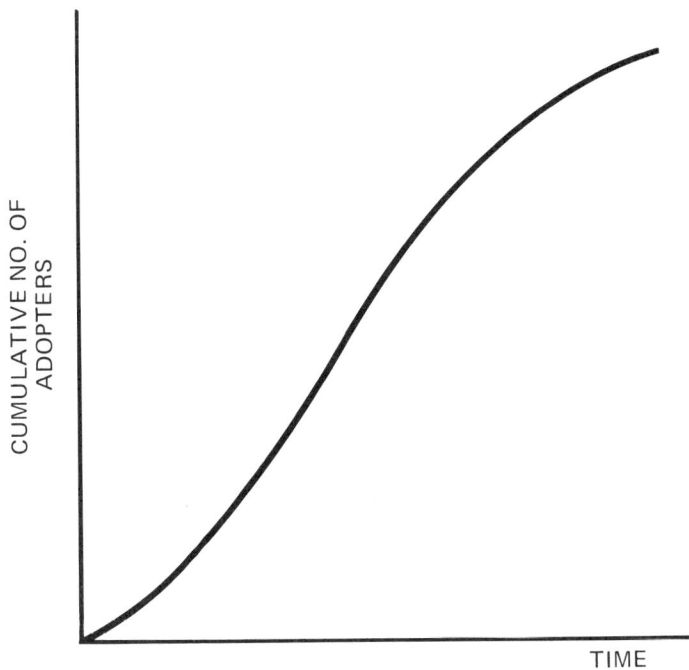

quite apart from any individual continuing to seek confirmation for his/her own adoption decision.

In discussing the important role of the interpersonal 'feedback' channels a useful hypothesis has been advanced by Mendez (1968). He argued that the shape of the adoption curve would depend on the extent of interpersonal communication in the particular social system. With low interpersonal communication (an individual only exerting influence on one other individual), the cumulative adoption curve will 'approximate a straight line'. In fact what was found by this, and other studies, is that the greater the degree of interpersonal communication the greater the divergence of the adoption curve from linearity, and the more rapid the rate of adoption — in other words the more pronounced the diffusion effect. Nearly all cumulative adoption curves are found to be S-shaped, and by inference this indicates the importance of the process of interpersonal communication.

Since Mendez studied societies with poorly developed, or non-existent, mass media channels, while we are concerned with more developed consumer markets, it might be instructive to develop his ideas a little further. To do this an extreme case is taken first.

Suppose there was zero interpersonal communication and that consumers obtained knowledge solely from the mass media (assumed to be a constant source). Further postulate that a constant fraction of 'new knowers' become 'new adopters'. Mathematically this situation is described by:

$$\frac{dk}{dt} = c_1$$

$$\text{and} \quad \frac{da}{dt} = c_2 \frac{dk}{dt}$$

where k is cumulative knowledge, a is cumulative adoption, t is time and c_1 and c_2 constants. Solving these produces:

$$k = c_1 t \qquad \text{(assuming } k = 0 \text{ at } t = 0\text{),}$$

$$\text{and} \quad a = c_2 c_1 (t - t_a)$$

where t_a is the time elapsed before the first adoption. Since c_2 must be less than c_1 then graphically these equations can be represented as in Figure 2.5.

Fig. 2.5: The Social Processes Assuming a Constant Media Source

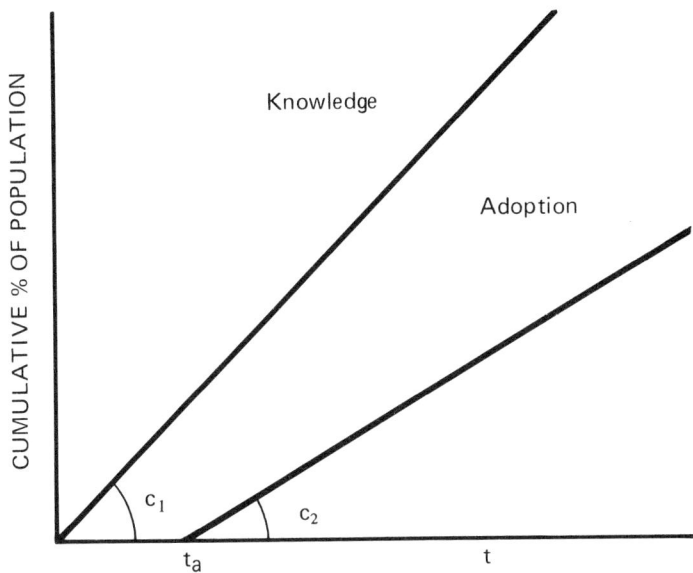

Fig. 2.6: The Diffusion Effect Assuming a Constant Media Source

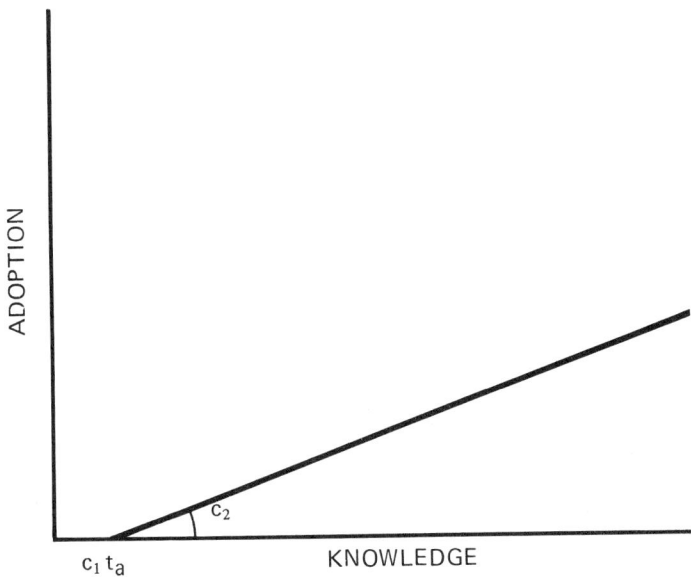

It will be noted that this is unlike any actual situation. Interestingly if the constant media source is replaced by the one-to-one interpersonal communication used by Mendez the result would be similar to Figure 2.5.[21]

The 'diffusion effect' corresponding to the above would be as Figure 2.6, and again unlike real world evidence, although it does have a sort of 'threshold' $(c_1 t_a)$.

However as soon as we make the assumption that interpersonal communication does exist then clearly the effect of people talking with each other will increase the aggregate knowledge in the system. At this point the case of interpersonal communication only could be treated, but it seems more relevant to leave the mass media in, as it were, and proceed by sophisticating the above. Therefore postulate that the increase in knowledge is the sum of the constant media source and the knowledge already in the system, viz:

$$\frac{dk}{dt} = c_1 + c_3 k$$

whence by simple integration:

$$k = \frac{c_1}{c_3} (e^{c_3 t} - 1)$$

and assuming the same relation between knowledge and adoption as before then:

$$a = \frac{c_2 c_1}{c_3} (e^{c_3 t} - 1)$$

which can be represented graphically as in Figure 2.7. The corresponding diffusion effect is as in Figure 2.8.

Now the author would be the first to admit that the above mathematical illustration is simplistic and therefore of limited use.[22] However it does show that once interpersonal communication is in some way introduced into the process the theoretical curves depart from linearity, and begin to resemble the actual phenomena found in reality. Thus there can be little doubt that observed adopter distributions are principally due to the effects of interpersonal communication. The above illustration gives theoretical justification for this conclusion, and the many studies in the area provide empirical backing. As will be detailed in Chapter 4 we also have evidence on the importance of interpersonal communication from studies using different, and

Fig. 2.7: The Social Processes Assuming a Constant Media Source and Simple Interpersonal Communication

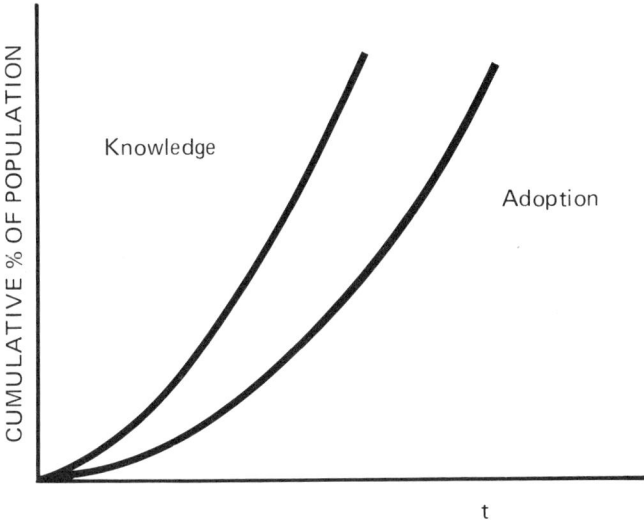

Fig. 2.8: The Diffusion Effect Assuming a Constant Media Source and Simple Interpersonal Communication

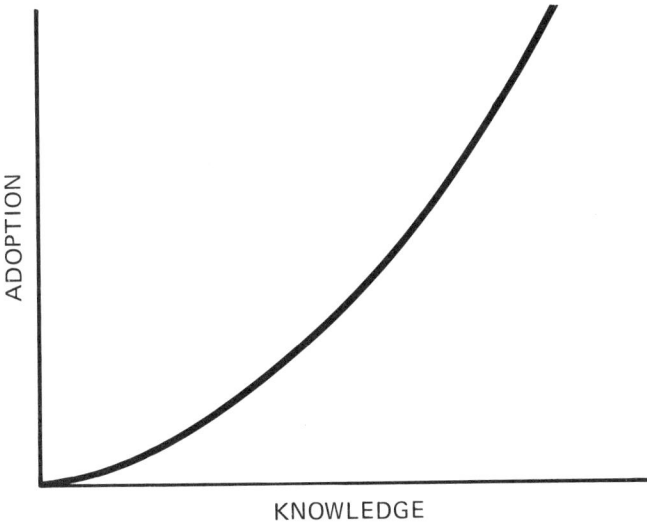

independent, methodologies from those discussed above.

The illustration given is simplistic not only because the exact mathematical formulation of these processes (which has yet to be found) might be expected to be considerably more complex, but also because a process has been omitted from the conceptualisation. To describe the situation adequately, and in accordance with the cognitive process model, it is necessary also to describe the spread of attitudes towards the innovation, and to suggest links between aggregate knowledge, aggregate attitudes and aggregate adoption.

Lastly it is also necessary to postulate that these attitudes can be favourable or unfavourable to the innovation, and hence lead to adoption or rejection. Since many new products fail we reasonably assume that unfavourable information and influence is a potent force. These topics will be developed in Chapter 4. I have also suggested a mathematical schema to describe such processes, and this will be discussed in Chapter 5.

What is indicated by the above is that it is perhaps better to view the mass media communications as being inputs to the system from the external environment, while interpersonal communications are the feedback channels within this system. Indeed research indicates that the mass media channels are more influential or important at the knowledge stage in the individual's cognitive processes, while interpersonal channels are more influential at the persuasion stage.[23]

Thus while the complexity of the social processes has by now become apparent, at the same time their respective roles have become clearer. People learn about the innovation from the mass media and their social contacts, are persuaded for or against this innovation primarily by their social contacts, and those who adopt transmit information which further increases the amount of knowledge in the system. If the knowledge is primarily favourable to the innovation then further adoption will occur and the process will continue to 'snowball' in this manner.

The role of the adopter has also become clearer, since it is his/her experience with the product which will be viewed as 'objective' by other members of the social system, and will add great weight to the sum total of knowledge for or against the innovation.[24]

At this stage the social processes of communication will be left, and the pertinent question raised of why these processes should be initiated as they depend so largely on feedback from the adopters. The simple answer is because people are different, and while the majority rely on interpersonally transmitted information some are prepared to

Fig. 2.9: Adopter Categories

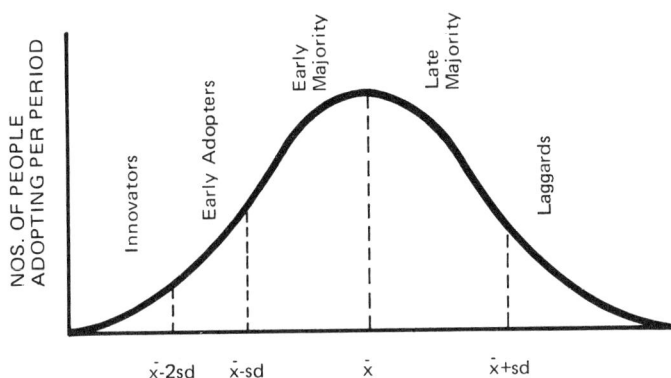

Source: Rogers and Shoemaker (1971), p.182, and used by permission of the
Free Press.

take a risk and adopt without such information. The last social
process to be discussed here is therefore that of the degree of
innovativeness individuals may exhibit.

In some ways this really relates to individual level cognitive processes,
but as the emphasis of diffusion research is on segmenting groups of
individuals on the basis of aggregate behaviour, innovativeness is termed
here a social process.[25]

Rogers and Shoemaker define innovativeness as 'the degree to which
an individual is relatively earlier in adopting new ideas than other
members of his system'.[26] In essence this is the point on the time
dimension at which an individual adopts, and the groups of individuals
are segmented by use of the bell-shaped form of the adopter

distribution. The mean time of adoption is computed, and the groups separated by laying off standard deviations from this mean, as in Figure 2.9.

It has been shown subsequently that when studied in terms of independent variables such as age, social class, attitudes, etc., all these groups do indeed have different characteristics. This topic will not be developed here as Chapter 3 is designed to cover this aspect of the diffusion of innovations. What it is relevant to say is that the innovators are those more likely to take risks, and less reliant on interpersonal communication as an influential source of information. They may be influenced to adopt by the mass media, or this event may occur by chance; whatever the case the last piece of the jigsaw can be slotted into place. The innovators are the independent spirits who first try the innovation, and they will transmit their perception of its performance to others. Should this perception be favourable then others will adopt, the diffusion effect come into operation, and the characteristic adoption curve begin to grow.

2.3 Summary

The origin and evolution of diffusion research has been outlined, and in particular the heritage and influence of rural sociology discussed. It has been demonstrated that the current schema is supported by the empirical evidence to some degree, and suggested that it may eventually develop into a unified theory of innovative behaviour.

The general schema has been divided into two components, individual level cognitive processes and macro-level social processes. It has been stated that while relatively little is known about the former, this does not in any way detract from the overall schema. Despite this it has also been argued that the cognitive process models throw useful light on the social processes, and will provide the most fruitful area for future theoretical developments.

Social processes, defined initially as 'patterns of social behaviour within a specific social system', have been discussed, and the crucial elements of the diffusion of innovations briefly outlined. The connection between this schema and more general communication models has been demonstrated, and the definition of social processes refined to 'procedures by which one mind may affect another within the overall communications environment'. It has been stressed that these processes all centre around verbal interpersonal communication.

The social processes relating to knowledge and adoption — the diffusion effect — have been analysed extensively and for good reason.

It has been conclusively demonstrated, by theoretical and empirical argument, that interpersonal communication, not the mass media, is responsible for the observed patterns of adoption. Were there no such 'word-of-mouth' communication, then while adoption would still occur it would exhibit a linear pattern, and increase at a far slower rate than actually arises.

It has been argued that mass media communication is more effective at the knowledge stage in an individual's cognitive process, while interpersonal communication is more effective at the persuasion stage. Therefore it is suggested that the mass media should be viewed as external inputs to the system, a system which principally operates by 'positive interpersonal feedback'. 'Feedback' which can be favourable or unfavourable to the innovation, and which originates with the experience of adopters.

Lastly the concept of innovativeness has been introduced, and a rationale advanced for the initiation of the process. The 'innovators' are the key to the early phases of the diffusion of innovations, and therefore determine the future course of events. We now turn to an investigation of these and other adopter categories in greater depth.

Notes

1. These terms being left undefined for the present.
2. Rogers and Shoemaker (1971), p.57.
3. Rogers and Shoemaker (1971), p.65.
4. Rogers and Shoemaker (1971), p.xvii.
5. The sociometric method will be described in detail in Chapter 4.
6. And in measuring time of adoption in this way the inaccuracy of recall methods was shown by actual comparison.
7. See Carlson (1968) for a critique of educational diffusion research.
8. The reason that 'translucid' boxes are preferable is basically that by specifying the contents of the box in this way the theory becomes more falsifiable.
9. Rogers and Shoemaker (1971), p.99.
10. The latter idea being due to Festinger (1957).
11. Rogers and Shoemaker (1971), p.103.
12. Since we remain relatively ignorant of the individual cognitive processes.
13. Rogers and Shoemaker (1971), p.18.
14. Shannon and Weaver (1949), p.xx.
15. Rogers and Shoemaker (1971), p.19.
16. Rogers and Shoemaker (1971), p.23.
17. Rogers and Shoemaker (1971), p.28.
18. Rogers and Shoemaker (1971), p.161.
19. Rogers and Shoemaker (1971), p.163.
20. See Rogers and Shoemaker (1971), p.179.
21. Since a one person to one person chain is effectively similar to a constant probability of obtaining 'knowledge'.

22. While simplistic, the analysis did raise some anomalies with regard to the diffusion effect as portrayed in Rogers and Shoemaker (1971, p.162). For instance is it possible to have adoption without knowledge, as Figure 2.2 indicates? This might be conceivable if the axes of this figure were 'rates' (that is dk/dt, da/dt) and it could therefore be said that the rate of adoption might decrease until the rate of knowledge had passed a threshold. However the authors define rate of adoption, for instance, as 'the number of receivers who adopt a new idea in a specific time' (p.157). Nonetheless while we might quarrel with the shape of the curve around the origin the overall concept of the diffusion effect remains extremely useful.
23. Rogers and Shoemaker (1971), p.382.
24. Which is why the diffusion of innovations may also be viewed as a learning process for society as a whole.
25. We also have the familiar problem of being able to predict from which groups of people adopters are likely to emerge at different stages in the adoption process, while remaining unable to predict the behaviour of individuals.
26. Rogers and Shoemaker (1971), p.27.

3 CONSUMER INNOVATIVENESS

3.1 The Measurement of Individual Innovativeness

Any attempt to understand consumer innovativeness must take into account its two main facets — the different demographic, socio-economic and psychological characteristics of the various categories of individuals depicted in Figure 2.9, and the ways in which the individual and aggregate behaviour of the more innovative individuals can 'affect the minds' of others. As innovativeness was previous classed as a social process, then the discussion will later concentrate on the communication aspects. However before proceeding to examine either of the above topics it is necessary to look at the ways innovativeness can be measured, and arising out of this measurement, how we can gain an understanding of just what is meant by the term 'innovativeness'. From this understanding, as expressed in a definition of the concept, it is possible to consider how the adopter categories may be formed, and whence the characteristics mentioned above determined. The scheme portrayed in Figure 2.9, while perhaps the most widely used outside the marketing area, has substantial drawbacks and will in fact not be used subsequently. Instead a modification will be employed, for the sole and pragmatic reason that it is the best available with which to discuss the research findings.

All categorisation schemes can be separated into two components. One of these is the measurement of individual innovativeness, and the other is the formation of the various categories of individuals — categories which represent differing degrees of innovativeness. All such schemes also associate the term 'innovators' with the highest degree of innovativeness, 'early adopters' or 'early majority' with the next highest, and so on down to the 'laggards'. While the actual terms used may differ, the basic concepts are remarkably similar. Furthermore all the schemes to be discussed here utilise the same fundamental measurement of individual innovativeness, and it is only in the second component — formation of categories — that differences emerge. It will subsequently be argued that all the schemes currently available involve an undesirable arbitrary element in this second component or procedure, and that a way has recently appeared by which such restrictive assumptions may be relaxed in the future. Before discussing these problems, the first procedure — the measurement of individual innovativeness — must be examined.

Innovativeness is assumed to be a trait possessed, to a greater or lesser degree, by all members of a society, and as such usually becomes a continuous dependent variable in research studies. Innovativeness relates to *when* an individual adopts the innovation as compared with when the society as a whole adopts it. If an individual adopts soon after the innovation appears, and before the bulk of the population adopts the innovation, then it will be readily appreciated that this individual is more innovative than one who only adopts after two-thirds of his fellows have already done so. Measurement of innovativeness is therefore accomplished by observing when individuals adopt, aggregating these individual adoptions into a distribution, and comparing any one individual's adoption date with the distribution. The first necessary items of information are the date an individual adopts, and the date the innovation was introduced. However this only provides a duration or elapsed time to adoption in isolation from other individuals, and says nothing about whether the individual was ahead or behind the majority. In order to effect this latter comparison, two other items are needed: the mean time of adoption for all individuals, and the standard deviation of the adopter distribution. The mean time of adoption is the arithmetical average of all the individual elapsed times to adoption, and provides a reference point with which to compare any particular individual's time of adoption. However the difference between the mean time and the individual time only indicates how far ahead or behind the average the individual was, and not how many other individuals were also equally far ahead or behind. In order to assess the latter a measure of the dispersion of individuals around the mean is needed, and the standard deviation is one such measure. In a new product context the measurement of an individual's innovativeness can be defined as follows.

Let t_i be the time elapsed between the introduction of the product onto the market and the i-th individual's first purchase of this product, m be the mean time elapsed for all n individuals, and s be the standard deviation associated with the adopter distribution.[1] The i-th individual's innovativeness, I_i, is then measured as:

$$I_i = \frac{m - t_i}{s}$$

This is a standardised measure in the sense that it no longer depends on the units of time used (in fact it is now expressed in units of the standard deviation), or how long it took for any specific innovation to be adopted by 50, 75 or 100 per cent of the population. Comparisons between different innovations are greatly facilitated by this procedure as they can now be made on the same basis. The only arbitrary elements of the measure shown above are that the mean has been chosen as the reference point, and that a high score has been equated with a high degree of innovativeness.[2]

This measure rests solely on the measurement of time, so it can be seen that the basis for the above is inherently very sound. The difficulty, of course, is in assessing (i) when the product was put on the market, and (ii) when any particular individual adopted it. The problems involved in making this assessment vary widely from market to market; for some products the exact date of introduction is known, and when individuals actually purchased can be determined from sales records. For mass consumer markets it may be impractical or impossible to collect these sales records, and therefore necessary to use some form of sample survey technique. Often questions are asked which rely on whether or not the respondent can recall when he or she first purchased the product. The disadvantages of such a methodology are obvious, in that most people are unable to remember dates accurately — unless the event was a recent one. Hence a longitudinal methodology where surveys are conducted at intervals, effectively reducing the period over which respondents have to remember, is more reliable. Unfortunately these surveys would have to be conducted throughout most of the adoption process, and this would be a costly approach.

As is now apparent, while the measurement is still one of time of adoption the accuracy of this measurement leaves something to be desired. In a bid to overcome the problems of recall surveys some researchers (Robertson and Myers, 1969; Summers, 1971) have used lists of new products, and asked respondents to indicate which they own at the time of the survey, the assumption being that those who own a greater proportion of the listed new products are more innovative than those who own a smaller fraction. While this assumption is no doubt valid it can readily be seen that such techniques are no longer measuring innovativeness directly, rather they are assessing a related variable, 'ownership of new products'. At the present time the relation between the latter and time of adoption is not at all clear. A further problem is that innovativeness often differs markedly across product categories; that is, the innovator for detergents may have completely different characteristics to the innovator for colour television. By showing a list composed of numerous new products such techniques may well obscure any meaningful findings. The author would argue that such procedures should be avoided wherever possible, and in favour of techniques which directly measure time of adoption.

Yet again in other fields not only is it difficult to assess when an individual adopted, but it is also difficult to determine when the innovation was first placed on the market. The most striking example of this lies in the field of fashion marketing, where it is often impossible to place an exact date on the appearance of a new style. For one thing there is often no such entity as an innovation, but rather a collection of related styles which are interpreted by designers for the mass market, and eventually evolve into an overall image. Assessing just when this more distinct image emerged is extremely difficult. However a number of authors have suggested ways round this problem. King (1963) used the recall survey technique on the purchase of any style out of those available for the season under study. Since this method was based on time of adoption it was potentially more reliable than that later used by Baumgarten (1974), who measured innovativeness by ownership of new styles. However, as Midgley and Wills (1974) have shown, the styles on sale for any one season are composed of both 'old' and 'new' innovations, and King's 'early adopters' may therefore have been a mixture of innovators and later adopters (buying the previous season's styles). Despite using an inherently weaker method, by focusing on newer styles Baumgarten may well have arrived at more valid conclusions.

Midgley (1974) advanced another technique based on the implicit hypothesis that what consumers perceive as a fashionable or unfashion-able style is in reality dependent on how long the style has been on the market. Therefore by asking respondents to rank pictures of the various available styles, according to how fashionable they thought they were, it was possible to form an overall scale measuring the perceived ages of the style images. By then placing an individual's expressed preference for, or last purchase of, one particular style onto this scale an indication of this individual's innovativeness could be obtained. The advantages of this technique, when applied to fashion innovations, are both that it obtains consumer perceptions, rather than those imposed by the outside observer, and that it measures time of adoption more directly than the 'list' method. The disadvantages are that for the technique to be practical (applicable to large samples) it is necessary to assume that fashion rankings can be transformed into an overall interval scale of fashion.[3]

It can be seen that the different measurement techniques outlined above may be more appropriate to different types of product, and the choice of any one method for a particular situation will depend on the type of product and the availability of data. It will obviously also depend on practical and financial constraints. However it must be stressed that the majority of the problems discussed above relate solely to the accuracy with which innovativeness is measured, and do not cast doubt on what is being measured. The researcher should strive to measure time of adoption by the most direct route feasible, and the closer this route to the 'exact date of purchase' technique the more accurate his measurement will be.

Once such a scale of innovativeness has been established then it is possible to proceed to the next phase of the process, the formation of categories. However at this point it will be noted that by measuring innovativeness in the previous manner, we have in no way defined exactly what innovativeness means. Therefore before looking at the adopter categories, the concept of innovativeness will be explored in a little more depth, and to do this it is necessary to look at the aggregate processes, that is to examine the adopter and innovativeness distributions.

3.2 The Meaning of Individual Innovativeness

To define precisely what the concept of innovativeness means, as opposed to what is measured, the phenomenon represented in Figure 2.9 is re-expressed in terms of the innovativeness measure or score developed in the preceding section. That is, instead of examining the number of adopters over time we look at the distribution of individuals with differing innovativeness scores. This distribution is presented in Figure 3.1.

It will easily be seen that all that has been done is to replace the time dimension by the standardised score. Yet again it is noted that although a normal distribution is shown here this is not necessary to the argument, which would hold for any empirical distribution.

Although at first sight this might appear a trivial change of axis, it in fact represents a major change of viewpoint. As can be seen, a temporal distribution of adopters has been transformed into the distribution of a trait amongst members of society, and one which can be thought of as essentially similar to any other, such as intelligence or extroversion. This is a key concept, as it implies that innovativeness is an innate expression of a person's psychological or sociological characteristics, and

Fig. 3.1: The Trait of Innovativeness

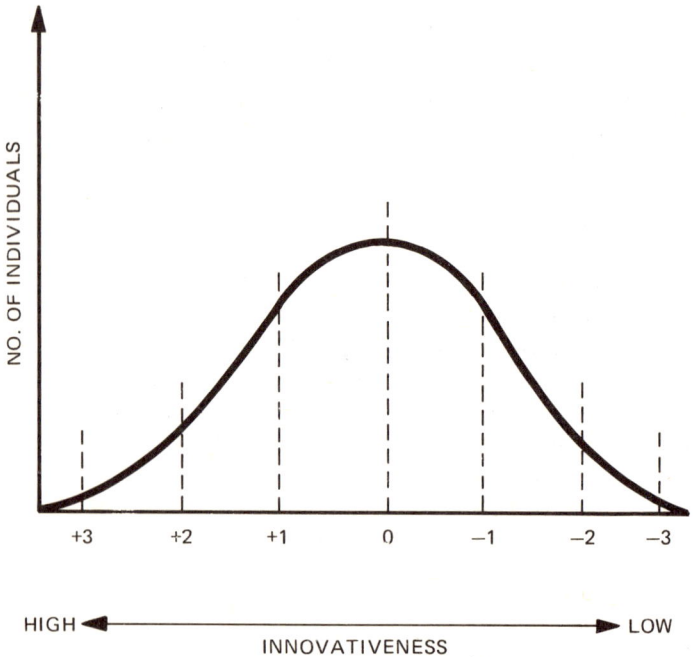

HIGH ◄─────────────────────────────► LOW
INNOVATIVENESS

might therefore be expected to show a strong relation to measurements of these other characteristics. A further implication, following directly from the above, is that a person's innovativeness is not confined merely to one specific innovation, but to a wider field — perhaps the product category, or several product categories. In other words the distribution shown in Figure 3.1 would be observed to be similar for several innovations, that is, would be similar with respect to the position particular individuals would hold in the process. It will subsequently become apparent that reality is a little more complex than this, and that it is not possible to state precisely which particular individuals will be innovators for a specific new product, but only to suggest which group the innovators may emerge from. The reasons for this are partly because of the situational nature of innovativeness, and partly because innovations differ in their degree of 'newness'. These aspects will be discussed in Section 3.4. However, what can be said here is that it is certainly not tenable to argue that the distribution is a mere manifestation of a random process, with the obvious corollary that the distribution of individuals would be unique to each innovation. The evidence suggests the opposite; a distinct type of person is more likely to be an innovator than any other.

The above also highlights the dual nature of the term 'innovativeness'. Is it a measurement of when all individuals adopt, or is it an expression of this individual's cognitive structure? In fact it is better viewed as the latter, and it would be as well to make a very clear distinction between the concept and the way we measure it. By defining innovativeness as 'the degree to which an individual is relatively earlier in adopting an innovation than other members of his system', Rogers and Shoemaker have defined the concept in terms of the measurement.[4] That is, innovativeness is what we measure, and what we measure is innovativeness. To avoid such tautologies it is suggested here that innovativeness is the degree to which an individual is willing to adopt without receiving favourable interpersonal information on the innovation's performance from his/her social contacts. Innovativeness therefore relates to the amount of such favourable information that an individual requires before accepting the risk of adoption. An 'innovator' is therefore the type of person who requires little or none of this social support, and is prepared to make his/her own independent decision on whether to adopt or not. The less innovative members of society feel the need for more support from people who have experience with the innovation, and such information comes from conversations with their friends. We measure innovativeness by when the individual adopts in comparison to others, but this is only because such measurements provide an indication of how independent the individual is. The author's definition of innovativeness is therefore as follows:

Innovativeness is the degree to which an individual makes innovation decisions independently of the communicated experience of others.

An important corollary is that, as less innovative individuals rely more on interpersonal communication, then there is a relationship between the receipt of this information and the time at which they adopt the innovation. Since a particular individual's receipt of the necessary information may be a chance or random event, then so might be their actual time of adoption. In other words while the 'innovators' (as a type) might be expected to be the first to adopt, the exact time at which another type of individual would adopt is less easy to predict. This thesis will be developed at greater length in Chapter 4.

In a sense the above definition has been arrived at by a circuitous route, as it would perhaps have been more logical to define the concept before defining its measurement. However it was necessary to proceed in, so to speak, the 'reverse' direction in order to develop an understanding of exactly what is meant by innovativeness. As such an understanding depends on the relationships between individuals it cannot be developed solely at the individual level, but only on the more aggregate level of adopter/innovativeness distributions. It is also obvious that it was necessary to develop the standardised innovativeness measure in order to effect the transformation between these two distributions.

The definition will be used subsequently, and has distinct advantages in that:

(i) it is not defined in terms of its measurement;
(ii) it emphasises the relation of innovativeness to individual cognitive structures, and hence to other measurable variables; and
(iii) it emphasises the relation between innovativeness and a particular type of interpersonal communication, particularly that the more innovative members of society need less information on how others have fared with the product in order to make their decision.

In essence innovativeness, when viewed as a variable (I), must be inversely proportional to the amount or extent of communicated experience the person needs to make a decision. Symbolically, if E represents this needed or desired threshold level of 'product' experience information then:

$$I_i \quad = \quad f\!\left(\frac{1}{E_i}\right)$$

Theoretically if the E_i of the individual could be measured then so, too, could his/her innovativeness. Unfortunately, quite apart from the difficulty of measuring the factor, we do not yet know what the relationship between I and E might be. Hence we rely on the person's relative time of adoption to indicate or measure I. Namely, and as before:

$$\tilde{I}_i \qquad \frac{m-t_i}{s}$$

Except that the tilde is used to distinguish between the measured and actual innovativeness. It is to be assumed that the nature of the relation between I and E is such that adoption closely follows receipt of this threshold level of information, and hence that $\widetilde{I}_i$ is equivalent to I_i. It can also be seen that the new definition makes explicit the situational nature of the innovativeness of the majority of individuals. Not only will the receipt of E_i be determined by the situation (occurrence and type of conversations), but the value of E_i may well fluctuate with the individual's own situation (finance, life style, etc.).

A distinction should also be made between the type of information being discussed here and 'information' in more general terms. As has been stated, 'communicated experience' is information on an individual's actual experience with the product, and communicated interpersonally between this individual and a potential adopter. Other types of information are mass media information and general interpersonal information about the innovation, the latter being factual or 'hearsay' information, and not based on actual experience with the product in question. It will be shown subsequently that the innovators are probably more exposed to the mass media, and general interpersonal information, than later adopters.

In the sense that they are different, (require less product information), the innovators are obviously of crucial importance to the whole process. They will try the innovation, and their experience of it will trigger the innovativeness of others or not, as the case may be. To progress any further with this exposition it is necessary to move from the individual to a more general level, and to do so requires that a method be found by which the innovators may be grouped into a discrete category.

Before attempting this, however, it is opportune to add a few less specific comments at this point. Firstly some writers move more rapidly into a discussion of the adopter categories and their characteristics, while here the concept of innovativeness has been dwelt on at considerable length. This is because I consider it vital to develop a clear understanding of innovativeness at the individual level, before any discussion of more general concepts. Without such an understanding it is not really possible to discuss the adopter categories, or more importantly to link these categories to various characteristics. A similar line of argument will be advanced in Chapter 4 where some time will be spent analysing the basic phenomena of interpersonal communication, before looking at the more global concepts and results. Furthermore the understanding of innovativeness which has been gained thus far provides a link between this concept and those of interpersonal communication.

It will also be noted that innovativeness has been discussed in the historical sense, that is looking at past innovations and their associated adopter distributions. This is because the main research findings have been established in this manner, and also because the phenomenon is clearer when viewed in this way. The problems of predicting innovativeness and the like, which are obviously of major managerial significance, will be largely deferred until Part III of the book.

3.3 Adopter/Innovativeness Categorisation Schemes

The importance of the innovators to the overall process has already been outlined, and the suggestion made that they form a distinct group in that they are self-reliant, or willing to take risks without receiving extensive social confirmation. It has also been argued that this is because their high degree of innovativeness is an innate expression of their personality, and therefore would be expected to relate to variables such as age, intelligence, cosmopolitanism, and so on. In order to determine whether this is supported by the evidence or not it is impractical to continue conceptualising the topic at the individual level, insofar that it is necessary to generalise beyond any one individual. This generalisation can only be achieved by forming categories. The focus will be on the innovators, as the observed innovativeness of other individuals is more dependent on the interaction of communication and personality factors than the above personal characteristics alone. Also as innovativeness has been conceptualised as a trait then this representation will be used rather than the over time representation of Figure 2.9.

To discuss the formation of the adopter or innovativeness categories it is necessary at this point to re-examine the assumption of the bell-shaped normal distribution of adopters. As outlined in Chapter 2 this assumption is usually made because the adopter distributions found in practice are quite often good approximations to the normal curve. Another reason is that this particular distribution has some desirable statistical properties. For instance it is symmetrical, and hence the mode, median and mean are identical. Therefore the highest rate of adoption occurs at the mean time of adoption, and this mean time divides the distribution into equal areas. Perhaps more relevantly, with a normal distribution the mean time of adoption represents the time by which 50 per cent of the population have adopted.

Using the normal distribution and the format developed here then Figure 2.9, which represents Rogers' (1962) categorisation scheme, becomes Figure 3.2.

The percentages denote the proportion of individuals in each

Fig. 3.2: Rogers' Adopter Categorisation Scheme

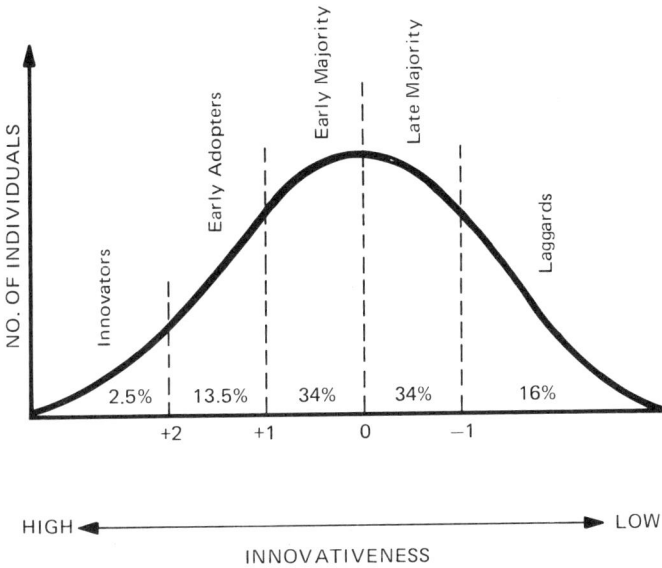

category. It should be stressed that these figures only hold for the
normal distribution or a good (moderately skewed) approximation to
it. This is the most commonly used categorisation scheme in rural
sociology, but has found little favour in the marketing area. The prime
reason for this is that most studies quite naturally focus on the
innovators, and if these are defined as 2.5 per cent of the adopting
population it is necessary to contact a very large number of respondents
in order to locate a statistically significant number of innovators.
Robertson (1971) points out that the 10 per cent definition has gained
prevalence in marketing simply because it makes sample survey methods
feasible.[5] Indeed in the later text Rogers and Shoemaker (1971), while
discussing the five categories in depth, present a high proportion of their
generalisations in terms of the 'earlier adopters', a category which
might be thought of as a combination of the 'innovators' and 'early
adopters'. Furthermore in the recent marketing literature Summers

(1971 and 1972) has explicitly used such a combination. Therefore the categorisation scheme proposed here, and the one I consider to be the best currently available, is shown in Figure 3.3. The scheme has the advantage of being compatible with the previous research, is more practical than the earlier one, and is simpler to use. The scheme also explicitly states that we are more interested in the innovators because of their independent nature, and less interested in the remainder because their innovativeness is communication dependent.

Fig. 3.3: A Simple Categorisation Scheme

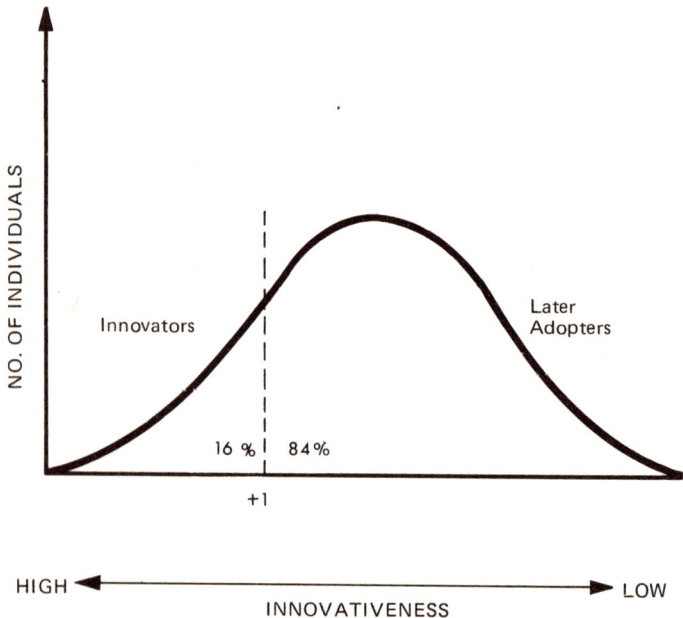

However it should be pointed out that while this scheme is slightly less arbitrary than those previously mentioned, it still has two arbitrary features. These are the assumption of normality, and the boundary between innovators and later adopters.

It can be stated that this assumption is not necessary in order to arrive at a categorisation scheme, and in the future it will become less desirable to make such a restrictive assumption. The measurement of innovativeness has been shown to be distribution-free, and hence the categorisation scheme should not force the innovators to be 16 per cent of the adopting population whatever the shape of the empirical distribution. It is of course possible to place the boundary at one standard deviation before the mean for any distribution, and therefore form a group whose size would depend on the shape of the distribution. However even this would be an arbitrary 'break-point', and Robertson has suggested that the boundaries should be placed where there is a distinct change in the characteristics of the individuals so categorised.[6] In the light of what has been said previously about the characteristics of innovators as opposed to the later adopters, this would appear to be a viable suggestion. Also it is possible that it may not be necessary to go to these lengths to achieve the same result. Petersen (1973) has indicated a method whereby categories may be formed on the basis of time of adoption alone. Petersen argues that any categorisation technique should mirror the categories which actually exist in the empirical distribution, and should not force this data into a preconceived number of categories, or a preconceived distribution form. The aim of his technique is therefore to form categories by maximising the between-group differences and minimising the within-group differences. The procedure employed is a clustering method, and determines the point at which the inclusion of one extra respondent increases rather than decreases the group variance.[7] Starting from an essentially arbitrary number of categories the technique produces the boundaries which result in the most homogeneous and distinct groups. By subsequently investigating whether one more category would decrease the within-group variances still further (that is, increase homogeneity) the method can be used to arrive at the 'optimal' number of categories as well as the 'optimal' size for these categories. However Petersen does suggest that care should be exercised in the latter phase as the 'optimal' number of categories 'does not consider either the theoretical aspects or the reliability of the categories derived'.[8] Here I would concur, and again suggest that the number of categories should be two. The innovativeness of the later adopters is probably more dependent on a combination of communication and personality factors, rather than on these personality factors alone. To divide the later adopters may well be an interesting exercise, but one which possibly says more about the flow of interpersonal communication than innovativeness *per se*. As the technique is relatively new little is known about the characteristics of individuals in 'optimal' adopter categories, as opposed to the more traditional kind. Much more research needs to be done in these areas before the technique can be applied with any confidence. Obviously another problem area is that the method produces categories specifically for each innovation, which makes comparisons with previous work difficult, and may therefore necessitate the development of new comparison procedures. Hence the scheme portrayed in Figure 3.3 must be used for the present, pending the development of a less arbitrary way of defining the boundary between innovators and later adopters.

3.4 The Characteristics of Innovators

In examining how the innovators differ from the rest of the population a convenient starting point is one of the earliest studies in the marketing area, that of Bell (1963). Bell surveyed some 5,000 households with a view to determining the demographic and socio-economic characteristics of the innovators, and contrasting these with the characteristics of the rest of the population. Innovators were defined as the first 10 per cent to purchase one or more of several consumer durable innovations. In turn these innovations were divided into two types, strategic and functional innovations. Strategic innovations were basically modifications to existing products (colour television, stereo equipment, etc.) while functional innovations were new solutions to old problems (dishwashers, food disposal units, etc.).

It was discovered that the innovators did differ significantly from other groups, in that they tended to be younger, more educated and to possess higher incomes. They were also more likely to belong to the professional and managerial classes, and to have greater exposure to the mass media. Perhaps more interestingly they were also of an independent frame of mind, in that 75 per cent of them did not consult anyone outside their family regarding their decision to purchase. This last result provides some confirmation for the previous arguments; the innovators are more self-reliant and less likely to seek out the advice and experience of others.

However if the innovators for strategic and functional innovations were contrasted with each other then it was found that they too differed significantly. The more radical the innovation (that is, functional as opposed to strategic), the more educated the innovators were, and the greater their income. This is the first intimation we have that the situation is more complex than might be thought at first glance. In some ways the innovation picks the innovators as well as the innovators selecting the innovation. This point will be returned to shortly.

Since 1963 several more studies have been conducted in the marketing area of diffusion studies, and quite a few have produced results of a similar nature. Here only the results that shed new light on the topic, and on the characteristics of the innovators, will be referred to.

Robertson and Kennedy (1968) studied the adoption of a small home appliance, and concluded that four variables were significant in determining whether an individual was an innovator or not. In order of importance these variables were, 'venturesomeness' or willingness to take risks, 'social mobility' or the degree of upward movement on the social scale, 'social integration' or degree of participation in the community, and 'privilegedness' or financial standing relative to the community. Once again these findings are consistent with the view of the innovator proposed earlier.

In a fascinating, and probably unique, look at the other end of the scale Uhl, Andrus and Poulsen (1970) investigated the characteristics of Rogers' 'laggards'. These authors found that the laggards had lower incomes than earlier adopters, a result which is in many ways striking as the products studied were low-cost grocery items. Uhl *et al* argued that the laggards 'may feel they have less money available for new products and hence prefer not to risk their limited funds until the products are accepted and proven by others'.[9] Furthermore they concluded that:

Innovators may seek to secure products which communicate 'new, first, original, futuristic, distinctively different', but our empirical inquiry suggests that laggards appear to cling to proven products. It may be that they are repelled by those products which appear to them to be too new, unproven and risky.[10]

It has already been suggested that later adopters (less innovative individuals) need information and confirmation from those who have already adopted. Uhl *et al* have provided some support for this suggestion.

For clothing innovations both Baumgarten (1974) and Midgley (1974) found that the innovators were more willing to take risks, and had a more favourable attitude to change. In both studies the innovators were also found to be more socially integrated, and to have greater exposure to the mass media than other individuals. Midgley (1974) also demonstrated that male clothing innovators were younger than later adopters.

On psychological characteristics Robertson (1967) found that the innovators of a consumer appliance were significantly more impulsive, active and dominant than other individuals. However Pizam (1972) in an extensive review of the literature on the psychological characteristics of innovators argues that the results in this area are at best inconclusive, and that further research is necessary before such relationships can be advanced with any certainty.

Haines (1966) reported that 15 per cent of his sample of purchasers of new supermarket products bought just because the products were 'new'. Midgley (1974) also noted the impulsive nature of the innovators of fashion items, finding that their purchase decision periods were much shorter than those of the later adopters.

Donnelly (1970) suggests that of the many personality characteristics which could be studied, Riesman's concept of social character has the most potential. Riesman (1950) advanced the idea that individuals could be classed as either inner-directed or other-directed. To quote Donnelly:

> The inner-directed person relies on his own internal standards and values to guide his behaviour; the other-directed individual tends to rely on the values of his contemporaries. Thus we can expect an individual's social character to fall somewhere between the two extremes of complete inner- or other-direction.[11]

By administering a scale designed to measure social character to purchasers and non-purchasers of new grocery products, Donnelly was able to show that the innovators were more inner-directed, that is were more able to make their 'own' decisions. In a later and perhaps more convincing study Donnelly and Ivancevich (1974) conducted a longitudinal investigation of the adoption of a new automobile. They were able to show a significant change in the proportions of inner- and other-directed individuals over the time period studied. Specifically the earlier purchasers (innovators) were predominantly inner-directed when compared with later purchasers. Interestingly the earlier purchasers of the new automobile were different to the purchasers of established makes, while the later purchasers of both were indistinguishable. That is, four year after its introduction the automobile was no longer perceived as an innovati

This concept of social character correlates closely with the concept of innovativeness advanced before. The innovator sets his/her own standards and makes his/her own decision with regard to the innovation. Later adopters rely on the values of others, values which reflect both attitudes toward and experience with the innovation in society as a whole.

It is also important to note that this relationship between inner- and other-directedness and innovativeness has been established for two quite different types of innovation. That is, for automobiles and grocery products. It will soon be discovered that this is not true of all such relationships, as it is normal to find quite large differences between the characteristics of innovators of differing types of innovation. Marketing as such represents only a small and relatively new contribution to diffusion studies as a whole, and it is therefore to be expected that a wider range of results are available in other areas. Indeed most of the postulated relationships originate from other areas such as rural sociology, and have often been applied to the new product situation with insufficient thought. It is crucial to realise that the concern of the rural sociologists or communications researchers is *major* innovations and not the kind of trivial product modification which is often found in supermarket products. It would therefore be surprising if all the relationships listed in Rogers and Shoemaker were applicable to products such as lemon-scented detergent. This is found not to be the case and will be discussed subsequently; first we address ourselves to the characteristics of the innovators of major innovations.

By 'major' is almost invariably meant products such as consumer durables (for the most part home appliances) and possibly, although with less certainty, new fashions in clothing. That is, products which entail a high financial or social risk to the innovator.[12] Rogers and Shoemaker have given numerous generalisations regarding the relationship between innovativeness and other factors, and there is only space here to list a few of the ones more relevant to the marketing of major product innovations.[13] Despite the fact that these generalisations were formed from a tremendous variety and range of empirical studies there is a remarkable consonance between the results found in the marketing area (for consumer durables and fashion items) and those found in other areas.

When stated in terms of the adopter categorisation scheme used herein the work of Rogers and Shoemaker suggests that, in comparison with later adopters, the innovators have the following characteristics. They are more educated, intelligent, rational, cosmopolitan, socially integrated and able to deal with abstractions. They are less dogmatic and fatalistic but possess greater social mobility and empathy. Further they have higher social status (and by implication higher incomes), achievement motivation, aspiration levels, and exposure to both mass media and interpersonal communication. They hold more favourable attitudes toward credit, education, risk, change and science, collect more information on the innovation and have shorter decision-making periods. In addition to these, they are more inner- than other-directed.

In a similar exercise, but one confined to the less extensive marketing literature, Robertson (1971) found support for most of the above, but only in the context of appliance innovations.

In the ten studies cited Robertson was unable to find support for the relationships with cosmopolitanism and inner-directedness, but as already mentioned the work of Donnelly (1970) and Donnelly and Ivancevich (1974) has supported the latter. Robertson also suggests an intuitively satisfying relationship between innovativeness and product category usage rate.[14] In other words heavy users of similar products are more likely to be innovators.

Robertson does not explicitly review the results for fashion items but a cursory analysis of three recent studies in the area (Baumgarten, 1974; Darden and Reynolds, 1974; Midgley, 1974) reveals support for nine of the twenty-five relationships listed thus far, namely those between innovativeness and greater social integration, social mobility and exposure to the mass media, together with more favourable attitudes to change, risk and credit, the collection of more information, shorter decision-making periods and higher product category usage rates. Neither Darden and Reynolds (1974) nor Midgley (1974) could find support for the relationship with education. Midgley also suggests that English male fashion innovators are more likely to come from the lower social classes. It should be pointed out that several of the remaining fourteen variables have yet to be studied in the field of fashion innovation.

It can be concluded that the majority of these findings, and particularly those relating to consumer durables, are consistent with the concept of the innovator developed earlier. The innovator is a competent and self-assured person, intelligent and educated enough to set his/her own standards, and to evaluate innovations against these criteria. They can comprehend the abstract implications of adopting major innovations, and furthermore have the financial resources to experiment. Above all else the innovators favour change and are willing to take risks. Thus they are inner-directed and do not need the experience, attitudes and values of others to mould their decisions for them. The fact that they receive more interpersonal and media information in no way contradicts this point of view, for the innovators assess this information against their own standards rather than let the information from others set the standards.[15] In short they innovate while the later adopters imitate.[16]

Hence it can be seen that we have a considerable degree of confidence in the research findings relating to the characteristics of the innovators of major innovations. If however we turn to minor innovations then this degree of confidence is much lower, and the picture less clear-cut. One reason for this situation is that it is necessary to rely on the relatively few studies conducted in the marketing area, for this is the only area in which such low risk, low cost innovations are encountered. Robertson (1971) was only able to find nine studies on grocery products, and to the author's knowledge there have only been two studies on similar products since these. The other reason is that the phenomenon would appear to be somewhat different, and it is not too difficult to suggest why this should be.

The adoption of a major innovation such as a consumer durable requires adequate finance, and entails considerable perceived and actual risk, whilst the adoption of a new grocery product raises no such problems. Not only is the outlay involved minimal, but if the product proves unsatisfactory then it need not be purchased again the next week, or whatever the purchase cycle is. On the other hand once a durable has been purchased the adopter may not be in the position to replace it for some considerable time. It can also be observed that durable products are often relatively very expensive in the early stages of their life cycle, until competition and increased demand lower unit costs.[17] The effect of these factors is to restrict the innovators to those who can view such risks with equanimity, that is, those individuals with higher disposable incomes. It can furthermore be noted that higher income nearly always correlates with other variables such as social status, education and so on. Therefore we might well expect that when studying low cost innovations most of the demographic and socio-economic variables would be of little relevance to the situation, and this is precisely what is found.

Out of the relationships discussed previously Robertson only found support for four in the context of grocery product innovations, these being that the innovators were more socially mobile, had more favourable attitudes to risk and change, and had higher product category usage rates.[18] Robertson also advances some support for a relationship which has not been discussed previously, but one which is of some importance. This is the relationship between innovativeness and perceived risk, in other words that innovators perceive less risk in adopting than later adopters. Perceived risk will be discussed in more detail shortly.

Two more recent studies provide support for the relationship between innovativeness and inner-directedness (Donnelly, 1970), and between innovativeness and exposure to the mass media (Summers, 1972). Both were conducted on grocery products, as well as other types of innovation in the case of Summers.

Therefore while the essential elements of the innovator (willingness to take risks, inner-directedness) are found in all situations, it can be seen that the other characteristics differ substantially between major and minor innovations. In particular the innovators for consumer durables appear to be distinct from the innovators for fashion items, who in turn are distinct from the innovators for supermarket products. However it must be stressed that this does not mean that the same individuals are always the innovators for all new appliances, for all new fashions or for all new grocery products.[19] The truth is more complex than this, and the research so far would suggest that it is better to view these three sets of characteristics as defining three groups of potential innovators, from which the actual innovators of any specific new product will emerge. Furthermore the factors which result in members of these groups of potential innovators actually innovating are connected more with the nature of the new product, and to each individual's personal situation, than their personal characteristics.

This point may be partially illustrated by looking at the research connected with the problem of whether individuals innovate across a wide field of products or not. Robertson and Myers (1969) and Summers (1971) are among the few research workers who have attempted to investigate this problem. Robertson and Myers concluded that although there was a slight tendency for individuals to innovate in closely related product categories, the evidence did not suggest the existence of generalised innovators. Using a larger sample and a greater number of product categories, Summers employed the 'list' technique to measure innovativeness with respect to 123 new products. These were divided into six categories: packaged food products; household cleansers and detergents; clothing; cosmetics; small appliances and large appliances. By comparing the observed overlap of an individual's innovativeness between various categories with that which would be expected to occur by chance alone Summers produced some interesting conclusions. Firstly, while approximately half the respondents only innovated with respect to one category there was a significant tendency for the remainder to innovate in several categories. Moreover this overlap was greatest between product categories involving similar consumer interests. That is, and in perfect agreement with previous arguments, between large and small appliances (consumer durables), between clothing and cosmetics (fashion goods), and between packaged food products and household cleansers (supermarket products).[20] Summers states that:

> The pattern of overlap (greater overlap between areas of similar interest and relatively low overlaps between small and large appliances and the other four areas) suggests that innovativeness may be a function of both situational variables, such as income and product involvement, and behavioural considerations. It may be that situational factors are unique to specific products and product categories and serve to constrain the individual's innovativeness to particular areas, while his behavioural (sociological,psychological, etc.) makeup influences his basic tendency to innovate.[21]

It can be inferred from Summers' results that many of these innovators, (whether for one or more than one product category), had only adopted a proportion of the available new products in each category.[22] Therefore not only do individuals restrict their innovativeness to certain areas, but within these areas only certain innovations are adopted by these individuals. It can be concluded that within each product category the particular new products that any innovator (as defined by a set of personal characteristics) adopts may also be dependent on situational effects.

Hence while we have profiles for the personality characteristics of the three main innovator types, in a predictive sense these profiles only inform us of which types of individuals are more likely to be the innovators of any particular new product. This is perhaps a not unexpected conclusion as it should be remembered that these profiles are generalisations from a wide and varied collection of *post hoc* studies. It would indeed be remarkable if such generalisations could be used to predict the actual behaviour of individuals toward future new products. They can, of course, be used to indicate target audiences or respondents for surveys, and this will be discussed in Part III of the book. However, to achieve more accurate predictions of actual innovative behaviour for specific products it is necessary to take into account the situational effects associated with each individual and each new product. It may seem obvious that the characteristics of the innovation should be investigated as well as those of the adopters, particularly in the light of the way the three innovator profiles were deduced, but it is only recently that attention has been focused on such aspects. Before discussing the results in this area it is first necessary to define just what is meant by the phrase 'situational effects'.

As Belk (1974) points out, the term 'situation' has a wide variety of meanings and usages in the literature. Here what have thus far been termed 'situational effects' can be separated into three distinct classes. That is individual situational effects, communication situational effects and the characteristics or attributes of the particular innovation.

The term individual situational effects merely denotes the fact that individuals encounter situations in the course of their everyday lives which have a pronounced effect on their purchase behaviour, but which could not be predicted from their personal characteristics. These situations could be a shortage of money, the need to cater for a dinner party, the breakdown of an existing product, the desire for a snack, and so on. Belk restricted his definition of situational effects to the individual case by saying that they are ' ... all those factors particular to a time and place of observation which do not follow from a knowledge of personal (intra-individual) and stimulus (choice alternative) attributes, and which have a demonstrable and systematic effect on current behaviour'.[23] At least for snack foods he was also able to show that these effects could explain quite a large percentage of observed purchase behaviour. Unfortunately this topic does not appear to have been investigated in a new product context.

Communication situational effects are those relating to the way individuals receive interpersonal information, and are perhaps more important to later adopters than innovators. They denote the fact that this information is received in a conversation or conversations, and that for the product to be discussed in this manner requires a certain type of situation. This topic will be discussed in Chapter 4, but again little work appears to have been done to date.

Therefore it is perhaps fortunate that our ways of measuring the third class of effects, that is the attributes of the innovation, take some implicit account of the first two effects. This is because we measure individuals' perception of these attributes, as will become apparent shortly.

Every new product is unique in some way, and every individual will have a unique perception of its characteristics or attributes. Therefore in investigating consumer innovativeness it is necessary to look at how individuals perceive different innovations, as well as studying the characteristics of these individuals. There are after all two sides to the story; an innovation implies innovators just as to be an innovator presupposes an innovation. Furthermore it has already been suggested that different types of innovations produce innovators with widely differing characteristics, and it might be surmised that this was in some way related to the innovators' perception of the innovations. The first question which arises is that of the nature of these perceptions, that is, what are the perceived attributes of an innovation.

Donnelly and Etzel (1973) consider that individuals primarily perceive a risk in adopting new products, and that the differences between 'genuinely' new and 'artificially' new products would be reflected in the degree of risk perceived. They also hypothesised that the perceived risk is related to the individual's category width. This category width is not to be confused with the product categories mentioned previously, and is in fact a psychological concept. Basically, a broad categoriser is an individual who 'tends to judge extreme instances of a category more distant from a central tendency value relative to the judgements of someone labelled as a narrow categorizer'.[24] In the context of new products the 'central tendency value' would be the existing products, and hence a broad categoriser would entertain wider deviations from this norm than a narrow categoriser. Essentially broad categorisers attempt to maximise their satisfaction (at the risk of adopting unsatisfactory products), while narrow categorisers attempt to minimise their dissatisfaction (at the risk of not adopting satisfactory products). Category width can be measured by a standard questionnaire. Donnelly and Etzel postulated that (i) individuals with broad category widths would be more likely to adopt genuinely new products, (ii) individuals with narrow category widths would be more likely to purchase artificially new products and (iii) individuals with medium category widths would show no particular preferences for either. Twenty new supermarket products were taken and classified into artificially (trivially) new, marginally new and genuinely new. As examples one of the artificially new products was 'lime dishwashing detergent' while one of the genuinely new products was 'frozen breakfast'. The classification was performed by independent experts. The hypotheses were substantially confirmed by the results of questioning purchasers of these products, and the authors concluded:

The results of the study seem to indicate that different groups of individuals may be 'innovators' for different products depending on the product's attributes, specifically, how similar or dissimilar the product is relative to previous offerings.[25]

This study demonstrates that individuals do perceive differences in the risks involved in adopting various new products, and that these risks are in some way related both to the 'newness' of the product, and to the personal characteristics of the person perceiving this product. Unfortunately this is all it does demonstrate, as Donnelly and Etzel do not present any findings for the personal characteristics of these individuals (other than category width) nor, more importantly, do they indicate what stage the adoption curve of each product had reached when the questionnaire was administered. It is therefore difficult to compare their research with any of the previous research in the area.[26] Hence all that has been established this far is that 'newness' and 'risk' are two possible attributes of an innovation, and it seems pertinent to question whether 'newness' is the only product dimension, or whether in fact there are several such dimensions.

Rogers and Shoemaker (1971) advance five attributes as uniqu·ly describing how an individual perceives an innovation. These are (i) relative advantage (the degree to which the new idea is perceived as better than the old), (ii) compatibility (the degree to which an innovation is perceived as being consistent with the values and needs of the consumer), (iii) complexity (the degree to which the innovation is perceived to be difficult to use), (iv) trialability (the degree to which an innovation may be experimented with on a limited basis), and (v) observability (the degree to which an innovation is visible to others).[27] It can readily be appreciated that observability relates more to later adopters, who need information on the performance of the innovation, than to innovators *per se*. It can also be seen that trialability provides one dimension with which to distinguish between major and minor innovations, in that items like consumer durables cannot always be tried on a limited basis.

'Relative advantage' appears closest to Donnelly and Etzel's 'newness' as it too measures dissimilarity to the existing products. Hence an artificially new product would have a lower relative advantage, while a genuinely new product would have a higher relative advantage.

Ostlund (1974) has specifically attempted to apply these concepts in a marketing context, and with good results. In the two studies reported he also added perceived risk to yield six attributes in all. In the first study a questionnaire designed to measure the six attributes was administered in a laboratory situation before the product in question was put on the market. Some two months after the product was launched, follow-up interviews were conducted with as many of the original respondents as could be found, with the aim of ascertaining who had purchased the product. The six attributes were then related to purchase behaviour by use of the technique of multiple discriminant analysis, and it was found that they correctly classified some 70 per cent of the innovators.[28] Ostlund also added personal characteristics to his set of predictor variables but found that these made little difference to the percentage correctly classified. However as the set of characteristics used was essentially that discussed earlier in the context of major innovations, and as Ostlund was studying low cost supermarket products, this result was hardly surprising.

The second study was conducted in similar manner but innovativeness was measured this time by recruiting a consumer panel prior to the product launch and then monitoring this panel for first purchases.[29] On this occasion the perceived innovation attributes correctly predicted 77 per cent of the eventual innovators. The relative importance of the various attributes in the discriminant function was, (ranked in order of decreasing importance), (i) relative advantage, (ii) perceived risk, (iii) complexity, (iv) compatibility, (v) observability and (vi) trialability. As the study concerned innovators the low ranking of observability was to be expected, and as the product in question was a low cost one then trialability was not a relevant concept.

It can therefore be seen that while 'risk' and 'newness' (relative advantage) are important to consumers they are not the only attributes of an innovation that they perceive. The situation is more complex, in that not only are there several such dimensions, but these dimensions 'pull' in different directions. For instance a product with a high relative advantage might also be highly complex. Since complexity is assumed to be negatively related to innovativeness, whilst relative advantage is positively related, then the individual would presumably have to form some compromise between advantage and complexity. Similarly risk is negatively related to innovativeness while compatibility, observability and trialability are positively related. A person's perceptions of an innovation could perhaps be represented as a point in some multi-dimensional perceptual or attribute space, but in the current state of knowledge such an illustration would not indicate which combinations of the various attributes represented acceptable propositions to any one individual.

What Ostlund's study does demonstrate is not only that the perception of any innovation is complex and multidimensional, but that this perception is dependent on the characteristics of the person making it as well as the actual (physical) attributes of the new product. For it can be inferred from the results that the innovators, who are characterised by their independence of mind and willingness to take risks, perceived the innovation more favourably than the rest of the sample (else why did they subsequently adopt the product). It can be postulated that if this product was successful in the market place then interpersonal communication would have caused shifts in the perceptions of the remainder, shifts which would have resulted in their subsequent adoption as well. And the determinant of success would be the innovators' perception of the product after they had used it.

The power of this approach in predicting innovativeness would therefore seem to be primarily because the measures of perception reflect both the individual's and the product's characteristics. It is known that an individual's perception of objects is dependent on personal factors; indeed many models of consumer behaviour make explicit use of this fact (Howard and Sheth, 1969; Engel, Kollat and Blackwell, 1973), and it is not difficult to speculate on the relationships between these factors and perception.[30] For instance a person's perception of the complexity of an innovation might well depend on their education and intelligence. It would obviously also depend on the nature of the innovation, and on situational effects such as information received from others, and so on. The following represent some tentative suggestions as to what the other relationships might be in the case of a major innovation.

Relative Advantage = f (product knowledge, attitude to change, product category usage rate, education, intelligence, rationality, the ability to deal with abstractions and situational effects)

Perceived Risk = f (product knowledge, attitude to risk, income, rationality and situational effects)

Complexity = f (product knowledge, product category usage rate, intelligence, education and situational effects)

Compatibility = f (product knowledge, cosmopolitanism, social integration, other-directedness, social mobility, achievement motivation and situational effects)

Observability = f (product knowledge, social integration and situational effects)

Trialability = f (product knowledge, income, ability to deal with abstractions, rationality and situational effects).

The phrase 'product knowledge' is a shorthand notation for the actual characteristics of the innovation (cost, function, etc.), as communicated to the individual by his/her own observation, and/or the mass media, and/or interpersonal communication. As such this also includes the communication situational effects, and hence the 'situational effects' noted elsewhere are solely those relating to the individual; that is they are as those defined by Belk (1974).

It should not be thought that the above are the only possible relationships. We have little knowledge in this area, and thus the ones shown are merely speculations on what seems plausible. Several variables have also been omitted for the sake of clarity.

These speculations do, however, illustrate neatly why Ostlund was able to predict the innovators of low cost new products relatively accurately. In this case it would be expected that the majority of the variables listed above would no longer be relevant, and that the relationships would simplify to something along the following lines:

Relative Advantage = f (product knowledge, attitude to change, product category usage rate, and situational effects)
Perceived Risk = f (product knowledge, attitude to risk and situational effects)
Complexity = f (product knowledge, product category usage rate and situational effects)
Compatibility = f (product knowledge, other-directedness, social mobility and situational effects)
Observability = f (product knowledge and situational effects)
Trialability = f (product knowledge and situational effects)

Furthermore for innovators the attributes observability and trialability would be of little importance.

By measuring the left hand sides of these expressions Ostlund has essentially measured the effects of personal characteristics, the product's attributes and the situational effects (at this point in time). If he had only measured personal characteristics, as in earlier methods, the other two effects would have been ignored and the predictions considerably less accurate. Therefore Ostlund was theoretically as well as empirically justified in concluding that 'perceptions of innovations by potential adopters can be very effective predictors of innovativeness'.[31] Given then that this perceived attribute approach appears to hold forth great promise, then at least two areas of further research suggest themselves.

First, attempts should be made to link perceptions of innovations to personal characteristics, and preferably over as wide a range of products as possible. Not only would this provide clearer insights into the whole process of adoption, but it would hopefully also provide support for the preceding arguments. If this was the case, and it seems likely, then more accurate predictions could be obtained from questioning potential adopters alone rather than a representative sample of the population as a whole, these potential adopters being identified on the basis of their personal characteristics. It does after all seem rather pointless to ask potential laggards for their perception of a product which is about to be launched, as the answers will neither be favourable nor meaningful. Furthermore if sufficient innovations can be studied in this manner then it may eventually be possible to link perceptions to levels of success or failure, and hence provide more rigorous product development procedures.

Second, it would be of great interest if the perceptions of individuals could be monitored over time, and the observed shifts in perception associated with communication and influence. It is to be expected that once a person adopts then product knowledge is replaced by product experience and his/her perception alters (favourably or unfavourably). This perception will be communicated to others, and persuade them for or against the innovation. By simultaneously observing the perceptions or attitudes of adopters and non-adopters at any point in time, a greater understanding of how individuals are persuaded to adopt could be gained.[32]

In conclusion it should also be pointed out that not all of the problems discussed above will be of major concern to the practising manager. It will be argued in Part III that such a person should build on the basic framework described here by developing his own set of criteria for predicting innovativeness. It is unfortunate that the innovators for different categories of products have different characteristics, but this is a fact which must be accepted. Nor does this cast any doubt on the validity or usefulness of diffusion theory; the crux of the matter is that the innovators of any new product are different from the rest of the adopting population, and must be treated as such.

3.5 Communication and the Innovators

It has already been stated that the innovators perform a vital role in the diffusion of an innovation in that they effectively test the new product, and it is on the basis of their findings that other individuals adopt or not. The innovators' initial perception of the product is modified by their experience of its actual performance, and it is this perception, favourable or unfavourable, which is relayed to others via interpersonal communication. However at this point it is necessary to demonstrate that we have some proof for this assertion, and once again the first study to be cited is that of Bell (1963).

As well as studying the characteristics of the innovators Bell also assessed the various information flows between these innovators and other individuals. He was able to demonstrate that the innovators directly influenced the behaviour of others, and concluded:

> Over 65 per cent of the innovators were asked for opinions of their products. Almost half the innovators were asked by friends and neighbours to see the innovistic product. Of the innovators who gave opinions or demonstrated the products, 68 per cent asserted that their questioning friends then purchased the innovation.[33]

Similar findings have been documented by Lazer and Bell (1966), and Engel, Kegerreis and Blackwell (1969). However most research in the area is conducted in the context of attempting to assess the degree to which innovators are also opinion leaders. The concept of opinion leadership will be developed in greater detail in Chapter 4 but basically it means, as Summers (1971) says, 'one who exerts disproportionate influence on others through interpersonal influence'.[34] Hence if a reasonable proportion of the innovators are also opinion leaders, and these individuals report favourably on their experience with the product, then further adoption is ensured.

Both within and without marketing, relationships between innovativeness and opinion leadership have been detected. The appropriate generalisation from Rogers and Shoemaker (1971) is: 'Earlier adopters have a higher degree of opinion leadership than later adopters.'[35]

Summers (1971) has conducted perhaps the most extensive investigation on this topic to be found within the current marketing literature. By measuring both innovativeness and opinion leadership for 972 individuals he was able to compute the actual overlap between the two, and compare this with that which might be expected as the result of chance alone. Furthermore these statistics were computed by product category, enabling comparisons between consumer durables, fashion goods and supermarket goods. Although Summers concluded that the actual overlaps were only slightly greater than would be expected, the results relevant to this discussion were that between approximately 26 per cent and 52 per cent of the product category innovators were also opinion leaders, (the lower figure being for small appliances and the higher for women's fashions).[36]

Summers apparently took this to mean that the relationship between opinion leadership and innovativeness was not significant (since for five product categories less than half the innovators were also opinion leaders.) Statistically this may or may not be the case, but in terms of their significance to the adoption process his figures prove exactly the opposite. This can quite easily be shown by manipulating the data Summers presents. The 'worst' case was for the small appliance product category where 14.8 per cent of his sample were innovators, 23.8 per cent opinion leaders and 3.8 per cent both innovators and opinion leaders. Hence 3.8 of 14.8 equals approximately 26 per cent of the innovators were opinion leaders. However suppose that each of these innovative opinion leaders persuaded one other person to adopt, then immediately the number of adopters would rise to 14.8 plus 3.8, that is 18.6 per cent of the population. If they each persuaded two other individuals to adopt then the total would rise to 22.4 per cent, and so on. In other words it is only necessary for a certain proportion of the innovators to also exert interpersonal influence in order for the diffusion effect to begin to operate, and the innovation to diffuse throughout the rest of society.[37]

As confirmation for some of the above results Midgley (1974), found that 30 per cent of his male fashion innovators were also opinion leaders, while Baumgarten (1974) reports 42 per cent for male and 31 per cent for female clothing. Baumgarten also suggests that future research might be better concentrated on these 'change agents', that is individuals who are both innovators and opinion leaders. However, this topic will not be pursued until later in Chapter 4, when a deeper understanding of the nature of interpersonal communication and opinion leadership will be provided.

Therefore it can be concluded at this point that there is little doubt as to the crucial role of the innovators. They test the innovation (whether it be major or minor), and depending on their comments as to its performance other individuals will be persuaded to adopt or not.

The final topic to be touched on in this chapter is that of where the innovators obtain their information on the innovation. Obviously, given the crucial role of the innovators, the topic of some importance to the new product manager is the question of it being possible to contact the innovators, and thereby influence them in favour of the new product. This discussion will also serve to clarify further the distinction made earlier between communicated experience, mass media information and general interpersonal information.

In the context of major innovations three generalisations were quoted in Section 3.4 that are relevant to the topic under discussion. They were that the innovators were (i) more exposed to mass media communication, (ii) more exposed to interpersonal communication and (iii) collected more information about the innovation. In the marketing area Bell (1963), found that over one third of the innovators of consumer durable products received information about the innovation from their friends. He also noted that most innovators had a substantial exposure to the mass media, particularly the printed media.

In the context of minor innovations only one of the above has been well supported to date, this being exposure to mass media communication. Summers (1972), using data from the study cited previously, found that the innovators of new products in six product categories were 'disproportionately more exposed to the mass media than non-innovators'.[38] However he also notes that this exposure was selective in that the innovators were more exposed to media with a content relevant to the product category. That is women's fashion innovators were more exposed to fashion magazines, appliance innovators more exposed to consumer information magazines, and all innovators (since his subjects were female), were more exposed to home magazines than non-innovators. Television and radio were found not to be particularly effective in contacting innovators.

A recent experimental study by Berning and Jacoby (1974) has also indicated that support may eventually be forthcoming for the other two generalisations in the context of supermarket products. Basically these researchers set up a mini-supermarket in a laboratory setting and represented sources of information by various printed cards. Respondents were then asked to make a purchase in each product category, and instructed to do so by following exactly the same procedure as they would normally use in the real world. The product categories were cake mixes, frozen vegetables, electric toasters, spray deodorants and lipsticks. Each contained both established products and one new product. To summarise the results, Berning and Jacoby found that innovators sought more information, primarily from 'friends'. While this is consistent with previous statements such studies would obviously have to be conducted in a more realistic setting before great reliance could be placed on these findings. However these authors did make the interesting comment that:

> The notion that innovators (by definition, the first to try new products) would seek information from other people may appear nonsensical at first. However, opinion leaders need not necessarily be innovators; they can be valid and knowledgeable sources of information for others including innovators, even though they never try the

product themselves.[39]

Which is almost, but not quite, the point made earlier when a distinction was drawn between communicated experience and information in general. The innovators do need information on the new product, and this they actively seek from the mass media and from their friends (who need not be opinion leaders). However this information is more 'factual', and is evaluated against the innovator's own internal standards. What they do not need is the reassurance of knowing that one of their friends has tried the product and found it satisfactory. Indeed it is unlikely that any of their friends or other social contacts will have tried the product. If, say, 10 per cent of the population had adopted then the chances are only one in ten that any of their social contacts would have already adopted the product (there being no evidence to suggest that innovators are members of the same clique). Thus this phenomenon relates more to the spread of knowledge and awareness about the innovation, which it will be remembered from Chapter 2 spreads ahead of actual adoption. However while both innovators and later adopters will become aware of the innovation in this manner the difference between them is that the innovators will, as it were, adopt on trust, while the later adopters will only adopt when they know some of their peers have already done so. Therefore, and as before, the innovators need little or no communicated experience.

3.6 Summary

This chapter has been concerned with illustrating both that a group or category of individuals known as innovators possess different personal characteristics to the rest of the population, and that these innovators have a profound effect on the future course of the innovation.

It was suggested that innovativeness is a trait possessed, to a greater or lesser degree, by all members of society, and that a clear distinction must be made between the ways this trait is measured, and its actual meaning. Measurement was shown to relate to when an individual adopted the innovation in comparison with other individuals, the comparison being effected by use of the mean and standard deviation of the adopter distribution. Hence the basis of the measurement is time, and various methods for determining time of adoption were discussed.

However in order to obtain a deeper understanding of the meaning of innovativeness, the temporal adopter distribution was transformed into the population distribution of the (innovation-specific) trait. From this latter distribution, innovativeness was defined as the degree to which an individual makes innovation decisions independently of the communicated experience of others. A distinction was then made between communicated experience and information (mass media and interpersonal) in general. Communicated experience is the perception of, or attitude toward, the innovation held by an individual who has adopted it, as expressed in interpersonal communication with a person who is as yet undecided. Innovators need little or none of this experience, while less innovative members of society need the reassurance of knowing that people like themselves find the innovation satisfactory.

The personal characteristics of these innovators were then examined at length, and it was concluded that the generalisations quoted by Rogers and Shoemaker (1971) were only applicable to major innovations. The innovators of fashion goods and supermarket products had distinct and different characteristics. However some characteristics were common to all innovators, namely the willingness to take risks, a favourable attitude toward change and inner-directedness.

It was stressed that while the characteristics of the three broad innovator types are known from *post hoc* studies, this does not mean that the same individuals will always be the innovators for future new products introduced into their respective product categories. Rather it was argued that these profiles should be thought of as indicating the potential innovators of a specific new product. Which members of these potential innovator groups actually innovate for a specific product is dependent more on situational effects than personal characteristics.

These effects were divided into individual situational effects, communication situational effects and, more obviously, the attributes of the innovation. While it was admitted that little was known about the first two effects, it was also pointed out that by measuring the perceived attributes of an innovation some account could be taken of them.

Lastly it was shown that the innovators communicated their experience of the product to other individuals, and hence formed a vital stage in the diffusion process. If the innovators find the product satisfactory, its chances of success are heightened; if they do not, then its failure is ensured.

In conclusion the innovators are different, and are more willing both to take risks and perhaps to be persuaded to try the product by the appropriate mass media. However if on trying the product it is found not to meet their needs, then the experience the innovators communicate will be unfavourable, and the less innovative members of society will not obtain the personal reassurance they require in order to adopt the product.

Notes

1.
$$m = \sum_{i=1}^{n} t_i/n \qquad \text{and} \qquad s^2 = \sum_{i=1}^{n} (t_i - m)^2/n$$

2. Rather than the usual statistical practice, which would be to let $I = t - m/s$ and would produce negative values for high innovativeness scores. It will also be noted that the measurement of innovativeness has been operationally defined without making any assumptions as to the shape or type of the adopter distribution. The case of the normal distribution will be discussed shortly but it is important to point out that it is not necessary to assume a particular distribution in order to compute a standardised measure of innovativeness.

3. That is that the rankings can be assumed to be interval data rather than ordinal. As Martilla and Carvey (1975) point out we are often forced into such assumptions by practical considerations. The technique of non-metric multidimensional scaling may eventually provide a solution to this problem (see Green and Tull, 1970).

4. Rogers and Shoemaker (1971), p.27.

5. Robertson (1971), p.85.

6. Robertson (1971), p.87.

7. The sum of the squared deviations about the group means.

8. Petersen (1973), p.327.

9. Uhl *et al* (1970), p.53.

10. Uhl *et al* (1970), p.54.

11. Donnelly (1970), p.11.

12. It will be argued later that what is important is consumer perception of how 'new' or 'major' the innovation is. However we do not appear to have any studies of major innovations in supermarket products and are therefore unable to assess whether these should be included with consumer durables etc. or not.

13. Rogers and Shoemaker (1971), pp.346-85.

14. Robertson (1971), p.102.

15. Furthermore as pointed out earlier this is 'general' information, and not 'communicated experience'. In other words the innovators do not need the reassurance of knowing that members of their social circle have adopted the innovation and found it satisfactory.

16. The relationships with age and opinion leadership have been omitted from this discussion. Robertson (1971) found no significant relationships between age and innovativeness while Rogers and Shoemaker (1971) report contradictory findings. The tendency, as far as new products are concerned, is for younger innovators but this may well depend on the type of innovation. The relationship between opinion leadership and innovativeness is discussed in the next section.

17. As one instance, the average price of 'cheap' colour television sets in the USA fell from \$500 in 1960 to \$300 in 1965 (no allowance for inflation). In 1954 when television was introduced the price of a set was \$900. Source: Ingman (1968).

18. Based on Robertson (1971), p.103.

19. This being a common but perhaps understandable misconception. If the same individuals were innovators for all products then there would be no new product marketing problems!
20. As further confirmation of previous statements it can be noted that Summers found only a small overlap between durable and non-durable products. A phenomenon which he, like the author, ascribes to income constraints. Summers observes that the appliance innovators had higher average incomes.
21. Summers (1971), p.316.
22. Summers (1971), in particular n.2, p.314.
23. Belk (1974), p.157.
24. Donnelly and Etzel (1973), p.296.
25. Donnelly and Etzel (1973), p.299.
26. If for instance the various products were at different stages then the 'innovators' cited would comprise different percentages of the population.
27. Rogers and Shoemaker (1971), pp.134-57.
28. Multiple discriminant analysis is a technique designed to determine which variables best discriminate between two dichotomous groups of individuals (in this case innovators and non-innovators). The discriminant function (that is the weighted set of variables which best discriminate) is normally developed on part of the sample (independent variables and purchase behaviour) and then used to classify the remainder of the sample into respective groups. Obviously a comparison between this classification and actual behaviour gives some indication of how well these variables explain the phenomenon in question (innovativeness). Extensions of the technique to more than two groups exist and an excellent review can be found in Green and Tull (1970).
29. Innovators were defined as those who purchased in the first three months. It can be seen that this provides a better measure than, say, that used by Donnelly and Etzel. However it still does not indicate what stage the adoption process was in, and hence as with Donnelly and Etzel makes it difficult to compare these 'innovators' with those defined earlier.
30. Interestingly enough the revised version of the Howard and Sheth model (Lehmann *et al*, 1974) shows 'innovativeness' directly affecting 'perceptual bias'.
31. Ostlund (1974), p.28.
32. The dynamic behaviour of the perceptions or attitudes for or against a new product are also the basis for a model of the diffusion process due to Midgley (1976). This model will be discussed in Chapter 5.
33. Bell (1963), p.93.
34. Summers (1971), p.313.
35. Rogers and Shoemaker (1971), p.375.
36. These and subsequent figures are based on Summers (1971), Table 1.
37. Indeed it is probably necessary that only a proportion of the innovators be opinion leaders, otherwise the diffusion process might be explosive! It should also be noted that just because the other fraction are not opinion leaders, in no way does this imply that they do not talk to, and thereby influence, other individuals. It merely implies that they do this on a smaller scale.
38. Summers (1972), p.45.
39. Berning and Jacoby (1974), p.21.

4 COMMUNICATION AND INFLUENCE

4.1 Opinion Change and Communication

In this chapter the discussion will centre around the key social process, that is around interpersonal communication and influence, and in particular the communication of experiences with the innovation in question. Initially the discussion will be at a general level, referring to the majority of the population rather than any one of its sub-groups. The aim is, then, to support the arguments presented in Chapter 2, and to further develop an understanding of interpersonal communication. Later sections of the chapter will relate this understanding of the process to the schema for the diffusion of innovations.

The first problem to be addressed is that of whether verbal communication can actually affect people's opinions, attitudes and behaviour. Now in many ways substantial evidence for this assertion was provided in Chapter 2, at both a theoretical and empirical level. It will be remembered that the conclusion reached was that a significant role for interpersonal communication was necessary in order to account for the observed shape of the adoption curves. Therefore in this section only complementary evidence will be cited, that is evidence gained by different, and independent, methodologies. In the main, studies from the field of marketing will be utilised, since it is an unfortunate fact that, for instance, communication researchers have concentrated on printed rather than verbal messages, and on artificial laboratory situations rather than the real world. Only a few relevant studies are to be found in the areas of communication and social psychology. Furthermore, whatever the academic origin of these studies, they have also tended to be conducted at one point in time, and therefore present a static picture of what is after all a dynamic process. This is perhaps the most damaging criticism of all, and one which will be raised again later in this chapter, and in Chapter 5.[1] We now turn to the evidence.

The first work to be examined is a comparatively old one, yet in some aspects it has not been surpassed to this day. This study is that due to Whyte, and was conducted in 1954. Whyte investigated the 'Web of Word of Mouth', 'word of mouth' or 'word of mouth advertising' being the terms used to denote interpersonal communication in the marketing literature. The methodology employed was unique and extremely powerful, although its efficiency rested upon the characteristics of the innovation in question, which was air-conditioning. Air-conditioning is a highly visible product requiring a 'box' attached to the owner's house, and Whyte put this visibility to good use by taking aerial photographs of several Philadelphia suburbs. The suburbs chosen were all homogeneous, that is, they contained very similar residents — mostly middle income white collar couples living in identical houses. The argument advanced, in the form of a null hypothesis, was that since all the residents were similar then conditioners ought to be equally or randomly distributed amongst the residents. In fact they were not, and an examination of the photographs revealed clearly discernible clusters of houses with conditioners. Why had these clusters formed, if all the residents had the same incomes, attitudes and life styles? By interviewing the owners of air-conditioners Whyte was able to conclude that the reason was a powerful network of interpersonal communication. Effectively, most people bought because they had discussed the product with a neighbour who already had one. The conversation 'tipped the balance' in favour of the innovation, and other factors such as price, advertising, sales promotion and even hot weather had only been of secondary relevance to the purchase decision (for instance most conditioners were bought in relatively 'cold' months).

This communication network was responsible for the 'contagious' growth of clusters of houses with air-conditioners, and from the photographs it was even possible to suggest which ways communications flowed between residents, a suggestion subsequently confirmed by interview research.

This is the first concrete and independent evidence for the fact that interpersonal communication can change behaviour (independent, that is, of the evidence given in Chapter 2). Since 1954 many other studies have been conducted on this topic, although it must be admitted that none have used as powerful a methodology. However before going on to consider later studies it is worth mentioning two other points relating to Whyte's work.

First, it has been suggested (Corkindale, Kennedy, Henry and Wills, 1974), that this and other early studies are no longer relevant to modern conditions. Shortly evidence will be presented to show that such speculations are essentially incorrect; what is more interesting is that one reason Whyte gives for initiating his work was that researchers in the 1950s were suggesting that word of mouth was not as powerful a force as it had been in the 1930s! More importantly the rationale Whyte puts forward for his conclusions is that increasing standards of living are presenting consumers with an increasing variety of choice, and therefore the need for independent advice is also increasing rather than decreasing. Interpersonal communication is perhaps the most prominent form of 'objective' opinion (that is, independent of the manufacturer), and it is therefore only natural that consumers should still be utilising it.[2] More recent models of consumer behaviour also explicitly recognise this need for, and search for, information on the product (Engel, Kollet and Blackwell, 1973; Hansen, 1974).

Second, Whyte also makes the point that trends in manufacturing and retailing are divorcing managers from the market place, and therefore from an understanding of word of mouth. This point is still of great, if not greater, import today.

Considerable space has been devoted to the above study, not only because it is unique and fascinating, but also because it highlights the major points relating to interpersonal communication — that is, it involves consumers talking to each other and thereby assisting potential purchasers in their decision processes.

Since 1954 there have been several other studies within the marketing tradition and at this point it is pertinent to mention some of them.

Arndt (1967a), for instance, indicates how exposure to favourable comments aided the acceptance of a new coffee product. He also notes that the main flow of information for this product was between would-be buyers. Engel, Blackwell and Kegerreis (1969) stress how word of mouth played a key role in the adoption of an automobile diagnostic centre, while Sheth (1971) discusses the role of interpersonal communication in the diffusion of stainless steel razor blades. This last work is worth considering in slightly more detail because while it may be obvious that interpersonal communication should be important for high cost, and therefore high risk, products, it is not so immediately obvious that it should be important in the purchase of a low risk product such as a razor blade.

Sheth explicitly set out to test the hypothesis that interpersonal communication was important in low risk innovations, having reviewed the literature and concluded that its importance for high risk products was well established. A total of 601 users of razor blades were interviewed and it was found that 36 per cent were made aware of the innovation by a personal source of information. More importantly, 48 per cent stated that they were influenced to adopt by such discussions, and 18 per cent indicated that they subsequently influenced someone else to adopt.

In other words despite the low cost nature of the product almost half the sample were influenced to purchase by discussions with another person, a fairly convincing demonstration of the power of interpersonal influence even in such situations.

Arndt (1967b) has reviewed the literature on interpersonal communication in the marketing area, and reached the following, wide-ranging conclusions:

> Still, word of mouth emerges as one of the most important, if not 'the' most importance source of information for the consumer. Word of mouth may both accelerate and slow up product acceptance, depending on factors like content of messages and group norms toward innovations ...

> The strength of word of mouth may be explained in terms of compliance and surveillance resulting from interpersonal relationships. A factor of at least equal importance is the unique characteristics of word of mouth which make this source particularly helpful to consumers involved in solving purchasing problems.[3]

Thus the argument given in Chapter 2 and that presented above lead to the same conclusion: that interpersonal communication is the key to the diffusion of innovations, and such a conclusion should cause little surprise. Man after all has evolved speech as a way of communicating with, and affecting the behaviour of, other members of his species. The question which now needs to be resolved is just how effective is interpersonal communication, and especially in relation to those communication techniques which the marketing manager can control — the mass media.

4.2 Interpersonal and Mass Media Communication

Thus far all that has been established in this chapter is some further evidence that interpersonal communication affects the behaviour of individuals. However it will be readily appreciated that to focus on interpersonal communication alone would be to take a somewhat limited and shortsighted view of the social processes. As indicated previously it is necessary to take some account of mass media communication and, it will be remembered, this form of communication was conceptualised as an external input to the social system. An input which assisted (but was not solely responsible for) the increase in aggregate knowledge of the innovation in question (Chapter 2). At this point it therefore becomes necessary to determine just what evidence there is for this point of view; in other words to investigate the role and impact of the mass media versus interpersonal communication. That is to develop the picture further, indicate the relative impact these two forms of communication have on individuals exposed to them, and assess whether they play similar or different parts in the social and cognitive processes.

In doing so an important distinction should be held in mind, the distinction between the type of message disseminated by these two communication 'channels'. Namely that interpersonal communication is communicated experience as defined earlier; that is the expressed opinions on, or perceptions of, the new product as held by the adopters of it. The mass media message is the perception of the product the manufacturer wishes to put before the individual. These two perceptions may be congruent, on the other hand they may be widely divergent, and any such discrepancy will affect the course of the innovation.

With this in mind the discussion begins by assessing the relative effectiveness of these two channels, and in making this assessment the first study of any note is that of Katz and Lazarsfeld (1955), the famous Decatur study.[4] This research was in fact a wide ranging programme, enquiring into the sources of influence on individuals in many different situations. However within the programme a study was also made on the effectiveness of various communication channels in persuading individuals to switch from their existing brand to some other one.[5] The items investigated were all of a low risk nature, that is soaps, cleansers, convenience foods, etc. Basically Katz and Lazarsfeld asked questions to ascertain which communication channels individuals had been exposed to, and whether the individuals concerned thought the information conveyed to them by a particular channel had been the most important factor in their decision (termed effective exposure), one of several factors in their decision (contributory exposure), or something they were only aware of (ineffective exposure). Their results are presented in Figure 4.1.

Within Figure 4.1. it can be seen that personal contacts (that is interpersonal communication) produced the greatest number of effectively exposed individuals (14.5 per cent) and therefore had the highest index of effectiveness. This latter being the ratio of effective exposure to total exposure for the channel in question (where total exposure is the sum of ineffective, contributory and effective exposure for that channel).

While representing a significant contribution, this particular study is by now fairly outdated, and it is therefore fortunate that a later study

Fig. 4.1: The Relative Effectiveness of Communication Channels (Supermarket Products) 1955

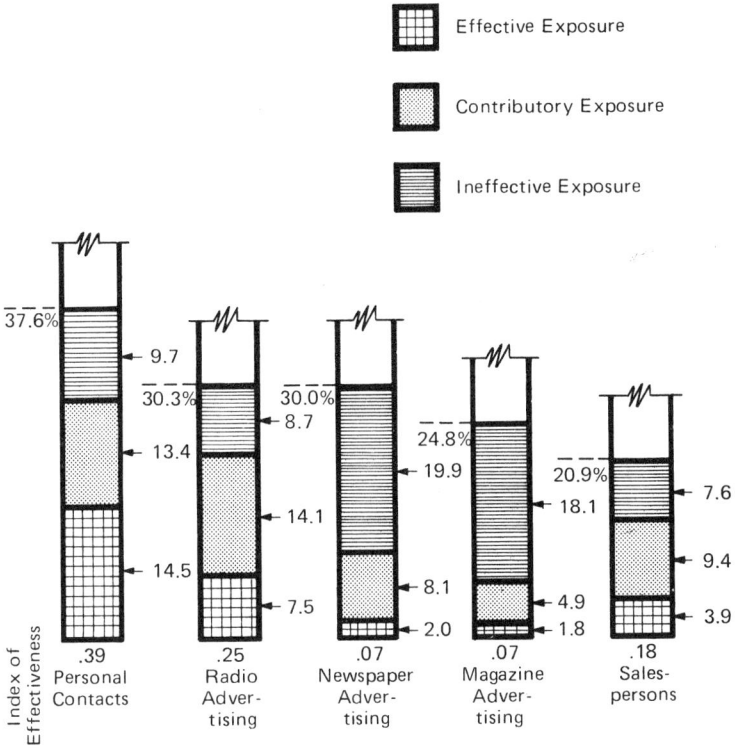

Source: Katz and Lazarsfeld (1955), p.176 and used by permission of the Free Press.

exists which is broadly similar. More importantly this work, by Haines (1966), was conducted with reference to new products. Effectively Haines repeated the Decatur study with the aim of assessing whether the situation had changed between 1955 and 1966, and also, of course, of assessing the relative effectiveness of the various channels used as of 1966. While he used a slightly different methodology, and presents the results in a different manner, there is sufficient similarity to allow comparisons. The findings are presented in Figure 4.2.

Fig 4.2.: The Relative Effectiveness of Communication Channels (Supermarket Products) 1966

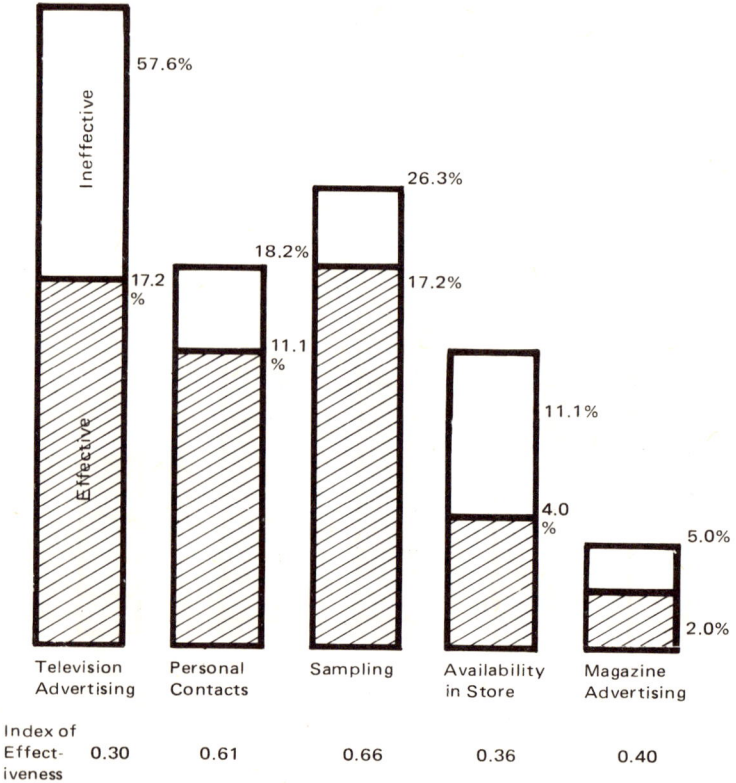

Source: G.H. Haines (1966), p.689, and used by permission of the American Marketing Association.

As might be expected, in this eleven year period some significant, and perhaps obvious, changes had occurred. Firstly television had emerged as a potent force for generating both awareness and changes in behaviour, although its index of effectiveness was the lowest of the five channels reported. Secondly the marketing technique of sampling (free samples, etc.) had emerged as the most effective 'channel' — which is not surprising given that this study too was concerned with low risk supermarket items. It can be noted, however, that interpersonal communication comes a very close second to sampling in terms of relative effectiveness.

Thus the growth of television, supermarket merchandising and mass marketing techniques has altered the picture considerably. However at this point it is worth raising the question of whether the above is an adequate picture, in other words does it accurately portray the market situation. It can be argued that it does not, and for the following reasons.

It can easily be seen that both the Katz and Lazarsfeld and the Haines studies represent aggregative views of the situation. That is aggregative not only in terms of summing over a group of individuals, but also over a group of (widely) different products. In the Haines study in particular, which dealt with new products, it can be seen that the effects of a set of different 'messages' have been grouped together. Remembering then that interpersonal communication in the context of an innovation is 'communicated experience' it can be argued that such pictures are altogether too simplistic. For one instance of the possibility of such differing messages in the above scheme it is necessary to assume that all the personal communications for all the products were uniformly and equally favourable (or conversely all unfavourable). If one product in the set was deficient in the eyes of the consumers then the interpersonal messages would be unfavourable to this product, further adoptions relatively few, and the 'effectiveness' of this channel correspondingly low. 'Effectiveness' as defined in both studies hinges on a favourable decision, that is purchase. Interpersonal communication could conceivably be working against purchase extremely effectively and efficiently, and yet be given a low 'index of effectiveness'. Unless, that is, we assume unfavourable influence creates purchasers! Thus by aggregating different products together several quite disparate communication situations may have been obscured. Note also that the mixed situation (simultaneous favourable and unfavourable influence) has not been discussed.

Thus for interpersonal communication it is not possible to separate the message from the perceived characteristics of the innovation, and such generalisations as presented above only have limited value. The matter of unfavourable versus favourable messages, a vital and relatively neglected topic, will be taken up in more detail in the next section. It is sufficient for the moment to indicate the difficulties.

Further while it can be assumed, for the present at least, that the mass media messages were 'favourable', in no way does either study take account of the objectives of those responsible for such messages. Were the aims of the advertising campaigns to persuade or make aware, and were they fixed over the launch period or did these aims, and therefore the message content, change over time? All of which would have a significant effect on the persuasive impact of the media campaign as measured in the above way.

This last point, of change over time, also raises a new set of problems with respect to both the interpersonal and mass media communication processes, although fortunately they are problems which in some way can be resolved. The studies presented so far in this section have been static in conception and execution, that is they give a cross-sectional rather than longitudinal view of the communication process. Since the whole thrust of the book so far is that the processes are dynamic, the adequacy of a static viewpoint is immediately called into question. Indeed the fact that the communication processes are dynamic has already been demonstrated in earlier chapters, where it was also indicated that different channels were more or less important at different stages in the individual's cognitive processes. At this point we can seek to broaden the scope of this section, and to resolve some of the problems raised by the static research studies, by examining the evidence relating to the operation of the communication processes over time.

In fact Katz and Lazarsfeld (1955) themselves initiated the resolution of such problems by asking their Decatur respondents to report the sequence in which they were exposed to each source of influence (communication channel). Undoubtedly this was too crude a method-ology; as they themselves note respondents often cannot remember such facts, and the results were not clear cut, serving mainly to highlight the research difficulties. However they did find that different channels appeared to be used for information at different stages in the decision process, and that this sequence might depend on the characteristics of the individual concerned.

Several other and more recent studies have been conducted in this area, and moreover these are studies specifically focusing on influence processes in the diffusion of innovations rather than influence processes in general.

Arndt in his review of the literature concluded that:

When the purchasing decision is broken down into sequential stages, the mass media have been found to dominate in the awareness stage, while word of mouth is the most frequently used source at the evaluation stage.[6]

Rather than cite all the relevant articles, and as before, we need look no further for support for the case advanced than Rogers and Shoemaker's exhaustive list of empirical generalisations. The ones pertaining to this discussion being:

> Mass media channels are relatively more important at the knowledge function and interpersonal channels are relatively more important at the persuasion function in the innovation-decision process.[7]

and

> Mass media channels are relatively more important than interpersonal channels for earlier than for later adopters.[8,9]

Taking the first generalisation it can be seen that this relates to the individual level cognitive process of knowledge→ persuasion→ decision→ confirmation, and suggests that the mass media are more important/ effective in the early stages of the sequence. On the other hand interpersonal communication is more important at the key persuasion stage, where the individual makes up his/her mind to adopt or not to adopt the innovation. This generalisation also implies that for most individuals, and in order for adoption to occur, exposure to both mass media *and* interpersonal messages is necessary.

The second generalisation bears a close relationship to the view of innovativeness advanced here, that is 'innovativeness is the degree to which an individual makes innovation decisions independently of the communicated experience of others' (p.49). We would therefore expect that highly innovative individuals − earlier adopters − would place less reliance on interpersonal channels, and together with the first generalisation above this suggests that the earlier adopters are exposed to the mass media at the knowledge stage, and are relatively unexposed to either at the persuasion stage. That is they make the decision independently.[10] The relationship between various forms of communication and the earlier adopters, or innovators as defined herein, has been discussed in detail in Chapter 3. The only pertinent point to repeat here is that of the distinction between the type of messages which innovators receive, that is general communications about the product rather than the specific product performance messages or 'communicated experience' that later adopters receive.

To summarise thus far, it can be seen that not only do the different communication channels have varying impacts on their total audience, but these impacts vary according to which stage in the cognitive process a particular individual has reached. Furthermore the reliance individuals place on each channel at each stage in the sequence will depend on how innovative each individual is. A picture of apparent simplicity has been replaced by a complex reality.

In the main these findings are supported by those emerging from social psychology and communication research. However before discussing these aspects a note of caution should be sounded. The generalisations listed above were culled primarily from the non-marketing literature and therefore, as was mentioned before in the context of the characteristics of innovators, might only apply to *major* innovations such as consumer durables. As far as the sequential influences of various channels in the diffusion of fashion items or low risk supermarket products are concerned, there would appear to have been very little research conducted.

Katz and Lazarsfeld (1955), present overall effectiveness indices for fashion items, and as shown in Figure 4.3 these demonstrate that a different mixture of channels is used by individuals in this situation as opposed to supermarket products. In a new fashion context both Midgley (1974) and Baumgarten (1974) suggest that visual and verbal influences still have considerable importance today. However none of these studies tell us anything about whether the mass media is used more frequently at the knowledge stage, and interpersonal at the evaluation stage, or indeed where visual influence fits into the process.

Similarly for low risk new products there is a dearth of useful information in the literature. Of the few people to have mentioned the problem, the work of Sheth (1971) suggests that some individuals adopted on becoming aware of the innovation from the mass media and did not utilise interpersonal communication. Others passed through the same sequence as for major innovations, that is became aware from the mass media (and other impersonal sources), and were persuaded to adopt by interpersonal communications. Yet again other individuals became aware from personal contacts, and were persuaded to adopt by these contacts. Sheth's findings are presented in Figure 4.4.

One study is insufficient to deduce any firm conclusions, but low risk products would appear to fit into the schema advanced, with the exception that the mass media may, for some individuals, have a relatively greater impact at the persuasion stage in the cognitive process.

Fig. 4.3: Relative Effectiveness of Communication Channels (Fashion Items)

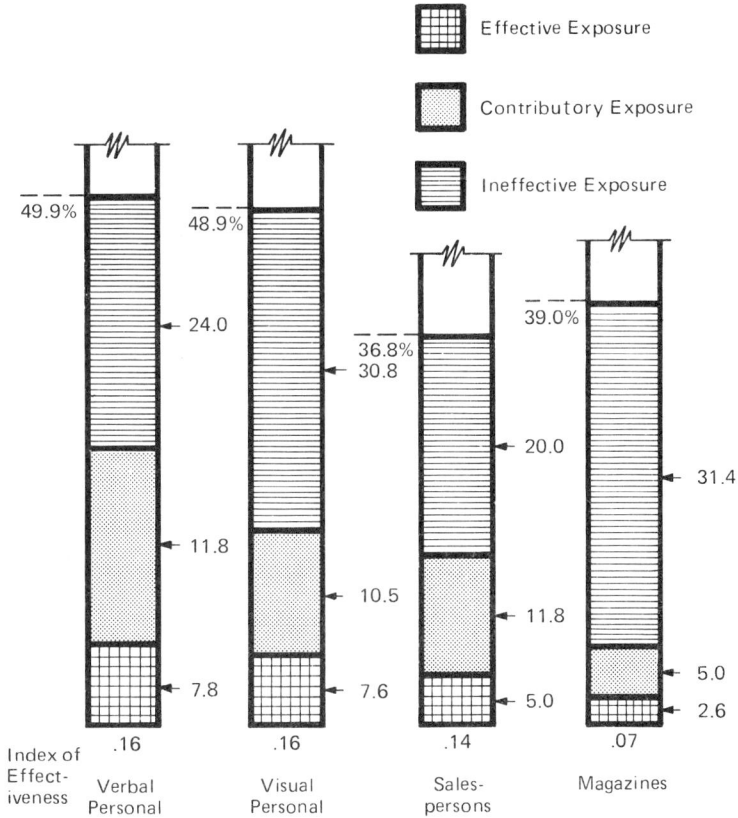

Source: Katz and Lazarsfeld (1955), p.181, and used by permission of the
Free Press.

This would seem to be a consequence of the fact that proportionately
more people are potential innovators of low risk products than of, say,
major innovations (see the arguments given in Chapter 3). Thus the key
factor in both the sequence and impact of the various channels on

Fig. 4.4: A Tree Diagram Representing the Importance of Word-of-Mouth In Diffusion of Stainless Steel Blades

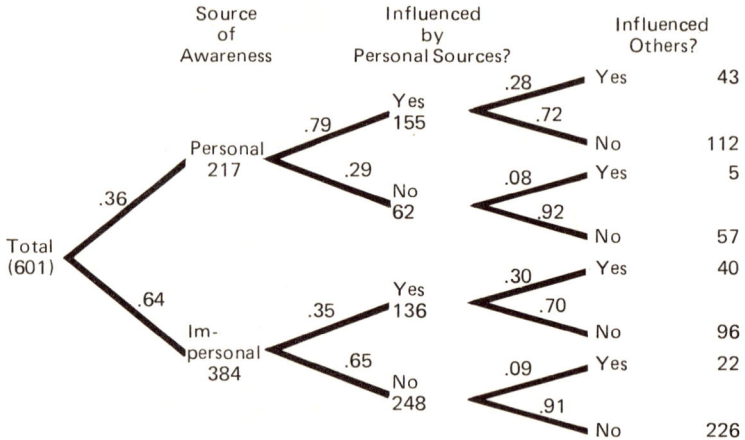

Source: Sheth (1971), p.18, and used by permission of the Journal of
    Advertising Research.

particular individuals would appear to be how innovative that individual is with respect to the innovation concerned.

The important role of mediating factors is something which has also emerged from the field of communication research. Klapper (1960) summarises the relevant research in the form of a generalisation:

> Mass communication 'ordinarily' does not serve as a necessary and sufficient cause of audience effects, but rather functions among and through a nexus of mediating factors ... and influences.[11]

In the case of new products the chief mediating factor is the innovativeness of the individual, which for the later adopters is in turn dependent on such things as situational effects.

Lastly the relatively greater importance of interpersonal communication at the persuasion stage, and for most individuals, receives some empirical and theoretical confirmation from the field of social psychology. McGuire (1969) in an extensive review of research on attitude change suggests the following reasons. First, face to face communication allows the receiver to communicate back, and therefore elicit the information he or she requires. Thus the messages become tailored to individual needs, and hence may well be more persuasive. Second, interpersonal communication gains greater attention because of social norms as to courtesy. The receiver cannot exercise selective avoidance of the message in the same way as he or she can with mass media communications.

To summarise the conclusions drawn from this section it must first be stressed that much more research is needed in this area, and in particular on the sequential use of the various channels by different individuals. Having said that, however, it would appear that there is a consensus as to this sequence for most individuals, and for major innovations. That is that the mass media are greater utilised at the knowledge stage in the cognitive process, whilst interpersonal channels are more important at the persuasion stage. For low risk innovations this picture may also be true for a large number of individuals, but there would appear to be some differences. The key factor is the innovativeness of the individual concerned, and the explanation of the latter findings may well be that more individuals can afford to be innovators for such new products. Thus a general or overall schema for these effects can be set up — dependent on the individual's innovativeness with respect to the particular innovation. This is presented in Figure 4.5 and by way of explanation it must be pointed out that when discussing interpersonal communication and the innovators, this is a different type of interpersonal communication to that for the later adopters. The latter utilise 'communicated experience' in their decision while the former utilise factual and less specific information (the rationale for this assertion was given on pp.72-74). Therefore in the diagrams interpersonal information has been separated into these two

Fig. 4.5: Innovativeness and Channel Importance

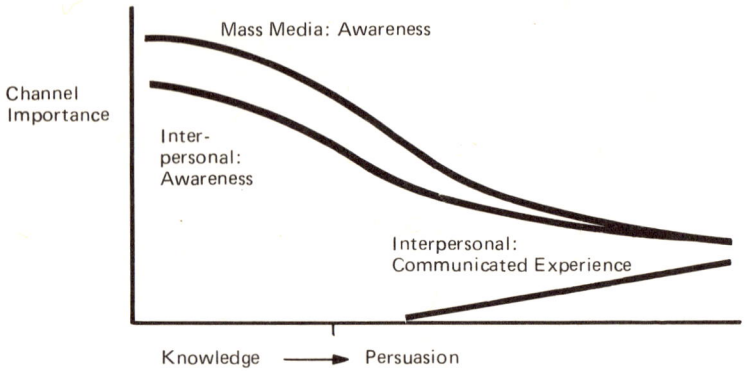

a) An Innovator

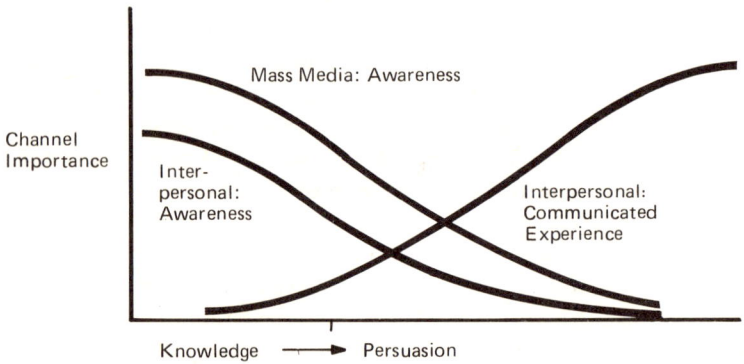

(b) A Later Adopter

types, that is 'communicated experience' and 'awareness'. It must be stressed that these are hypothetical constructs and need further empirical verification.

Perhaps the most important conclusion, at least as far as further research and development of our conceptual framework is concerned, is also highlighted by Figure 4.5. A static picture of channel importance or effectiveness is extremely limiting; the phenomenon is dynamic and must be treated as such. Furthermore the content of the messages transmitted down these channels is dependent on the product in question, and for interpersonal communication especially, aggregative studies (several innovations) can be misleading. The problem is whether the message is favourable or unfavourable and it is to this problem, coupled with the dynamic nature of the process, we address ourselves in the next section.

One final point: the author has resisted the temptation to digress into the numerous studies on mass media persuasion and advertising in general. This book is not aimed at how to advertise your products, although the importance of advertising in the new product context is treated. The interested reader will find an excellent summary of research into persuasion in general in Karlins and Abelson (1970), and an overview of the advertising process in Corkindale, Kennedy, Henry and Wills (1974).

4.3 Favourable and Unfavourable Influence – An Unexplored Area

It has already been suggested at several points that the information transmitted through interpersonal channels of communication can be for or against the innovation in question. The transmitted perceptions of the product – communicated experience – need not necessarily work in favour of further adoption. An individual who has had a disagreeable experience with the product, or found its performance unsatisfactory, is not likely to urge others to try it, quite the contrary. Further since most new products are unsuccessful we may speculate that unfavourable information and influence is a common phenomenon. It is therefore regrettable that the number of publications which mention the phenomenon, let alone present empirical findings on it, can be enumerated on the fingers of one hand. In the marketing literature only Arndt (1967a) has, to my knowledge, conducted research on this topic, finding not surprisingly that unfavourable comments may hinder the diffusion of a new product. Arndt concludes, in his review of this and other literature (1967b), that:

Word of mouth may both accelerate and slow up product acceptance, depending on factors like content of messages and group norms toward innovation. While word of mouth may be a carrot to marketers offering good products, it may also function as a stick should the products fall short of consumers' expectations.[12]

Similarly Robertson states: 'Interpersonal communication can be dysfunctional in (1) recommending against adoption, (2) being unreliable in content, and (3) being unfavourably perceived.'[13]

Lastly, in the whole of Rogers and Shoemaker's (1971) otherwise admirable list of generalisations not one is to be found on this crucial distinction between favourable and unfavourable messages. Furthermore scant reference is made to this topic in the bulk of their text. Surely to aggregate information (and its consequent influence) for and against the innovation into total interpersonal communication is too naive a viewpoint. As the previous section suggests it is necessary to conceptualise each as being different, and moreover to allow for the fact that the processes involved are dynamic. Hence the ratio between unfavourable and favourable influence in the social system at one point in time may be completely different at another. To represent the process more realistically we introduce time as a dimension, and also make the assertion that in terms of the success or failure of the innovation the relevant concept is the behaviour over time of the total amount of unfavourable or favourable influence in the system. Two hypothetical representations are given in Figure 4.6. In one we have an initial growth of favourable influence, which is later destroyed by an upsurge of unfavourable information. In the other we perhaps have the picture of a more successful innovation. The horizontal axis is time whereas the vertical, 'total influence', could perhaps be thought of as the number of messages (for or against) in the system at any point in time.

However the representation has certain deficiencies, not the least of which is the practical impossibility of measuring the total number of messages in the system. More importantly, and in line with the concept of communicated experience, it is more relevant to stress the numbers of people involved in communication. Interpersonal communication. means people talking to each other and it can be readily accepted that the variable of interest is the proportion expressing a favourable as opposed to an unfavourable perception of the new product. Thus, for instance, Figure 4.6(b) can be modified and depicted as in Figure 4.7.

This is one possible outcome and there must be an infinite number of others, dependent on the characteristics of individual innovations

Fig. 4.6: A Dynamic Representation of Interpersonal Influence

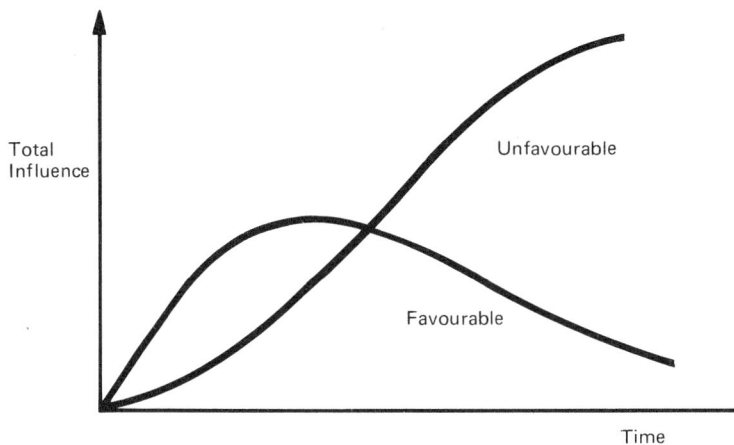

a) An Unsuccessful Innovation?

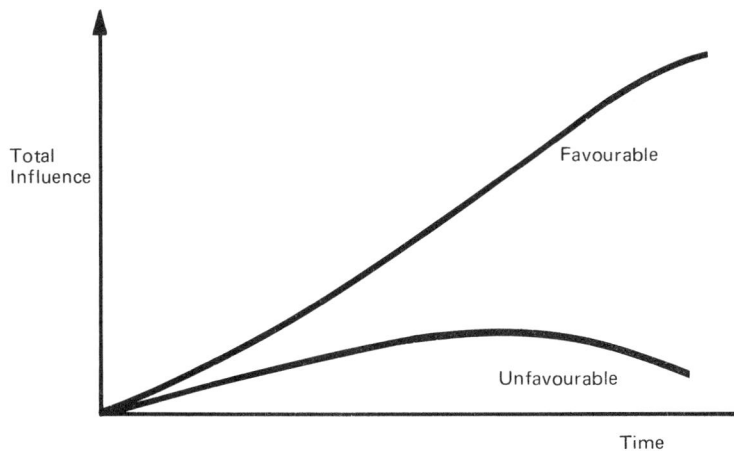

b) A Successful Innovation?

Fig. 4.7: The Communication of Experience Over Time

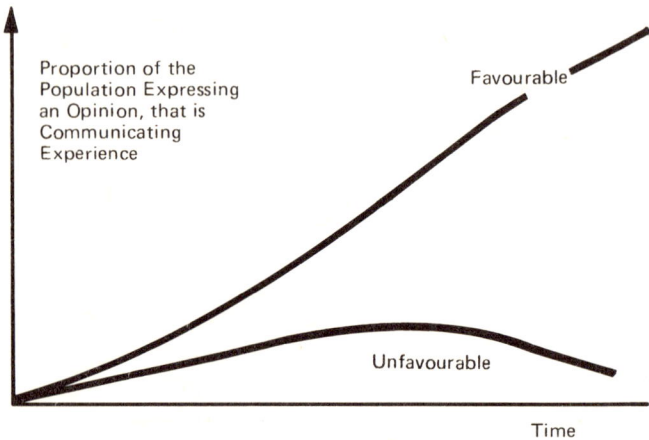

and the perceptions of those adopting them. However we will conclude this section by noting that the above implies an equal weighting between individuals, and therefore before this conceptual framework can be developed further it is necessary to investigate whether some individuals have proportionately more influence than others. That is, the notion of opinion leadership.

4.4 Opinion Leadership: Concept and Characteristics

The idea of an opinion leader, or as Summers (1971) defines the term 'one who exerts disproportionate influence on others through interpersonal communication', originated with the work of Lazarsfeld, Berelson and Gaudet (1948), and was applied to marketing situations by Katz and Lazarsfeld in the Decatur study cited previously. Opinion leadership was measured simply by asking respondents whether they had given or been asked for advice on the topic or product in question. On the basis of a simple cross-tabulation of the exposure of leaders and non-leaders to the mass media the concept of a two-step flow of mass communication was derived. That is that the opinion leaders obtained their information from the media and then in turn disseminated this information verbally to the rest of society. Now as Cerha (1967) points out the data from the earlier studies simply does not support any such conclusion, while in the 1955 Decatur study Katz and Lazarsfeld themselves conclude: ' ... several channels of influence impinge on the leaders in much the same way as they do upon the non-leaders'.[14] Cerha concludes that 'the two-step flow of mass communication and pertaining concept of opinion leadership has never been scientifically documented'.[15]

Nicosia (1964) too saw no validity for the concept of an opinion leader as this concept is used in the two-step hypothesis. Instead he postulates several types of opinion leader according to whether they had been exposed to the mass media or not.

Given then that the subject of opinion leadership got off to such an inherently shaky start it is somewhat mystifying that probably a greater proportion of effort has been expended on this subject, at least in the marketing field, than on other and equally important facets of innovative behaviour. While, in my view, the work done has yet to prove conclusively the utility of the concept of opinion leadership, it has provided valuable insights into the processes of interpersonal communication, and as such is therefore worth considering. However before doing so we should bury the myth of a two-step flow of communication.

Without going into the literature in any great depth a cursory re-examination of the findings reported in Section 4.2 will serve to meet this end. For instance the work of Sheth (1971) as presented in Figure 4.4 indicates that some individuals became aware of the innovation by means of interpersonal communication, were influenced to adopt by interpersonal communication, and in turn personally influenced others to adopt. This does not fit easily into the two-step hypothesis; Sheth himself suggests a three-or-more-step flow of communication. As mentioned on p.88 the situation is too complex for simplistic conceptualisations. For those interested, Rogers and Shoemaker list six shortcomings of the two-step model, and conclude that a multi-step model is more in accordance with reality, a model which:

   does not call for any particular number of steps nor does it specify that the message must emanate from a source by mass media channels. This model suggests that there are a variable number of relays in the communication flow from a source to a large audience.[16]

A multi-step model is effectively what has been presented in Sections 4.2 and 4.3, and will be further developed in both Section 4.5 and Chapter 5.

In discussing opinion leadership we must commence by looking at how it is measured, since by and large, and somewhat in common with innovativeness, what is meant by the term opinion leadership has come to be what is 'measured' as opinion leadership. Basically there are three ways of measuring this variable, the sociometric method, informants' ratings and the self-designating technique.

The sociometric technique is probably the most valid but requires the researcher to perform a census on the social system, or at least to locate a large and related proportion of this system. The method consists of asking the respondents with whom they discuss the matter in question, and from the answers obtained building up a picture of the communication network. Individuals who serve as nodes or focal points in this network can then be identified as opinion leaders. Because of the practical difficulties involved this method has been little used in the marketing area, one notable exception being Coleman, Katz and Menzel's (1957) study of the diffusion of the use of a new drug among medical practitioners.

The use of informants also requires the identification of a manageable social system, except that in this case key informants or judges are asked who are the opinion leaders within the system. Again this method has found little application in the marketing area.

The self-designating method is the one almost invariably used in the marketing area, since it lends itself to the sample survey method. Effectively respondents are asked whether they consider themselves to be influential in the eyes of their social contacts. Quite often a battery of six questions devised by Rogers and Cartano (1962) is used, which (hopefully) yields at least an ordinal scale of opinion leadership. Normally a cut-off point is then determined, those above this point being designated leaders and those below non-leaders.

However at this point the problems begin to appear, since as Nicosia (1964) points out not only have researchers used different definitions of opinion leadership, but also different methods of analysis, and therefore made comparison extremely hazardous. In recent years researchers, while they may or may not agree on the definition, have at least focused on one methodology, that of Rogers and Cartano mentioned above, and to some extent this has allowed greater comparability. Nonetheless there would still appear to be difficulties in this area, and considerable controversy over what the results mean. However before we investigate these problems the main findings of the recent past will be examined, findings which fall into two main classes. Firstly we will examine the supposed characteristics of these opinion leaders, and secondly whether some individuals are opinion leaders with respect to more than one product, that is are generalised opinion leaders.

Rogers and Shoemaker cite opinion leaders as having greater exposure to the mass media, greater change agent contact and greater social participation. Further, they are considered to be more cosmopolitan, to have a higher social status and to be more innovative than non-leaders. However, remembering that such generalisations are largely based on major innovations it is necessary to examine the marketing literature for evidence on low risk and fashion innovations.

In this literature it will be found that the picture is much less clear cut; for instance Robertson (1971) considers that most existing results are somewhat tentative, suggesting that only social participation and innovativeness are general indicators of opinion leadership. He concluded:

> Age varies by product category; social status is most often the same as that of advisers; high gregariousness is uniformly the case; cosmopolitanism, or orientation beyond the local community, is generally cited, but has not been tested explicity for consumer goods; knowledge is generally greater; no distinguishing personality features exist; norm adherence is greater; and higher innovativeness is found.[17]

Probably more research has been conducted for fashion innovations than for supermarket products, although again with contradictory and somewhat disappointing results. Summers (1970) considers that female fashion opinion leaders were more likely to be young, and have a higher income, education and social status. They were also more socially active and cosmopolitan, but perhaps of greater relevance is the fact that they were more involved and interested in fashion. As another nail in the coffin of the two-step hypothesis it can be noted that 88 per cent of the leaders received information from (and thereby were influenced by) other members of the community.

In a similar study Baumgarten (1974) was only able to find support for some aspects of social participation being determinants of female campus opinion leadership, whilst this variable and social status were related to male opinion leadership in the fashion area. Again for male fashions Darden and Reynolds (1972) were only able to detect 'interest in fashion' and 'venturesomeness' as general predictors of opinion leadership. Further when they subdivided their sample into different social situations they found (by stepwise multiple regression) that different sets of characteristics explained opinion leadership in each situation.

The topic of fashion innovation will be discussed at length in Chapter 7; here the important conclusions are that, (i) opinion leaders may be influenced by communications from others and (ii) which individual is an opinion leader is dependent on the social situation or setting.

Both these conclusions are also apparent in the area of supermarket products, and it is safe to suggest that a standardised set of characteristics for an opinion leader does not exist across different product categories, any more than it exists across major and minor innovations.

It can also be noted that, as discussed in Chapter 3, the strong and consistent relationship is between opinion leadership and innovativeness — a crucial point which we will take up again shortly.

The fact that different product categories produce opinion leaders with widely divergent characteristics leads us to the second main area of research — generalised opinion leadership. In other words whether an individual can be an opinion leader in more than one product category, and irrespective of personal characteristics. Opinion leaders who only exercise their leadership within one area or sphere of interest are termed monomorphic, whereas those who are leaders in several areas are termed polymorphic. It can be pointed out that there is yet to be any agreement in the literature as to what an 'area' or 'category' is.

The appropriate generalisation is: 'When the norms of a system are modern, opinion leadership is more monomorphic.'[18] Therefore we would expect that for new products, opinion leadership would be more likely to be monomorphic. However a study of the recent literature neither confirms nor refutes this hypothesis.

For instance Silk examined opinion leadership for the product categories of electric toothbrushes, regular toothbrushes, toothpastes, mouthwashes and dentists. That is, all within the general area of dental care. He investigated whether individuals designated themselves in two or more areas, and then ascertained whether there were mor of these general leaders than might be expected to occur by chance alone. He concluded:

> These data for dental products and services give no clear indication that the degree of overlap of opinion leadership is greater than that expected if opinion leadership in one area is entirely independent of that in another.[19]

On the other hand King and Summers report a significant number of generalised opinion leaders. These authors:

> explored the dynamics of new product adoption across a range of product categories including packaged foods, household cleaners and detergents, women's fashions, cosmetics and personal grooming aids, drugs and pharmaceutical products, clothing materials, and large and small appliances.[20]

The following main conclusions were reached, namely that opinion leadership was a common phenomenon, 69 per cent of respondents qualifying as leaders for at least one product category. Further overlap across product categories was 'high', 49 per cent qualifying in two or more categories, 28 per cent in three or more, etc. Lastly it appeared that the overlap was more likely to be among categories involving similar interests, that is between large and small appliances, fashions and cosmetics, etc. Subsequently Montgomery and Silk (1971) have extended this last point and gained further evidence on the relationship between overlap and consumer interests.

However before we conclude that the controversy has been resolved in favour of generalised opinion leaders it is as well to question exactly what King and Summers (1970) did. By their own admission the 'seven question opinion leadership battery was prepared for each broad product category studied'.[21] In other words, respondents designated themselves as leaders for a category such as 'large appliances'. Whatever else this study was about it was not about 'new product adoption'. Surely to study opinion leadership as it relates to new products it is necessary to measure this variable in the context of specific innovations.

As Silk notes:

> The inconclusiveness of each area studied affects the likelihood that generalised opinion leaders will be found. The more broadly defined

each area is, the greater the chances are that an individual will exert influence in more than one such area. This factor alone may account for any generalised opinion leaders that are found in one study and not another.[22]

To paraphrase the argument in a simplistic manner, if we ask people two questions — 'have you discussed politics recently' and 'have you discussed the weather recently' — we are likely to get a large proportion of people answering yes to both! In a new product context, and in order to measure influence in the process, it is necessary to determine who were the leaders for a specific innovation. Given the laws of chance and the situational (random) nature of the diffusion process it is unlikely that we would find the same 'leaders' for several innovations.

We may also question whether the very concept of a 'leader' is relevant in the case of the diffusion of a particular innovation. King and Summers' work indicates that more than two thirds of the population can be opinion leaders in a specific context.[23] Further the other cited works suggest that these 'leaders' will have been influenced by other individuals — which begs the whole question of who is 'leading' who.

These and other studies of similar ilk are also static and lack the dynamic perspective. Are we really expected to believe that an opinion leader will still exert the same influence next week, next month or next year? If the process is as situationally dependent as some of the research suggests, then a 'leader' today may be a 'non-leader' tomorrow.

The author would therefore argue that the current concept of opinion leadership is of little utility in explaining the diffusion of an innovation. It may explain more global and general aspects of human behaviour but as employed at present it has no connection with the transmission of messages about a new product, that is the communication of experience. The problem would appear to be both definitional and methodological: definitional because different researchers apply the concept to different types of messages, and messages usually of far wider scope than is relevant to diffusion studies, and methodological because of the inherent shortcomings of the self-designating technique (as normally deployed). Substantial progress could be made if the method was used in a longitudinal manner, therefore detecting the dynamic aspects, and if the distinction was made between favourable and unfavourable information. The latter only entails an extra question in the scale but has wide reaching implications for the results.

However one seemingly intractable difficulty would remain — the self-designating method, unlike the sociometric approach, provides no easy link to overt purchasing behaviour. Therefore the implicit assumption is made that those who disseminate greater amounts of information exert more influence or leadership than the remainder of the population. This assumption should be questioned since undeniably the content of the messages has some relevance to the matter. Is someone who transmits one message about the product's deficiencies more or less influential than someone who transmits two messages about its advantages, or someone who transmits ten messages based on hearsay? To discover this we need to assess whether favourable messages cause adoption, and unfavourable messages rejection. In other words to link information to changes in opinions, attitudes and, preferably, behaviour. Throughout the text the term 'information' in general, and 'communicated experience' in particular has meant messages which caused such changes. By only looking at the transmission of messages and not their effect on the recipients of these messages the self-designating measure of opinion leadership provides less than half the story.

Lastly some explanation of the apparent strong relationship between innovativeness and opinion leadership should be offered. One rationale, in terms of the concept of innovativeness developed here, is that the innovators will be highly visible to other, more cautious individuals and may be asked for their opinion. They may also have the psychological need to display publicly the fact that they have innovated, and therefore be more likely to initiate conversations about the new product. The crucial role of the innovators has been discussed previously, and in particular the role of the opinion leaders amongst the innovators was highlighted in Chapter 3. While some doubt has been expressed as to the usefulness of the concept of opinion leadership the importance of the above finding has not been decreased by this in any way. Research has shown that a large proportion of innovators are involved in transmitting information about the innovation (Bell, 1963; Engel *et al*, 1969). Given the broad definition of opinion leadership generally employed then it is not surprising that the innovators designate themselves as high on the opinion leadership scales. Again what is desirable is that future research investigate whether this 'leadership' was for or against the product, and whether this 'leadership' affected the behaviour of others. It also seems necessary to ascertain whether the individual concerned has adopted the innovation before communicating experiences about it. That is whether only immediate experience communicated between an adopter and a non-adopter will be influential, or whether such experience can be passed on through a chain of individuals who have yet to adopt. Rationally, and in line with the developed schema, it would appear likely that only the adopter-potential adopter conversation would have a major impact on the behaviour of the latter individual, and this will be the assumption made in the following pages. Certainly this assumption would be in line with research in the marketing area (see Katz and Lazarsfeld, 1955), and in social psychology (see Karlins and Abelson, 1970). However it must be admitted that relatively little research has been conducted on this aspect to date, particularly in the context of new product marketing.

To conclude, the research on opinion leadership has demonstrated that the flow of information and influence is complex, reaching different individuals via different channels, and via different series of channels. It has also been demonstrated that the transmission and reception of interpersonally communicated information is in some ways situationally dependent, an argument that will be extended shortly. However the present definitions of opinion leadership, and methods for measuring it, tell us relatively little about whether some individuals have a disproportionate amount of influence in the adoption of a specific innovation. Given the nature of the interpersonal communication process, and in particular the fact that such so-called 'leaders' may have been influenced to adopt by others, then it appears more plausible to study all those individuals who are disseminating information for or against the innovation, without making subjective and hazardous judgements as to which are 'leaders' and which 'non-leaders'.

4.5 Innovativeness and Communication — A Further Analysis

Thus far in the chapter a schema for the relative importance of the various communication channels to individuals with differing degrees of innovativeness has been established (see Figure 4.5). This figure demonstrates the inter-relation between innovativeness and communication, and links back to Chapter 3, particularly Section 3.4. In extending the concept of innovativeness developed therein, it was noted that the exact point in time at which a particular individual adopted is dependent on the receipt of a required level or magnitude of communicated experience, and this in turn is dependent on various factors relating to that individual's situation. With every individual placing differing weights on the importance of the various channels at differing points in his/her cognitive process, then adoption will be very much dependent on the right combination of messages arriving at any one time. For the majority of the population the most important type

Fig. 4.8: The Operation of Communicated Experience

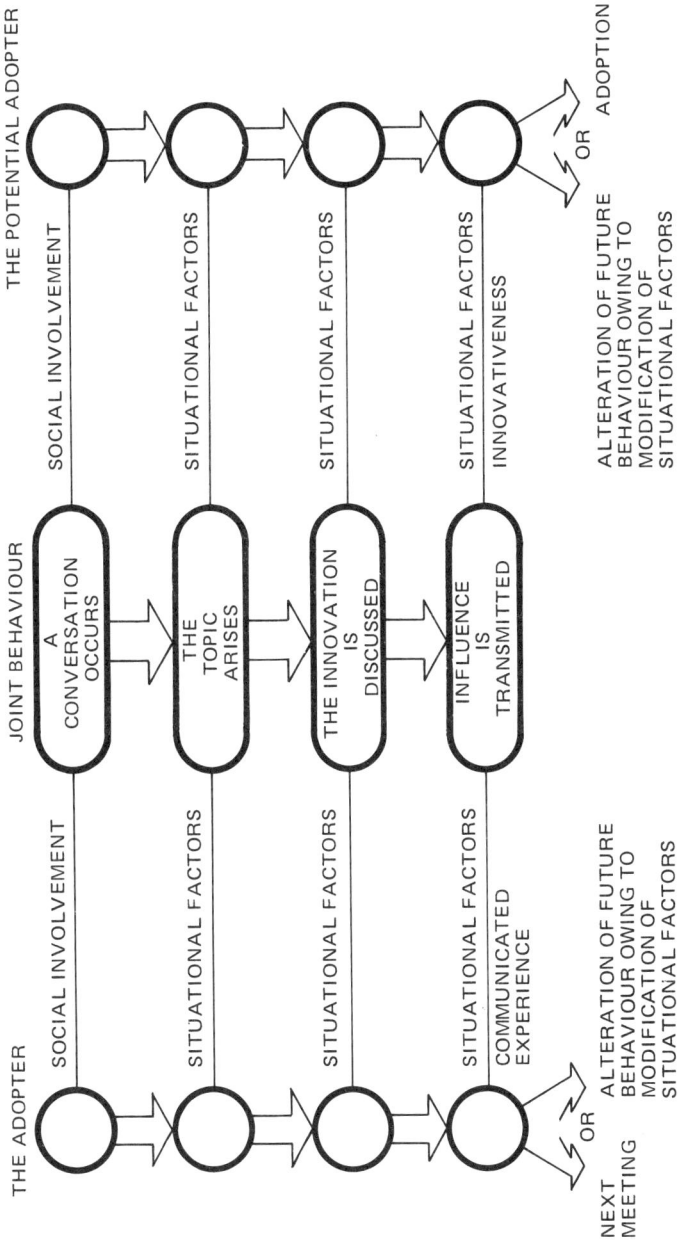

THE ADOPTER   JOINT BEHAVIOUR   THE POTENTIAL ADOPTER

SOCIAL INVOLVEMENT   A CONVERSATION OCCURS   SOCIAL INVOLVEMENT

SITUATIONAL FACTORS   THE TOPIC ARISES   SITUATIONAL FACTORS

SITUATIONAL FACTORS   THE INNOVATION IS DISCUSSED   SITUATIONAL FACTORS

SITUATIONAL FACTORS   INFLUENCE IS TRANSMITTED   SITUATIONAL FACTORS
COMMUNICATED EXPERIENCE   INNOVATIVENESS

NEXT MEETING   OR   ADOPTION

OR   ALTERATION OF FUTURE BEHAVIOUR OWING TO MODIFICATION OF SITUATIONAL FACTORS

ALTERATION OF FUTURE BEHAVIOUR OWING TO MODIFICATION OF SITUATIONAL FACTORS

Source: Adapted from Midgley (1975), p.99.

of information will be communicated experience, and for these individuals to receive their threshold level of this information it is necessary for one or more of their social contacts both to have adopted the product, and to have discussed it with the individual in question. Thus for later adopters the time of adoption is a function of the unique network or chain of interpersonally communicated messages in society ('unique' because this network will be different for each and every innovation).

For any individual act of adoption some form of sequence such as that depicted in Figure 4.8 is necessary, dependent at each stage on situational and therefore random factors. It is also necessary that the potential adopter shown in the figure is at the persuasion stage in his/her cognitive process.

Hence if we were to return to the distribution of innovativeness amongst the population developed in an earlier chapter, and shown here as Figure 4.9, an explanation of some observed facets of this distribution is possible.

Fig. 4.9: The Trait of Innovativeness

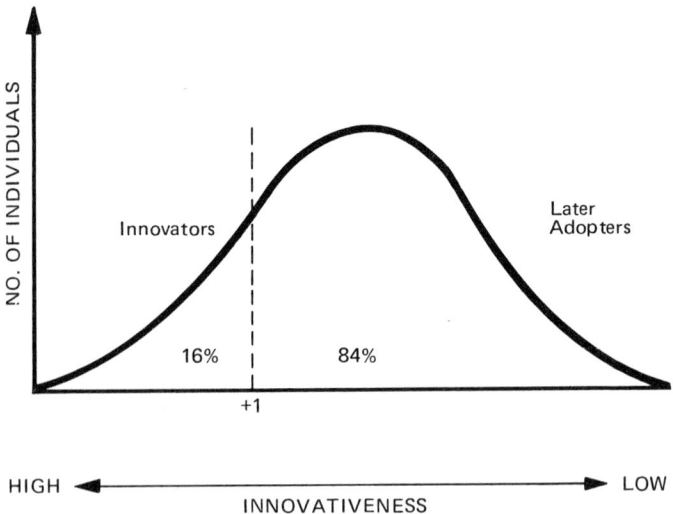

It can be noted that the innovators require little or no communicated experience and are therefore not as dependent on the unique network of messages. As suggested in Chapter 3 the innovators as a distinct group will always be more likely to appear in the left hand tail of the distribution. Or put more realistically it would appear probable that what exists is a pool of potential innovators out of which the innovators of a particular innovation will emerge.[24] Situational factors will still be important but relatively less so than for the later adopters. Therefore the left hand tail of the distribution, the first 16 per cent of the population, is less a manifestation of a random process than is the remainder.[25] For individuals in this remaining 84 per cent then their observed position is largely a manifestation of a random process, a process determined by the unique network of messages about the new product.

At this point it is possible to add the final dimension to the concept of innovativeness being advanced in this text.[26] What is being discussed above is observed innovativeness and not the distribution of an innate trait of all human beings. The vital dimension to add is that of communication, and the consequent difference between an individual's innate innovativeness and the innovativeness he or she displays with respect to a particular innovation, the latter being the innovativeness which can be measured by time of adoption. Communicated experience is the variable intervening between potential innovativeness and observed behaviour. Figure 4.10 illustrates this distinction between innate innovativeness and observed or actualised innovativeness. This figure also demonstrates that while communicated experience is relatively unimportant for innovators and therefore causes little difference between their innate and actualised innovativeness, this intervening variable can effect a marked discrepancy between the positions of later adopters, according to the amount of information and the time at which it is received. The reader should realise that due to space considerations only some possible events are shown. The upper distribution is shown as larger than the lower in order to indicate that all individuals do not automatically adopt *every* innovation. For a specific new product there may be many, both innate innovators and innate later adopters, who never actualise their innovativeness before the product is withdrawn from the market. The discrepancy between the distributions is dependent on the nature of the experiences communicated, that is, on how well the product satisfies consumer needs.

Therefore what is measured by $\widetilde{I}_i = \dfrac{m - t_i}{s}$ (p.50) may not be

Fig. 4.10: The Role of Communicated Experience

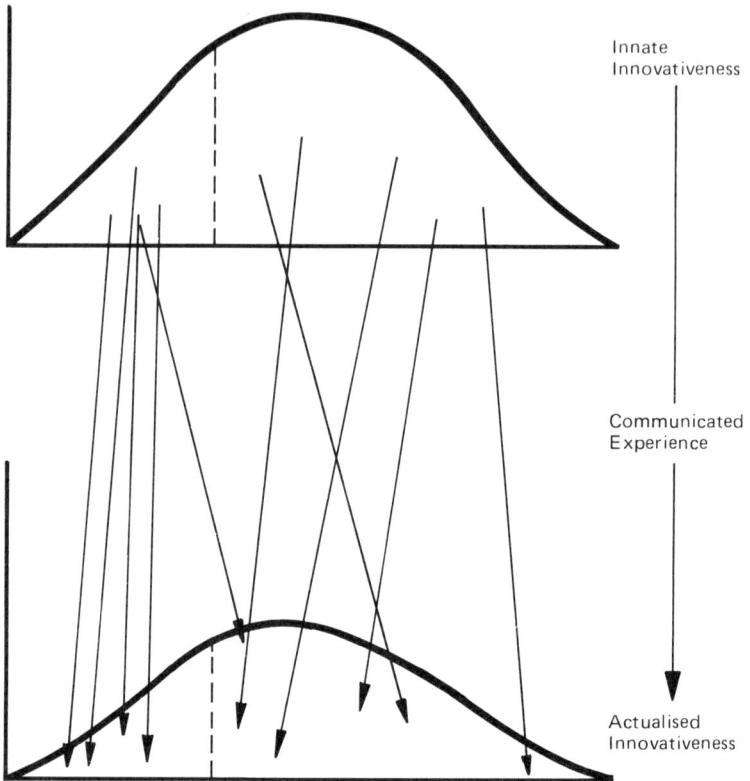

the individual's innate innovativeness score, especially if the individual is a later adopter. Now in terms of studying one innovation in isolation this distinction is not of great relevance; its importance lies where characteristics of individuals are to be determined, and on the basis of studies of many innovations. While it might be expected that those individuals who are innately innovative would be more likely to be the actual innovators observed across several innovations, which in turn would allow empirical determination of their personal characteristics, this would be less true for those innately 'later' adopters. These latter individuals would display different innovativeness in relation to different innovations and thus in turn make determination of their characteristics difficult, if not impossible, In the author's opinion the categorisation scheme presented by Rogers and Shoemaker is therefore unlikely to be a useful conceptual and empirical device.[27]

Nor is Figure 4.10 a complete conceptualisation; for one thing, no mention has been made of another important factor − the type of innovation, major or minor. This could either be handled as a further intervening variable which would modify the innate distribution to two intermediate distributions, before communication produced the final distributions, or by suggesting that there are two innate distributions. In the lack of sufficient empirical evidence it is proposed to do no more here than raise the matter in the reader's mind. The other limitation is that no distinction has been made between favourable and unfavourable information; according to the proportions of, and dynamic behaviour of, these quantities we might expect to get radically different final distributions. However no attempt will be made to discuss this aspect at this point, and for the following reason.

Effectively it can be argued that we have reached the point at which it is no longer possible to manipulate the concepts and phenomena in an essentially verbal manner. The interaction of situations, favourable and unfavourable information, individuals and innovations can produce a myriad of possible outcomes − a complexity which it is only feasible to describe and manipulate mathematically. In Chapter 5 a mathematical theory of innovative behaviour will be presented and discussed. The remainder of this chapter will therefore be used to complete the basic framework of concepts for this theory.

Thus communication of opinions on, perceptions of, or experiences with, the innovation are the key to observed adoption patterns, and Section 4.4 was concluded by suggesting that the way to conceptualise this process was to look at those individuals disseminating information for or against the innovation. Which also refers back to earlier comments, and in particular to Figure 4.7, which presented a possible picture of this favourable and unfavourable information. Remembering that earlier a distinction was drawn between communicated experience and awareness then by also allowing for the fact that some individuals may not communicate their experiences to others, that is can be termed passive, then the framework can be completed and presented as Figure 4.11. This represents the numbers of people aware, passive or communicating favourable/unfavourable experiences for one possible hypothetical diffusion of an innovation.

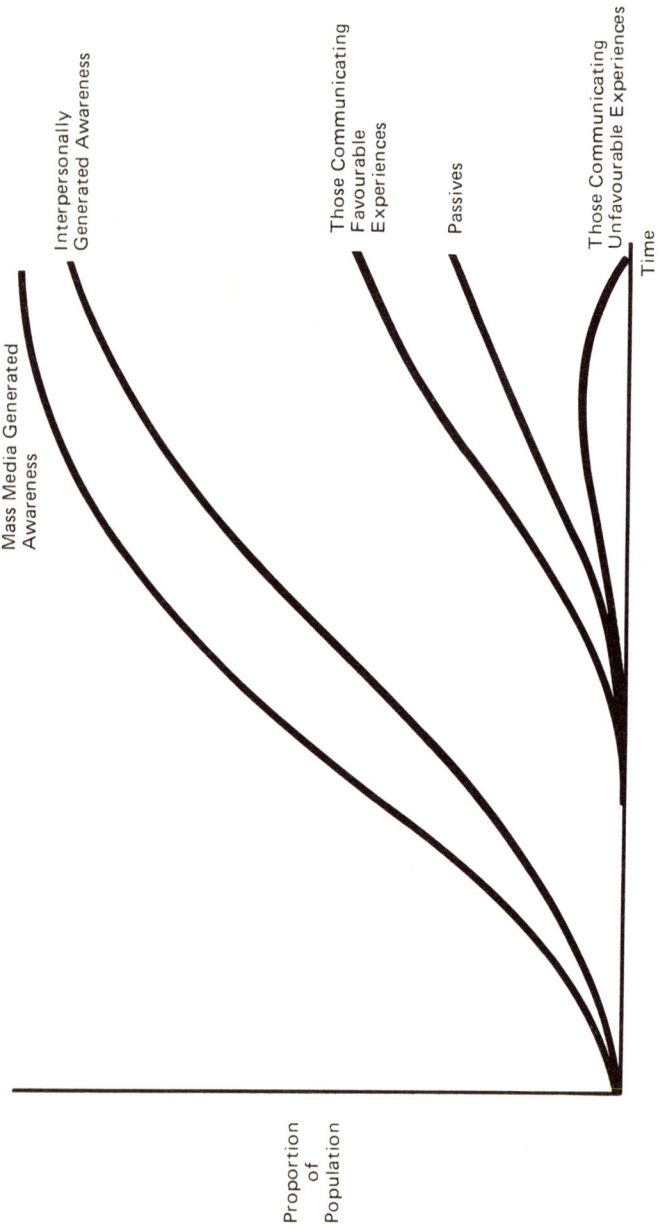

Fig. 4.11: The Communication Processes for a Hypothetical Innovation

Proportion
of
Population

Mass Media Generated Awareness

Interpersonally Generated Awareness

Those Communicating Favourable Experiences

Passives

Those Communicating Unfavourable Experiences

Time

A few concluding remarks are in order here. Firstly, on the basis of the evidence given in Rogers and Shoemaker (1971), it is assumed that awareness/knowledge diffuses ahead of actual adoption. Robertson (1967) provides some support for this within a marketing context. Secondly no attempt has been made to further subdivide awareness/ knowledge into favourable or unfavourable categories. Given that the persuasive meetings are between adopters and non-adopters, and the outcomes of these meetings dependent on what type of experiences are communicated, then the effectiveness of communicated experiences (in changing behaviour) far outweighs that of the awareness-generating channels. It therefore seems less relevant to subdivide the latter. Individuals may have received more or less favourable knowledge of the innovation, but in the majority of cases their ultimate adoption/non-adoption will be dependent on what experiences are communicated to them by adopters of the new product. Lastly, as yet nothing has been said about how the adopters come to adopt — most likely this was because of the experience of others, but it may also have been due to the mass media. In order to discuss this topic it is necessary to formulate a mathematical theory of the total diffusion process.

4.6 Summary

In this chapter the various communication processes were examined, the processes that lie at the centre of the diffusion of innovations. In particular we focused on interpersonal communication, and especially the communication of experience, as this was hypothesised to be the main determinant in the observed changes in individual behaviour. Some time was spent examining whether interpersonal communication can be regarded as an effective mechanism for behaviour change, an exercise seen as complementary to earlier arguments. The overwhelming mass of evidence suggests that such verbal communication is a powerful and effective source of influence on individual behaviour. However in then examining the relative effectiveness of interpersonal and mass media communication, difficulties were encountered. It was noted that several studies purported to measure this relative effectiveness, but in fact made no allowance for two vital factors. First, both information channels are not static in operation but dynamic, and therefore the relative effectiveness of each might be expected to display marked changes over time. Second, and perhaps more important, past and current methodologies make no allowance for, or distinction between, favourable and unfavourable information.

From the dynamic or longitudinal studies which have been conducted it was possible to conclude that, for major innovations, the mass media was relatively more important at the knowledge stage, while interpersonal communication was relatively more important at the persuasion stage in the individual's cognitive processes. However the evidence for minor innovations was less clear-cut, suggesting that the sequence may be different for different individuals, and in different situations. It was concluded that the likely key to the sequence of, and relative effectiveness, of the various communication channels was the innovativeness of the individual concerned. A diagrammatic schema was then set up relating channel importance to the innovativeness of the individual with respect to the particular innovation. Within this schema information was separated into awareness and communicated experience.

In a discussion of favourable and unfavourable influence it was concluded that the generation of unfavourable information about the new product is a common occurrence, which makes the lack of research in the area difficult to understand. It was further argued that the success or failure of the innovation was dependent on the relative proportion of favourable to unfavourable information in the system, as this varied over time. Again this concept proved susceptible to a diagrammatic representation, effectively in terms of the numbers of people communicating experiences for or against the innovation and over time.

The next topic was that of opinion leadership and the first step taken was to replace the simplistic two-step flow of communication model with the more realistic multi-step model. From there the measurement of opinion leadership was outlined, the characteristics of these persons listed, and the problem of generalised opinion leadership examined. Broadly speaking it was discovered that the characteristics of opinion leaders were dependent on the social situation or setting. However only when the concept of generalised opinion leaders was examined did the difficulties in this area become more apparent.

It was argued that the wide and arbitrary definition of product 'categories' had been such as to render most of the research meaningless, and that it was necessary in the future to study opinion leadership as it relates to specific innovations. It was considered that while some methodological problems could be rectified, the widely used self-designating method would still entail considerable difficulties. The most severe limitation being that it did not measure reception of information, that is overt behaviour changes, and was therefore difficult to relate to actual diffusion processes. This section was concluded by stressing again that what should be studied is the behaviour of individuals transmitting information about the innovation (favourable or unfavourable), without arbitrarily defining some to be leaders and some not.

The relationship between innovativeness and communication was then re-examined, and the role of communicated experience stressed again. It was noted that most individuals require the receipt of a certain amount of such information, and this receipt will be dependent on a situational, and therefore largely random, process. Innovators were assumed to be different in that, lacking this need for the experience of others, then their adoption was not dependent on a complex, random network of messages. A vital distinction was then made between an individual's innate innovativeness and his/her actualised innovativeness. The intervening variable being communicated experience. It was suggested that this distinction was a plausible explanation of several facets of the process.

Since communicated experience is the key to observed phenomena this concept was re-examined, and a final diagrammatic schema presented — a schema illustrating the dynamic behaviour of the various forms of information. It was then argued that verbal explanations could go no further and it was necessary to turn to mathematical formulations in order to progress.

Notes

1. However it is also true, at least to some extent, that marketing professionals have made the same fundamental mistake.
2. It is interesting to speculate that consumer associations and magazines are another manifestation of this need.
3. Arndt (1967b), pp.70-1.
4. Named after the place where the fieldwork was conducted.
5. Which is therefore not quite the same as a new product situation, but as will become apparent the situations are sufficiently comparable to allow the argument to be developed.
6. Arndt (1967b), p.71.
7. Rogers and Shoemaker (1971), p.382.
8. Rogers and Shoemaker (1971), p.383.
9. Remembering that what is termed here an earlier adopter has been defined in the context of this text as an innovator.
10. It should be noted that the close relationship is a result of the definition of innovativeness used here, this definition being formed on the basis of the above.
11. Klapper (1960), p.8.
12. Arndt (1967b), p.70.
13. Robertson (1971), p.164.
14. Katz and Lazarsfeld (1955), p.318.
15. Cerha (1967), p.304.
16. Rogers and Shoemaker (1971), p.209.

17. Robertson (1971), p.179.
18. Rogers and Shoemaker (1971), p.380.
19. Silk (1966), p.257.
20. King and Summers (1970), p.45.
21. King and Summers (1970), p.46.
22. Silk (1966), p.259.
23. A figure which might, presumably, be increased if a greater variety of product categories was used.
24. Remembering also that the characteristics of the pool will vary according to whether the innovation is a major or minor one.
25. Using the proportions given in Figure 3.3 but noting that these are in some ways arbitary. See pp.53-54.
26. Continuing the argument from p.49.
27. Rogers and Shoemaker (1971), p.182.

5 MATHEMATICAL THEORIES OF THE SOCIAL PROCESSES

5.1 An Overview

In this chapter an attempt is made both to provide a mathematical theory of innovative behaviour, and then to demonstrate the power of such an approach — by reference to actual case studies. First a synthesis of all that has gone before is made. In effect this is a general theory of innovative behaviour, and this theory forms not only the conceptual schema for the rest of this chapter but also the theoretical background for Part III of the book. There a framework for new product management is to be advanced. Hence the general theory is the core of the thesis, essentially a particular viewpoint on the diffusion of innovations, and specifically new consumer and industrial products.[1]

Having advocated this point of view the discussion then turns to how the general theory might be formulated mathematically. It proves that this is not completely possible at the present time, except for certain restricted cases. Nonetheless these cases are not only interesting in themselves but of great relevance to new product marketing. One case in particular is expressed mathematically and then solved for six new consumer products. The results prove highly significant.

To conclude, the fact that the application of this restricted or special case to empirical data proves successful lends considerable support to the author's arguments. That is, it lends credence to the general theory. A conclusion which needs to be stressed here, for extensive use is made of the general theory in Part III. Thus the conceptual schema advanced in Section 5.2 is not merely an academic or theoretical exercise, it also represents an extremely powerful operational framework for new product marketing. In essence the general theory of innovative behaviour is a dynamic causal model of consumer attitudes. Irrespective of subsequent mathematical extensions a manager could derive substantial benefits solely from an orientation to this picture of market behaviour. The general theory not only shows how the market behaves but it also suggests why. It is the latter which provides the vital link between our concepts of innovative behaviour and improved management practice.

5.2 A General Theory of Innovative Behaviour

By 'innovative behaviour' is meant the manifest behaviour of social
systems towards innovations, and by using the indefinite article it is
intended to convey the message that this is just one of the many alternative
general theories which could be formulated, one which follows logically
from previous arguments, and one which could be considered the most
realistic. It should be indicated though, that different points of view are
possible, and may be equally valid.

The starting point for the construction of a general theory is
Figure 4.11 in Chapter 4. If the types of adopter portrayed there are
examined it is possible to discern three distinct categories of individual.
These categories may be named and defined as follows.

1. *Favourables:* Those who have tried the product and who will
   communicate favourable experiences of it should the situation arise.
2. *Rejectors:* Those who have tried the product, found it deficient, and
   who will communicate unfavourable experiences of it should the
   situation arise.
3. *Passives:* Those who have tried the product but who do not
   communicate their experiences of it.

These categories arise directly from the arguments given in Chapter 4.
As a further extrapolation from Figure 4.11 it may also be noted that
at least two other categories are necessary to describe the situation
completely, that is those aware of the innovation but yet to adopt it,
and those as yet unaware of the innovation.

It is the main thrust of this text, and Chapter 4 in particular, that
the numbers of people in these categories may, and indeed do, change
over time. Thus Figure 4.11 is really a portrayal of the manifest
behaviour of a dynamic system, and in order to formulate a general
theory the next logical step is to specify the system, and the ways or
mechanisms by which people may move from one category to
another. That is, and for one example, how an individual becomes
aware, then a favourable, and then subsequently perhaps a rejector or
passive.

Again some of these mechanisms have already been discussed in
some detail, specifically those relating to interpersonal communication
and the mass media. It could be argued that these provide the sole
means by which individuals are influenced to 'change category'.
However, it can be suggested that there are other mechanisms by which
such transfers may occur.

For instance in discussing the change of status from aware to adopter then for many products this change may be brought about by a free sample. Regardless of whether a monetary exchange takes place the fact that a person has tried the product gives them the necessary experience to communicate. Lest it be thought this only applies to low risk products it should also be pointed out that the familiar device of a free trial period extends this argument to more expensive and durable products.

Next, and perhaps of greater importance, it does not seem logical to insist that once a person is a favourable, rejector or passive then they continue as such indefinitely. Surely they may have a subsequent change of heart, or perhaps cease to venture opinions on the topic. Changes of this nature might be due to subsequent experience with the product, or perhaps just boredom with the subject. Equally well such a transfer might be brought about on hearing of the disagreeable experiences of others, or being re-educated on how to better use the product by conversations with other adopters. Hence there appear to be two basic ways by which adopters may repeatedly change their state of mind, and thus change the direction of the influence they exert on others. One way is some form of internal and individual experience while the other is a variant of the interpersonal mechanism discussed previously. A variety of explanations seem plausible, but the important conclusion is that the system remains dynamic even when the majority of the population have adopted the product. As will be seen later these concepts provide some suggestions as to how the theory might be extended to include repeat purchasing as well.

To specify the system the population has been divided into five categories (unaware, aware, favourable, rejector, passive) and four basic mechanisms proposed for effecting transfers between these categories. The mechanisms being: interpersonal communication of experience; mass media communication; other marketing activities; individual experiences. To standardise the terminology the five categories will be referred to as states and the four mechanisms as state transfer mechanisms.

Given all the above then it is apparent that Figure 4.11 is the manifestation of a system such as that shown in Figure 5.1. Some comments are necessary to explain Figure 5.1, which is the first step in constructing the general theory.

It should be reiterated that this is a dynamic system – which is also of course a little difficult to represent diagrammatically. Some transfers can only be unidirectional, that is unaware to aware, aware to adopter,

Fig. 5.1: A First Step Toward a General Theory of Innovative Behaviour

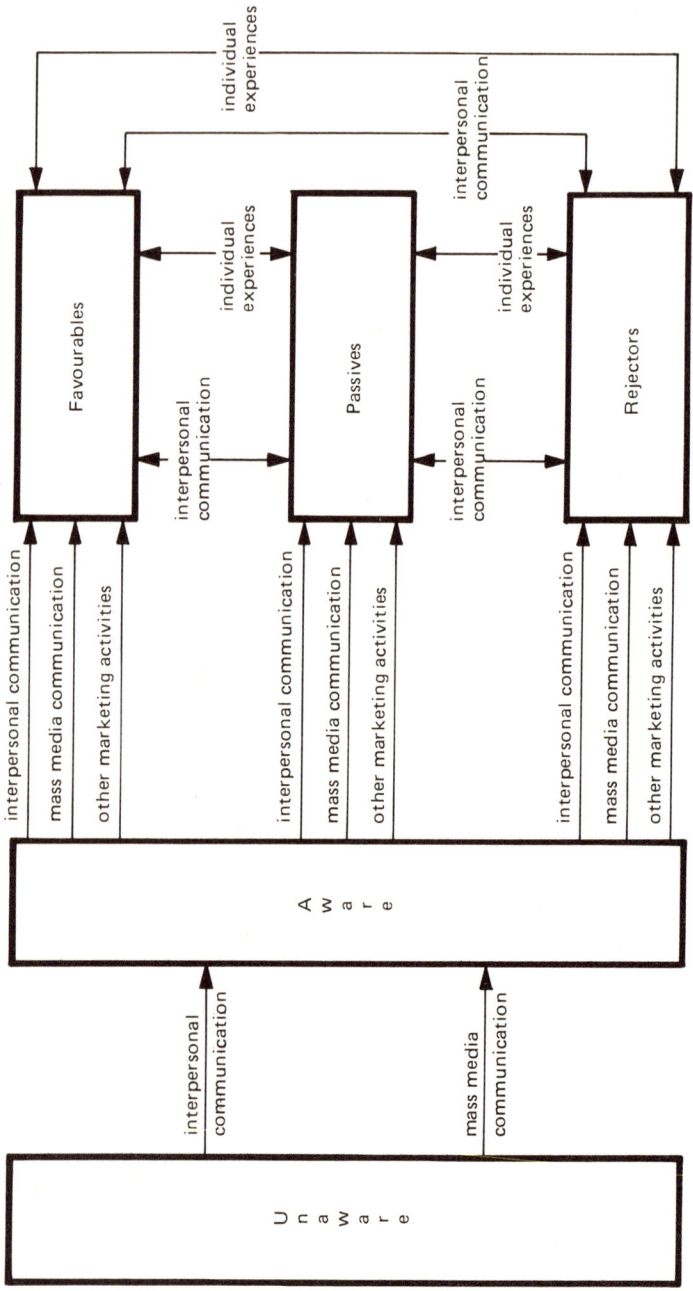

while the remainder, that is between adopter states, can be in both directions. This is denoted by the arrows on the diagram.

When the innovation first appears the total population would be in the unaware state. Subsequently some individuals would become aware and, in the course of time, adoption would begin. According, then, to what sort of experiences were communicated the interpersonal state transfer mechanism would accelerate or retard the growth of the adoption of the innovation. Obviously a large proportion of favourables would persuade a significant number of others to adopt, and if these individuals found the product satisfactory they in turn would persuade yet more people to try the product, leading to the well-known S-shaped adoption curve.

In discussing the interpersonal state transfer mechanisms it would seem logical that only the favourables are responsible for influencing others to adopt. The passives have no role in interpersonal communication and it would be somewhat perverse to allow those individuals with unfavourable opinions of the product, the rejectors, to persuade people to try it. The difficulty with Figure 5.1 is that while the role of the favourables is fairly self-evident, the role of the rejectors is less so. Figure 5.1 only outlines the state changes, and as such does not attempt to describe the communication flows which caused these changes. This is an important distinction and worth expanding in more detail.

The general theory which we are formulating quite naturally seeks to explain the adoption of innovations. It therefore focuses on changes in overt behaviour (state transfers) and its chief concepts are the states and the state transfer mechanisms, which are depicted in Figure 5.1. The theory does not attempt to describe all the information flows in the population but only those relevant to state transfers. The rejectors cause no change in overt behaviour; in essence they persuade other individuals not to do anything, that is not to adopt. In other words the rejectors cannot cause state transfers, and therefore their role cannot be portrayed in Figure 5.1.

However there is no doubt that this role is vitally important to the process, and it becomes necessary to question how this role might be incorporated into the theory. In fact this is quite easily achieved if we move from an individual level conceptualisation to an aggregate level conceptualisation. At the individual level a person either adopts or does not adopt, at the aggregate level we may speak of favourable information accelerating the rate of adoption whilst unfavourable information retards this rate. We will therefore proceed by examining the state transfer mechanisms at these two levels, express them quasi-mathematically, and then subsequently reformulate Figure 5.1. To conclude: as it stands, Figure 5.1 provides only the basic frame for the theory, and we now need to add the theoretical 'machinery' in order to describe and explain the phenomenon more completely.

While it has been stated that there are four basic state transfer mechanisms, an inspection of Figure 5.1 leads to the conclusion that some of these mechanisms operate in more than one situation. For instance, the interpersonal mechanism is involved in transfers (i) from unaware to aware, (ii) from aware to adopter and (iii) between adopters themselves. Let us now examine each of the mechanisms in the situations in which each operates, commencing with the one at the centre of these arguments, that is the interpersonally generated transfer from merely being aware to actually adopting. This examination starts at the individual level, and by reference to earlier comments.

It will be remembered that innovativeness was discussed and defined in terms of communicated experience. Specifically:

$$I_i \quad = \quad f \left(\frac{1}{E_i} \right) \qquad (p.50)$$

which states that the more communicated experience (E_i) an individual i requires in order to adopt, the less innovative they are. Hence if we were to study any one individual we would find that they received messages from others until, at some point in time, the required level of experience has been accumulated and they adopt. Thus whether or not a person has adopted by time T is some function of their innovativeness and the experience that has been communicated to them up to time T. However this is not the whole story as the experience could be favourable or unfavourable to the product concerned. Presumably the individual makes some assessment of the conflicting evidence before reaching a decision. The distinction here is between information received from the favourables, and that received from the rejectors. If the former is denoted by $E_f(T)$ and the latter by $E_r(T)$ then whether or not an individual i adopts may be expressed as the function:

$$a_i(T) \quad = \quad f_i \left[I_i , \int_o^T E_f(T) \ dT , \int_o^T E_r(T) \ dT \right]$$

The notation T indicates that the quantities concerned vary over time. The function relates the person's innovativeness (itself a function of required levels of communicated experience) and the total amounts of favourable and unfavourable information conveyed to this individual by others up to time T. The latter being both expressed as integrals from T = 0 to T = T. Obviously for any one individual this is a binary function: either they have adopted as at time T or they have not. That is a = 1 or a = 0 respectively. Hence an individual who received largely unfavourable information would probably not make the transfer of state from aware to adopter.

If we now aggregate all the (different) individual functions we obtain the general form of the (interpersonal) state transfer mechanism between two states, namely:

$$-\left(\frac{dA}{dT}\right)_{ab} = f_{ab}\left[I(T), \int_0^T E_f(T)dT, \int_0^T E_r(T)dT\right]$$

where $-(dA/dT)$ is the rate af which individuals leave state a for state b.[2] I is an aggregate function of the innovativeness of the individuals in state a. This could be thought of as:

$$I(T) = \int_{i=0}^{i=A(T)} I(i)di$$

However the important point is that as the number of individuals in state a varies with time, then the aggregate I also varies with time. The number of individuals in state a is denoted by A, henceforth capital letters will be used for numbers of people and lower case letters for identifying the respective states and state transfers. E_f and E_r have become the total amounts of information for and against the product generated by the adopters.

In the aggregate form above the state transfer mechanism is continuous, rather than binary as before, and clearly demonstrates the role of the favourables and rejectors. If

$$\int_{T=0}^{T=T} E_f(T)dT > \int_{T=0}^{T=T} E_r(T)dT$$

then we may expect dA/dT to be high, that is a large number of individuals to be changing from state a to state b, at time T. If, however,

$$\int_{T=0}^{T=T} E_f(T)dT < \int_{T=0}^{T=T} E_r(T)dT$$

then dA/dT will be low, that is the rejectors will be retarding the state transfer. To relate these comments to earlier work, let state a be that of being aware, and state b that of being an adopter. It can also be seen that the above effect is mediated or influenced by the innovativeness of the people in the aware state a. In the early stages of the diffusion process the aggregate innovativeness I of this group will be higher than in the later stages, when for example all the more innovative individuals will have adopted and only the less innovative are left in the aware state. Since we now see that I, E_r and E_f are all likely to fluctuate over the course of the innovation then it may be appreciated just how complex the behaviour of dA/dT will be. Furthermore the value of dA/dT at one instant in time determines how many adopters there are subsequently, which in turn affects E_f and E_r, and hence dA/dT in later periods. The process is therefore in the nature of a feedback system, but one of considerable complexity.

In applying this state transfer mechanism to Figure 5.1 it should be noted that there are three possible interpersonally caused state transfers from aware to adopter: that is aware to favourable, aware to rejector and aware to passive. Therefore three such expressions will be needed in the reformulation.

Individuals are thus allowed to adopt and then immediately express an opinion on the product's performance. This seems more realistic than any other possible schema — such as only allowing entry through the favourable state and thereby constraining individuals to be, at least initially, in favour of the product. It is more likely that on trying the innovation the adopter can speak his/her mind on the topic, or of course remain passively silent.

It was pointed out in Chapter 3 that it was difficult to measure E, dependent as this is on a host of factors. A pertinent question then is whether or not it is possible to work with more accessible measures and variables. It can be stated that the receipt of a certain amount of communicated experience is quite obviously dependent on the number of meetings a person has with adopters, and on whether the innovation is discussed in these conversations or not. This is the argument given in Chapter 4, the essential features of which are summarised in Figure 4.8. The process is a highly situational one in that the meetings have to occur and the innovation has to be discussed. Obviously also the chance of meeting an adopter within one's social circle depends on what one's social circle is, and on how many adopters there are at that point in time.

Put in aggregate terms

$$\int_{T=0}^{T=T} E_f(T)dT \quad \text{and} \quad \int_{T=0}^{T=T} E_r(T)dT$$

are related in some quite complex fashion to how many adopters and awares there are at time T, and on some equally complex aggregation of all the individual situational effects — say S(T). The latter are a reflection of the structure of society and the chance of product related conversations occurring. However since the adopters have been split into favourables, rejectors and passives (who do not enter into this process) then if the number of favourables is F(T), the numbers of rejectors R(T) and the number of awares A(T) we have:

$$-\left(\frac{dA}{dT}\right)_{af} = \left(\frac{dF}{dT}\right)_{af} = f_{af}\left[I(T), A(T), R(T), F(T), S(T)\right]$$

where the subscript af denotes the state transfer aware to favourable. It should be pointed out there are similar expressions for the corresponding transfers aware to passive, and aware to rejector. The expression states that the rate of decrease of the aware state is equal to the rate of increase of the favourable state and both are some function of the variables listed.[3] While the precise nature or form of this function is, and will remain, fairly vague and general it is possible to specify it a little more rigorously. If we have a total of X people in group x and Y people in group y then the total possible number of meetings between members of the two groups is XY.[4] Thus the above expression may be rewritten:

$$-\left(\frac{dA}{dT}\right)_{af} = \left(\frac{dF}{dT}\right)_{af} = f_{af}\left[I(T), A(T)\ F(T), A(T)\ R(T), S(T)\right]$$

As a final point on the form of the mechanism for transfers between the aware and the adopter states, it should be noted that there are three such state transfer mechanisms, namely f_{af}, f_{ar} and f_{ap}. Hence in f_{af} and f_{ar} some implicit allowance has been made for differing perceptions of the product's performance, since the favourables are impressed with the innovation and the rejectors not. Any one of these transfers is therefore due to a combination of persuasion and subsequent trial of the product. However rather than complicate the form of the expression by adding a separate product performance term this factor will be viewed as one component of S(T), that is of the aggregated situational term. Intuitively this would seem to be a reasonable step as an individual's use of the product, and hence perceptions of it, will be to at least some, if not a great, extent situationally determined. For the mechanism f_{ap} there are no such complications, the passives' silence is presumably some function of their social situation, rather than directly connected with the product concerned.

The other interpersonal state transfer mechanisms may be dealt with quite quickly. First, the transfer mechanisms between adopter states are similar to the above, with the exception that as these individuals have adopted then their innovativeness is no longer relevant. The expressions are also simpler in that fewer groups of people are involved. As one example the transition from the favourable to the passive state can be expressed:

$$-\left(\frac{dF}{dT}\right)_{fp} = \left(\frac{dP}{dT}\right)_{fp} = f_{fp}\left[\, F(T)\, R(T)\, ,\, S(T)\,\right]$$

With appropriate change of subscript this expression would be identical for the transfers rejector to passive, favourable to rejector and rejector to favourable.

Note that the passives have no role in the above; if however we discuss the transfer passive to rejector they do have a role, albeit still a neutral one. The relevant expression is:

$$-\left(\frac{dP}{dT}\right)_{pr} = \left(\frac{dR}{dT}\right)_{pr} = f_{pr}\left[\, P(T)\, R(T)\, ,\, S(T)\,\right]$$

Here the rejectors are persuading some of the passives to become vocal, persuasion which occurs in meetings between passives and rejectors. It is therefore clear that only favourables and rejectors play active roles in the interpersonal communication process, exerting influence in meetings with members of the other states.

For the state transfer unaware, ua, to aware, a, then the expression is quite simply a function of how many people are already aware (which includes adopters) and how many are unaware. That is:

$$-\left(\frac{dU}{dT}\right)_{uaa} = \left(\frac{dA}{dT}\right)_{uaa} = f_{uaa}\left[\, U(T)\, \left\{A(T) + F(T) + R(T)\right\}\, ,\, S(T)\,\right]$$

Note that the 'awares' have been allowed to diffuse further awareness, on the grounds that while they may not exert influence (more precisely communicate experience) there seems no good reason why they should not disseminate the message that the product exists. The total number of possible meetings is therefore $U(T) \left\{ A(T) + F(T) + R(T) \right\}$. The passives are again allowed no role in this process, a decision which does raise a slight and obvious difficulty. While this problem could be resolved by separating the aware state into 'actively aware' and 'passively aware', for a variety of reasons which will be discussed shortly it has been decided not to take this route.

Next we have the mass media initiated changes of state. Obviously these are in part dependent on the nature and extent of the advertising campaign, and in part on the situations in which individuals receive these advertising messages. However for the transfer between the aware state and the adopter state the state transfer mechanism is again a function of some aggregated index of innovativeness. This is because individuals' innovativeness determines how much interpersonally communicated experience they require, and hence conversely how susceptible they are to advertising alone. The media initiated transition from aware to favourable may be written:

$$ -\left(\frac{dA}{dT}\right)_{af} = \left(\frac{dF}{dT}\right)_{af} = f_{af}^{*} \left[I(T) , A(T) , M(T) , S^{*}(T) \right] $$

where $M(T)$ is the aggregate media exposure and $*$ is used to signify that the form of these functions is different to those for the interpersonal case.[5] Where the transition is from unaware to aware as before $I(T)$ is eliminated from the expression.

The other marketing controlled state transfer mechanism would appear to be merely a function of the promotional campaign and individual situational effects. Innovativeness is not involved because, for one instance, the individual has no control over the receipt of a free sample. The expression may therefore be written:

$$ -\left(\frac{dA}{dT}\right)_{af} = \left(\frac{dF}{dT}\right)_{af} = f_{af}^{**} \left[P(T) , A(T) , S^{**}(T) \right] $$

$P(T)$ denoting a promotional campaign.[6] It should be noted that while this expression is part of the general theory, many products are launched without such promotional campaigns. In these specific cases the expression would, of course, be redundant. Note also that this form of state transfer is only allowed between the aware and the adopter states, not between unaware and adopter. Since the consensus of the evidence is that awareness spreads ahead of adoption, and since receipt of a free sample is defined here as 'adoption', then there is no good reason for allowing any role for this mechanism other than that discussed above.

Lastly we have those transfers which occur between adopter states, and which are not caused by interpersonal communication. These are due to factors such as boredom, or individual experiences with the product. Experiences which occur subsequent to the initial formation of opinion, and which may lead to the individual disseminating the opposite point of view from their initial stance. The form of this expression is dependent on individual situations, and how many people there are in the relevant category to have such experiences. That is:

$$- \left(\frac{dF}{dT}\right)_{fr} = \left(\frac{dR}{dT}\right)_{fr} = f_{fr}^{***} \left[F(T), S^{***}(T) \right]$$

This completes the preliminary exposition of the state transfer mechanisms, and allows Figure 5.1 to be restated as Figure 5.2.

A few words are necessary by way of explanation of Figure 5.2. It will be seen that, in comparison to the earlier figure, the number of transfers between adopter categories has increased. This is because it has been deduced that these transfers depend on the meetings between people in two states (interpersonal mechanisms) or the number of people in one state (individual experience mechanisms). Therefore to allow for the various combinations the number of transfers is effectively doubled. The one exception is the interpersonal state transfer between the favourable and the rejector state. In either 'direction' this is dependent on the number of meetings between favourables and rejectors and thus this is left as one 'transfer', with the proviso that the aggregate net flow will be in one direction or the other.

All the above is a direct consequence of only allowing the favourables and rejectors to communicate experience. Despite the apparent complexity of Figure 5.2 the only permitted transfers are those which follow logically from the behavioural theory expounded in Chapters 2, 3 and 4. A close inspection of this figure will reveal that the general theory is not simply a collection of all possible combinations of five states and four mechanisms but a rigorously specified logical construct.

At this point the reader may entertain the possibility of simplifying the theory by grouping the three mechanisms for transferring individuals from the aware state to one of the adopter states into one global expression. The rationale for this being that people adopt due to a combination of the three effects and not one alone. However, it could

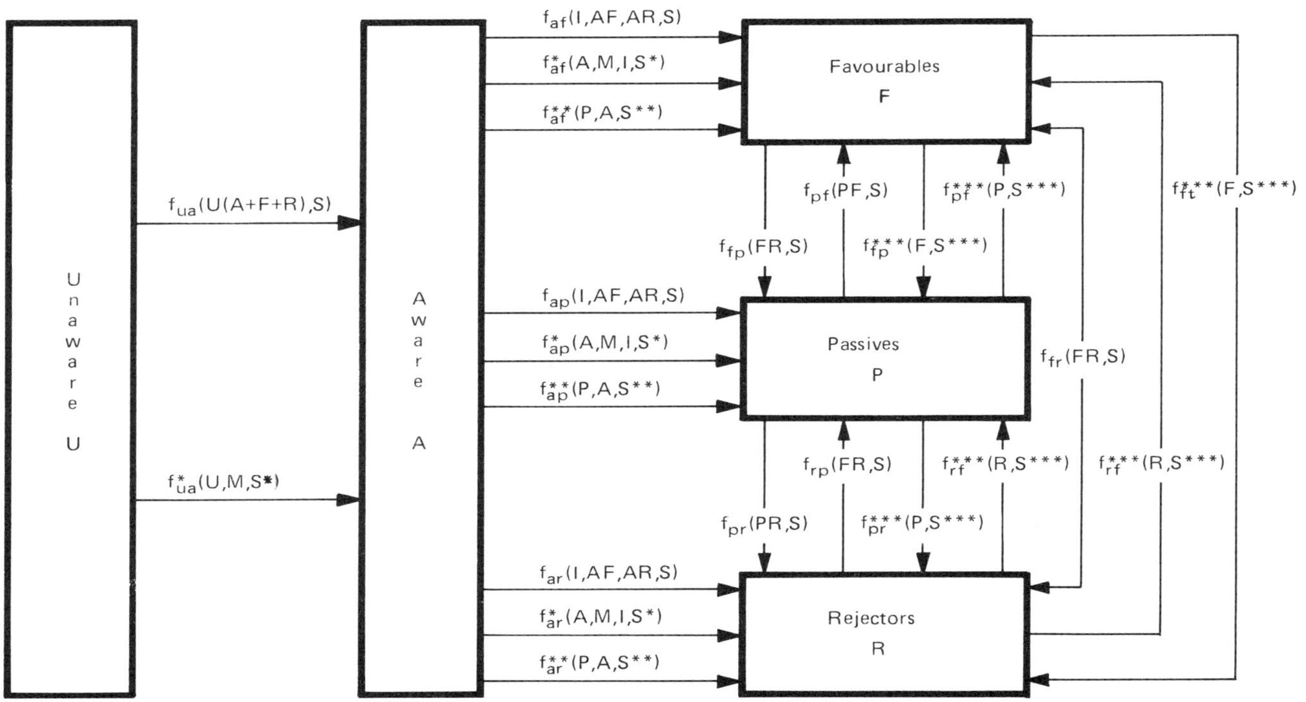

Fig. 5.2: A General Theory of Innovative Behaviour — System Diagram

be argued that the evidence is against this rationale. In the crucial persuasion stage individuals would appear to be influenced either by their social contacts or in isolation by the marketing channels. Remember the theory focuses on the moment of persuasion, the point when the requisite amount of communicated experience is acquired. Thus the majority of individuals would be expected to adopt because of interpersonal influence. The individuals who enter the adopter states by the media initiated route are those more innovative members of the population (which is consistent with the evidence showing that innovators are more exposed to the mass media given on p.73). It would therefore be expected that in the early stages of the diffusion process the rate of transfer via the media mechanism would be higher than that via the interpersonal mechanism. Indeed initially the interpersonal rate of transfer is zero (until some adopters exist) and the media mechanisms are necessary in order to start the process.[7] As the innovators adopt and as favourables and rejectors are created the rate of transfer via the media mechanism will show a relative and absolute decline, with most subsequent adoptions being due to interpersonal communication. Shortly evidence will be given showing this to be the actual case.

The role of the mass media is therefore twofold, first to create awareness and second to stimulate the innovators to adopt. This would appear consistent with the available evidence. It is known that the innovators are more exposed to the media, and that a proportion of the population are directly influenced to adopt by such impersonal sources (see Sheth, 1971). The innovators require little or no 'communicated experience' in the system. It therefore seems logical to ascribe this initial role to the media. It should also be pointed out that the form of the mass media state transfer mechanism could be such as to accommodate individuals who adopt directly upon becoming aware — perhaps solely because the product is 'new'. This eliminates the need to complicate the theory any further.

Before discussing how the general theory operates it is desirable to repeat the key assumption of this formulation. Now it is possible to conceive of a more complex version of the theory, specifically by dividing the aware state into favourably aware, unfavourably aware and passively aware. These new states might then be given a role in the total process. However it was noted in Chapter 4 that only adopters are effective in changing the behaviour of others. Provided that people without first-hand experience of the product are ineffective in changing attitudes and/or behaviour then the given formulation is adequate. The key assumption is therefore summarised as — *only those who have experience with the product may influence others.*

The operation of the proposed system is really quite simple. Commencing with all the population in the unaware state then the media campaign accompanying the product launch will generate awareness. Of course once some individuals are aware then further awareness may also be generated by interpersonal communication. From the aware state the more innovative members of the population will be stimulated to adopt by the media (there may also be a promotional campaign which would lead to a more complex situation). Then, and according to the product's perceived performance, some of these adopters will begin to communicate experience. If most are disseminating favourable information then more individuals will be persuaded to adopt and the now familiar 'snowball' effect will occur, leading to a rapid growth in the adoption curve. Should some adopters, however, be disseminating unfavourable information then not only will the adoption rate be lowered directly, but also the rejectors may persuade the favourables to change their opinion and hence state. In this situation there would be a dramatic fall in the rate of adoption. Such an effect might also transpire if originally favourable individuals subsequently had disagreeable experiences with the product. Indeed any event whereby the number of favourables is decreased relative to the number of rejectors will lower the adoption rate. Note, however, that the adoption curve may still continue to rise, albeit slowly, because of the presence of the media mechanism. According, then, to the dynamic behaviour of the number of people in each of the five states an infinite variety of event sequences may be generated, a variety which parallels that found empirically.

To achieve a complete formulation of the general theory, and one which demonstrates its dynamic nature, the system diagram may be expressed as a set of symbolic simultaneous differential equations. These are shown in Figure 5.3 and illustrate how the rate of change of the number of individuals in any one state at time T is dependent on the state transfer mechanisms. The total number of adopters at time T is $F + R + P$, and a solution of these equations for this quantity would yield the adoption curve.

However thus far all that has been achieved is to specify the theoretical system in symbolic terms. To progress any further mathematically, and thereby solve the equations, it is necessary to determine the precise form of the functions, that is f, f*, f** and f*** (and in each state transfer). For the general theory this cannot be achieved directly

Fig. 5.3: The Symbolic Equations for the General Theory of Innovative Behaviour

$$-\frac{dU}{dT} = f_{ua}(U \quad A+F+R \quad ,S) + f_{ua}^{*}(U,M,S^{*}) \qquad . \qquad . \qquad . \qquad (I)$$

$$\frac{dA}{dT} = f_{ua}(U \quad A+F+R \quad ,S) + f_{ua}^{*}(U,M,S^{*}) - f_{af}(I,AF,AR,S) - f_{af}^{*}(A,M,I,S^{*}) - f_{af}^{**}(P,A,S^{**})$$
$$- f_{ap}(I,AF,AR,S) - f_{ap}^{*}(A,I,M,S^{*}) - f_{ap}^{**}(P,A,S^{**}) - f_{ar}(I,AF,AR,S) - f_{ar}^{*}(A,I,M,S^{*})$$
$$- f_{ar}^{**}(P,A,S^{**}) \qquad . \qquad . \qquad . \qquad (II)$$

$$\frac{dF}{dT} = f_{af}(I,AF,AR,S) + f_{af}^{*}(A,M,I,S^{*}) + f_{af}^{**}(P,A,S^{**})$$
$$+ f_{pf}(PF,S) + f_{pf}^{***}(P,S^{***}) + f_{rf}^{***}(R,S^{***}) - f_{fp}(FR,S)$$
$$- f_{fp}^{***}(F,S^{***}) - f_{fr}^{***}(F,S^{***}) \pm f_{fr}(FR,S) \qquad . \qquad . \qquad . \qquad (III)$$

$$\frac{dP}{dT} = f_{ap}(I,AF,AR,S) + f_{ap}^{*}(A,I,M,S^{*}) + f_{ap}^{**}(P,A,S^{**}) + f_{fp}(FR,S) + f_{fp}^{***}(F,S^{***})$$
$$+ f_{rp}(FR,S) + f_{rp}^{***}(R,S^{***}) - f_{pf}(PF,S) - f_{pf}^{***}(P,S^{***})$$
$$- f_{pr}(PR,S) - f_{pr}^{***}(P,S^{***}) \qquad . \qquad . \qquad . \qquad (IV)$$

$$\frac{dR}{dT} = f_{ar}(I,AF,AR,S) + f_{ar}^{*}(A,I,M,S^{*}) + f_{ar}^{**}(P,A,S^{**}) + f_{pr}(PR,S) + f_{pr}^{***}(P,S^{***})$$
$$+ f_{fr}^{***}(F,S^{***}) - f_{rp}(FR,S) - f_{rp}^{***}(R,S^{***}) - f_{rf}^{***}(R,S^{***}) \mp f_{rf}(FR,S) \qquad . \qquad . \qquad . \qquad (V)$$

Notation f refers to the general function for interpersonal state transfers, similarly f^{*} is the general function for mass media transfers, f^{**} for the other marketing transfers, and f^{***} for transfers due to individual experiences (adopters only). The subscripts refer to the specific form of the function for one state transfer mechanism, that is f_{ap}^{*} refers to the mass media state transfer mechanism between the aware and the passive state.

$\frac{dF}{dT}$ is the rate of change of the numbers in the favourable state, and so on.

at the present time, since the requisite empirical knowledge does not exist. Nor would it be entirely desirable thus to operationalise the general theory. The likely result would be mathematically very difficult to solve, and extremely unwieldy when applied to a *specific* innovation. A more fruitful line of progress would appear to be *a priori* to hypothesise simpler functions (thus eliminating mathematical difficulties) and to modify the general theory as appropriate to the type of innovation it is wished to study (thus allowing it to be applied to specific situations). By assessing the performance of a restricted or simplified version in explaining empirical data then insights may be gained into more realistic forms for the functions, and so on. It will subsequently also be indicated how such simpler versions may be used to study the behaviour of the state transfer mechanisms. However it must be stressed that the general theory remains the core of the endeavour; it is not possible, or at least it is dangerous, to proceed directly to simpler forms. The general theory is needed to suggest what the appropriate simple or special model might be in any specific situation. It can also be noted that while a simple model will, in a scientific sense, always be more testable than the general theory (because the predictions of the former are more specific) it will always involve a greater number of restrictive assumptions, and therefore be less realistic than the general theory.

To date, only one restricted case of this general theory has been solved. However despite the fact that only relatively simple expressions were used for the state transfer mechanisms the results obtained, in conjunction with empirical data, were interesting and encouraging. The evidence presented by Midgley (1976), goes some considerable way to supporting the arguments advanced in this text. This evidence will now be discussed in detail, for quite apart from its theoretical significance it has great importance for the management of new products.

5.3 A Special Mathematical Theory of Innovative Behaviour

In an article entitled 'A Simple Mathematical Theory of Innovative Behaviour', the author presents a model for low risk products, a model which is in fact a restricted version of the general theory.[8] The first simplifying assumption made was that all the population was already aware of the new product. Given the nature of low risk innovations, which are normally introduced with massive advertising campaigns, this was thought to be a reasonable assumption. With widespread media advertising and the high level of initial distribution usually obtained by such products (making them immediately visible to most housewives), it is

Fig. 5.4: A Special Theory of Innovative Behaviour for Low Risk Products

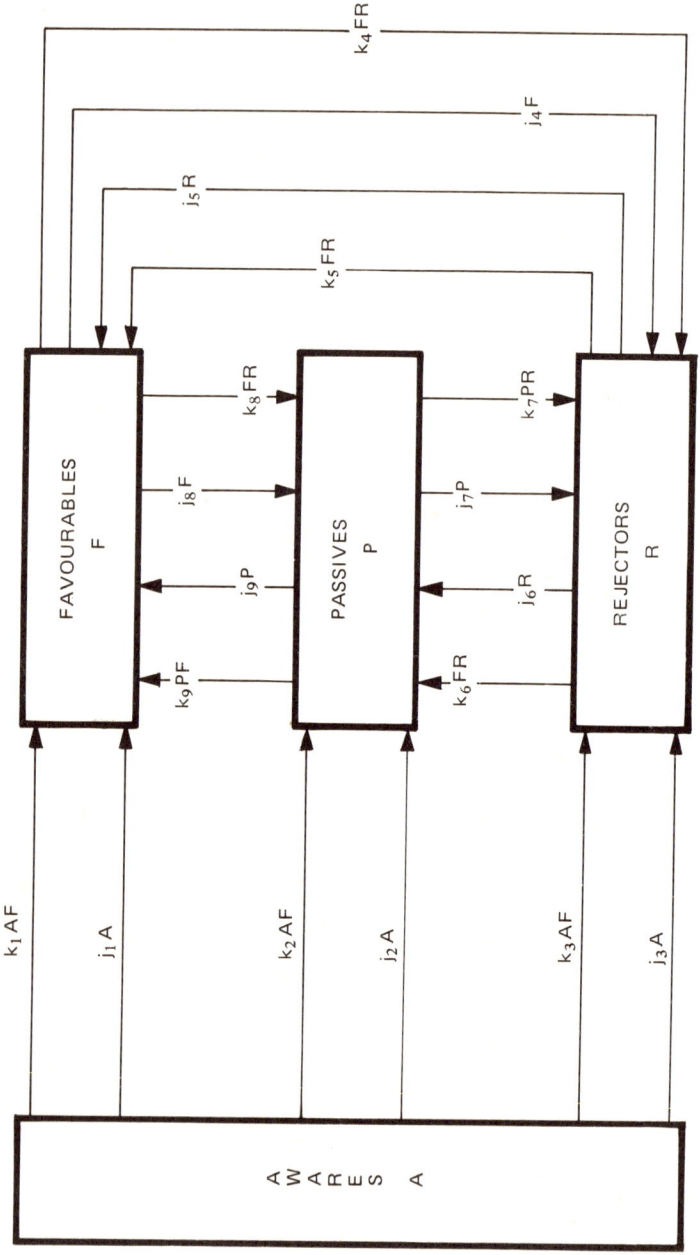

Source: Adapted from Midgley (1976), and used by permission of the Journal of Consumer Research.

plausible that the majority of individuals know of the product's existence within two or three weeks, and certainly in a far shorter time than the product takes to reach, say, 5 per cent adoption. This type of product takes of the order of a year to a year and a half to be adopted by the majority of the population.[9]

The next assumptions were made to reduce or eliminate any possible mathematical difficulties, and consisted of specifying simple forms for the various functions. The media and other marketing mechanisms were aggregated into one function of the form $j_e A$, where j_e is a constant. This form was also used for the individual experience mechanisms, for instance $j_m R$. The subscripts denote that a different value was assumed for the constant in each state transfer mechanism. The interpersonal mechanisms were all of the form $k_n AF$, where k_n is again a constant.[10] The system diagram comparable to Figure 5.2 is that displayed in Figure 5.4.

This leads to the following set of non-linear simultaneous differential equations:

$$-\frac{dA}{dT} = AF(k_1+k_2+k_3) + A(j_1+j_2+j_3) \qquad . \qquad . \qquad . \qquad (I)$$

$$\frac{dF}{dT} = k_1 AF + j_1 A + k_5 FR + j_5 R + k_9 PF$$
$$+ j_9 P - k_4 FR - j_4 F - k_8 FR - j_8 F \qquad . \qquad . \qquad (II)$$

$$\frac{dP}{dT} = k_2 AF + j_2 A + k_8 FR + j_8 F + k_6 FR + j_6 R$$
$$- k_9 PF - j_9 P - j_7 P - k_7 PR \qquad . \qquad . \qquad . \qquad (III)$$

$$\frac{dR}{dT} = k_3 AF + j_3 F + k_4 FR + j_4 F$$
$$+ k_7 PR + j_7 P - k_5 FR - j_5 R$$
$$- k_6 FR - j_6 R \qquad . \qquad . \qquad . \qquad . \qquad . \qquad (IV)$$

Once again as this is a closed system, that is $A + F + P + R$ = population size, then one of these equations is redundant. If the variables are stated as *percentages* then at the moment of product launch ($T = 0$), $A = 100\%$ and $F = P = R = 0\%$.

To contrast the above state transfer mechanisms with the general case two examples will be taken. These are the interpersonal and mass media transfer mechanisms for the state change aware to favourable. In the general case the mechanisms are $f_{af}(I,AF,AR,S)$ and $f_{af}^*(I,A, M,S^*)$ respectively, while above they are k_1AF and j_1A respectively. Hence it may be noted that k_1 is equivalent to some function of I,AR and S, and j_1 to some function of I,M,S^*. Functions which may be expected to vary over time and thus render the assumption of constancy invalid. However it can be pointed out that the method by which the special theory is fitted to empirical data produces estimates for the k's and j's which are effectively averages over the population over time. Thus the k's and j's can be considered as the mean values of the above functions.[11] Symbolically, and for the two examples:

$$k_1 = \overline{f(I,AR,S)}$$

$$j_1 = \overline{f(I,M,S^*)}$$

It must also be stressed that the form of these reduced functions would be different to that of the original expressions.

Because of the relationship depicted above the special theory provides a series of measurements on aspects of the general theory; in particular it indicates the relative average magnitudes of the various state transfer mechanisms.[12] Furthermore the relative simplicity of the mathematics allows us to make these measurements in relation to actual case histories of new product introductions. *Hence the special theory provides an empirical test of the conceptualisation advanced here.*

Given values for the constants the solution of equations I to IV is a trivial exercise in numerical integration. However no *a priori* knowledge of these values exists and we must therefore proceed as follows. Arbitrary numbers are assigned to the k and j constants, equations I to IV numerically integrated over the appropriate number of time periods and an adoption curve generated (from F + P + R).[13] This theoretical curve may then be compared with actual data.[14] The arbitrary values are then adjusted and another comparison produced; if this comparison is more favourable we repeat the successful pattern of adjustments and solve the equations again. If not, we try another set or pattern of adjustments. The process is repeated until we achieve the 'best fit' between the theoretical and empirical adoption curves, that is the set of values for the constants which produce the closest agreement between the theoretical and empirical curves. Fuller details of this iterative procedure, termed a direct search optimisation technique, are given in Midgley (1976).

In this manner values may be obtained for the k and j constants, and, of greater interest, a complete solution for the special theory, a solution illustrating the dynamic behaviour of the adopter states, and considered to be a good representation of real world events.

5.4 The Results for Six New Product Launches*

In this section we will be concerned first with the two fundamental tests applied to this, and any other, theory. That is, whether it is consistent with the actual data, and whether it can predict the future. We will then explore the nature of the solutions, particularly as far as these yield empirical support for the behaviour of the adopter states proposed earlier.

The consistency between theory and data was assessed by fitting the equations to the maximum amount of data available for each of six low risk non-durable products. The results are set out in Table 5.1. The figures quoted for the Kolmogorov-Smirnov test represent the probability of occurrence, under the null hypothesis, of a value of the statistic greater than or equal to that observed. The null hypothesis is, of course, the theory, and the respective probability levels were computed from the tables of Smirnov (1948). In essence the Kolmogorov-Smirnov test relates to whether the largest discrepancy observed between the theoretical and empirical adoption curve can reasonably be thought of as a chance fluctuation from the theoretical distribution. The test is discussed in Massey (1951) and Siegal (1956). The test applied to the residuals or remaining differences between theory and data was that due to Durbin and Watson (1951). *A priori* it was expected that the residuals of the cumulated series would be positively autocorrelated, while those of the first difference series would be independent. These hypotheses were supported by the results.

A good deal of support is provided for the special theory by Table 5.1; the average squared errors are small, the correlations high and it appears probable that any discrepancies between theory and data are merely chance fluctuations. However, consistency is only the first step in assessing a theory's value. It is also necessary to ask whether it can predict future events. Hence various exercises were conducted in which the theory was fitted to part of the data and then a forecast made of the remaining portion of the empirical adoption curve. With the data it was possible to obtain, such forecasting exercises could only

---

* Section 5.4 is based in part on Midgley, D.F., 'A Simple Theory of Innovative Behaviour', *Journal of Consumer Research,* Vol.3, No.1 (1976), and used there with modifications by permission of the *Journal of Consumer Research.*

Table 5.1: Testing the Theory against Panel Data: Values Obtained for the Statistics

Product Number	Product Type	Number of Observations (weeks)	Average Squared Error ($\%^2$ per week)	Correlation Coefficient	Kolmogorov-Smirnov Probability Level	Results of the Durbin-Watson Test on the Residuals (0.05 level)		Total Panel Size
						Cumulative Series	First Difference Series	
1	Toothpaste	42	0.188	0.998	89.3	positive	independent	368
2	Confectionary	20	0.049	0.998	99.9	positive	independent	545
3	Detergent	26	1.026	0.998	53.3	positive	independent	490
4	Detergent	23	3.286	0.994	20.0	positive	independent	438
5	Toothpaste	27	0.131	0.996	49.8	positive	independent	652
6	Biscuit	35	0.465	0.999	40.0	positive	independent	835

Source: Based on Midgley (1976), and used by permission of the Journal of Consumer Research.

meaningfully be performed for two of the products. With 18 constants to be estimated, 20 observations (that is weeks of data here), are necessary for one spare degree of freedom. Table 5.2 presents the results of these exercises, and as can be seen one was an extremely accurate prediction while the other was less successful.

However subsequent analysis reveals that the reason for the latter probably lies in the data rather than the theory. The consumer panel used to generate the data for Product 1 was the smallest of the six panels cited, and this, together with a low initial rate of market penetration meant that the number of adopters was very small in the early phases of the product launch. Apart from its relevance to the discussion here this result also raises an important point with respect to the management control of new product launches, namely that any consumer panel used to monitor such a launch must be large enough to allow reliable estimation and prediction. The statement applies regardless of whether sophisticated models (such as that above) or simpler forecasting methods (such as curve fitting) are being used.

The special theory demonstrates a reasonable degree of predictive ability with respect to the cumulative adoption curve. However the emphasis here is on the behaviour of the various adopter states proposed earlier, that is the favourables, rejectors and passives. In Figures 5.5 and 5.6 the solutions for two of the products are presented; the first being one which might be considered a 'successful' innovation while the second might be thought of as an 'unsuccessful' innovation.

Now it must be pointed out that as yet there is no direct empirical evidence for the behaviour of the three time series depicted in these figures. The theoretical model was fitted to the summation of these three categories, that is to the cumulative adoption curve, and not to each category individually. Indeed to collect data for these categories would require the development of new survey-based methodologies. However there is some evidence, of a circumstantial nature, which relates to these pictures, and is based on managerial perceptions of what actually happened.

Thus in the case of Product 4 the theoretical solution depicts the continued rise of those in favour of, or neutral toward, the product, while those against it remain a very small proportion of the population. In managerial perception this product was a 'success', generating a high level of repeat purchasing and exhibiting a healthy growth in sales.

On the other hand the management involved in Product 3's launch perceived it as a 'failure', with a low repeat purchase rate and continued problems. This is also the conclusion which would be drawn from the

Table 5.2: Forecasting Exercises

Product number	Forecast estimation period (weeks)	Total period forecast (weeks)	Average squared error over forecast period	Correlation coefficient over forecast period	Kolmogorov-Smirnov probability level over forecast period	Results of the Durbin-Watson test on the residuals	
						Cumulative series	First differrence series
1	20	42	6.08	0.988	very small	positive	positive
6	20	35	0.69	0.998	54.9	positive	independent

Source: Midgley (1976), and used by permission of the Journal of Consumer Research.

Fig. 5.5: Adopter State Behaviour for Product 4

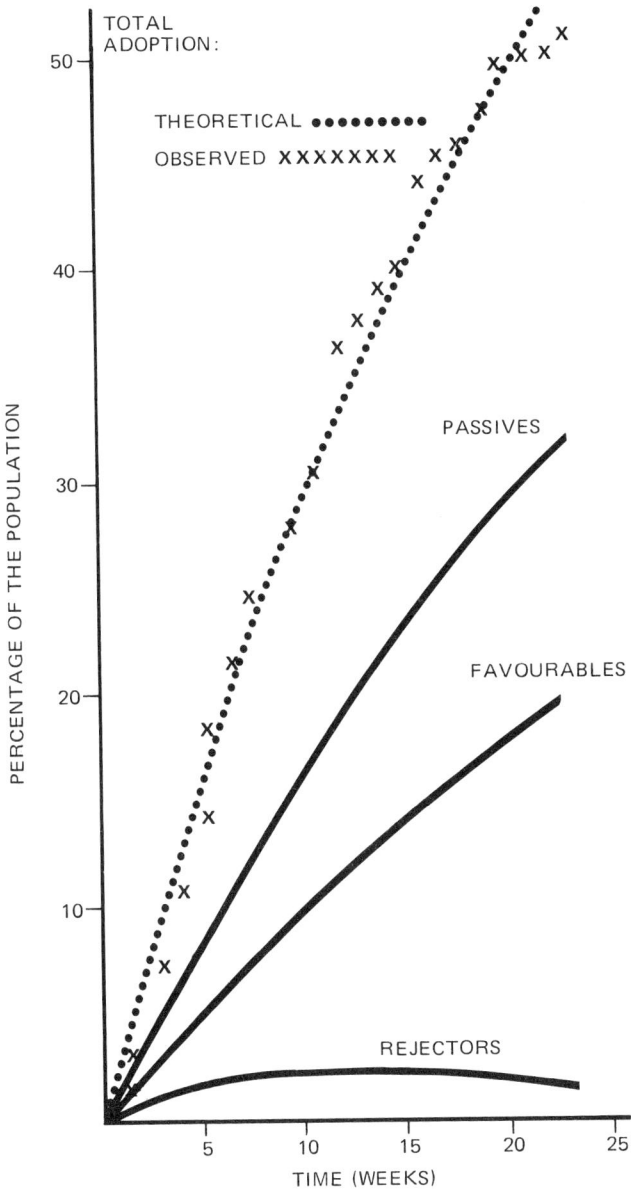

Source: Midgley (1976), and used by permission of the Journal of Consumer Research.

Fig. 5.6: Adopter State Behaviour for Product 3

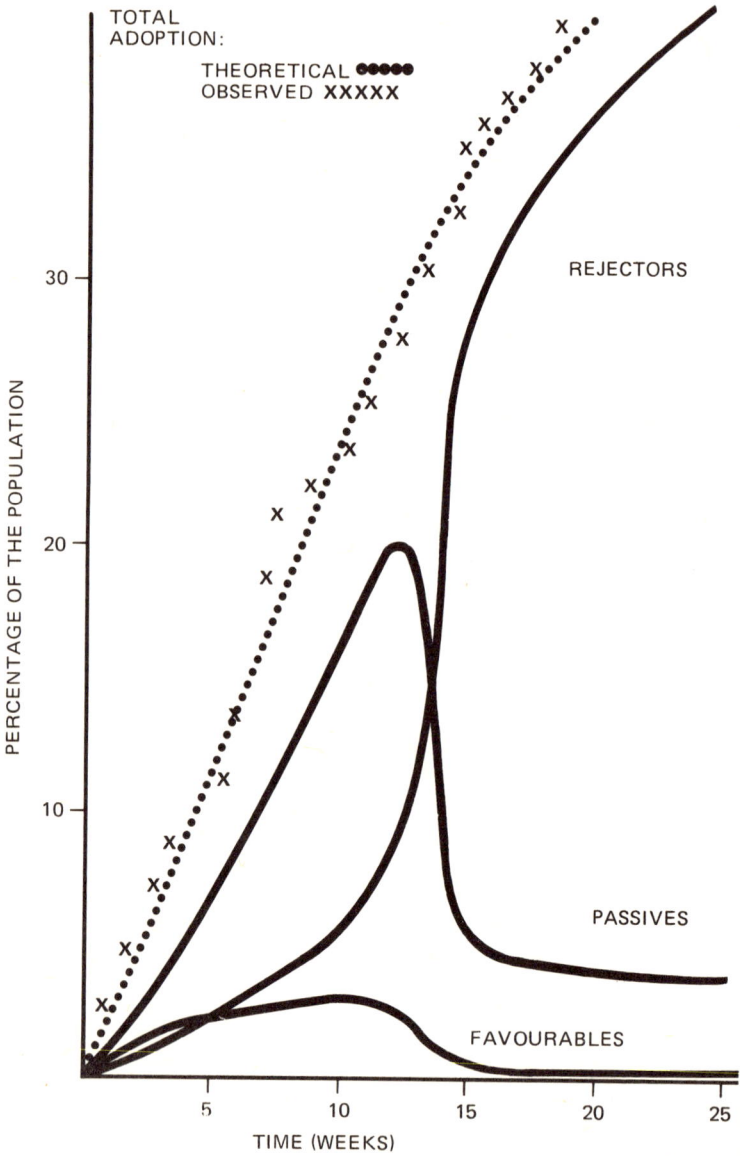

Fig. 5.7: Adopter State Behaviour for Product 6

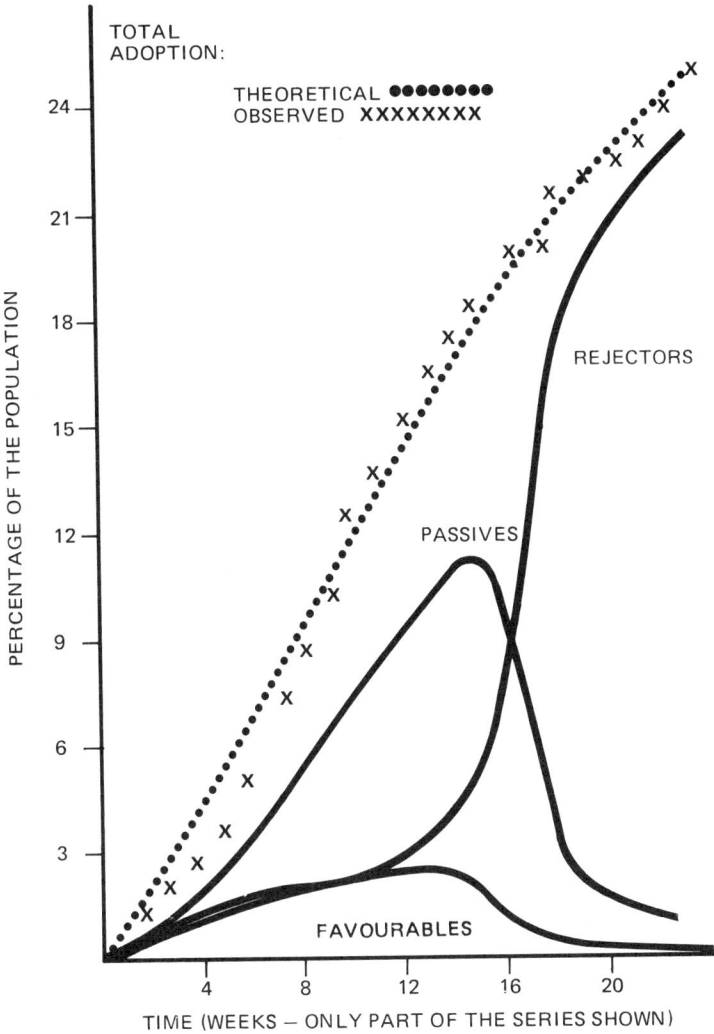

Source: Midgley (1976), and used by permission of the Journal of Consumer Research.

theoretical solution detailed in Figure 5.6. There, initial success can be seen to give way to failure as the number of those actively against the product exhibits a dramatic increase from week 5 onwards. In this case the theory would imply what actually occurred in practice, that is a low level of repeat purchasing.

Thus the theoretical solutions generated from the consumer panel data have immediate and recognisable connections with managements' perceptions of real events, and this is even more strikingly evidenced by the solution for Product 6, given in Figure 5.7.

In that figure it can be seen that what was initially a fairly successful launch turned into failure. The numbers of those people in favour of the product peak and go into decline after week 12; those neutral toward it decline after week 15. On the other hand the growth of the rejectors accelerates after week 12.

Now it is known that, while initially a success, this product encountered distribution problems around the point in time shown in Figure 5.7. The fact that there were insufficient quantities of the product on the supermarket shelf did indeed result in an adverse consumer reaction, and one which took some time to rectify.[15]

Thus the pattern of dynamic behaviour for the various adopter categories or states which was hypothesised in this and other chapters has been tested in actual situations, and has been shown to have distinct connections with the real world. The special theory is consistent with empirical data, capable of yielding accurate predictions, and provides new and deeper insight into the acceptance and rejection of new products by the population. The benefits of a mathematical formulation, albeit one based on limited assumptions, are therefore clearly demonstrated. By the use of such a formulation the theory has become more testable, since it now provides a quantitative prediction of the dynamic behaviour of the social system. Furthermore the theory caters for the compexity of the phenomenon known as the diffusion of innovations in a way no purely verbal treatment can.

5.5 The Derived Measure of Communication Effectiveness

That the k and j constants provide a measure of communication effectiveness is fairly self-evident. In the simple form of the interpersonal state transfer mechanism we have $k_1 AF$ for instance. AF represents the total number of meetings between awares and favourables, which may be thought of as the most important component of the general form of the mechanism, and k_1 therefore represents the effectiveness of these meetings in persuading individuals to adopt. Similarly in $j_1 A$ then j_1

represents the effectiveness of the media in creating favourable adopters.[16]

In this section we will therefore discuss the values obtained for these constants in the six cases, and then subsequently the total state transfers observed in each of these cases. Essentially the constants of the special theory provide a summary picture of the effectiveness of all the various information transfers, and as such provide better measurements of these processes than have hitherto been possible. However before proceeding any further one important comment should be added.

While it is feasible to compare the k constants among themselves, or the j constants among themselves, difficulties arise if attempts are made to compare the value of a k constant with that of a j. The k constants relate to interpersonal communication/influence and as such are multiplied by the product of two variables, that is the number of meetings between individuals in two different states. On the other hand the j constants are only multiplied by one variable. Hence while the absolute values of the k constants are often much smaller than the corresponding j values this should not be taken to mean that their relative effectiveness was also much smaller ('relative effectiveness' in terms of state transfers). In fact, depending on the magnitude of the variables in question, this transfer is often much larger than that generated by the j constant — because of the multiplying effect of the second variable.

Therefore, while it is possible to discuss the individual values of the two types of constants, when it comes to making comparisons between the two (effectively between interpersonal influence and all other processes), then these must be made on the basis of the flows between categories which the respective constants generated. In turn these flows are dependent on the magnitude of the various variables at any point in time and thus another method is needed to make such comparisons. This will be discussed shortly; for the moment we will concentrate on the individual constant values. These values are given in Table 5.3 together with the relative accuracies to which these values, and those of the associated squared error functions, were determined.

Taking the values in Table 5.3 then these fall into logical groups. Obviously k_1 to k_3 and j_1 to j_3 relate to the persuasion of people to adopt, and are of prime importance in gaining initial acceptance for the product. For a successful launch k_1 to k_2 should be greater than k_3, similarly j_1 and j_2 should be greater than j_3. This would imply that most people were giving favourable opinions of the product, and that the advertising was creating more such favourable adopters. On the other hand if k_3 or j_3 were larger

Table 5.3: The Values Obtained for the Constants

Constant	Product 1	Product 2	Product 3	Product 4	Product 5	Product 6
k_1	0.0002649	0.0026657	0.0000046203	0.0	0.0031586	0.0011522
k_2	0.00014715	0.00017043	0.0037724	0.0	0.0	0.00053173
k_3	0.0	0.025922	0.0033824	0.0	0.000063772	0.00058022
k_4	0.0	0.15977	0.24998	0.17	1.0708	0.9509
k_5	1.8675	0.53491	0.58996	0.85	0.51314	0.99937
k_6	0.21877	0.0	0.71995	0.79	0.0040077	0.99937
k_7	0.60487	0.29157	0.1156	0.62	0.5385	0.1318
k_8	0.0023652	0.83766	0.55736	0.33	0.86016	0.95055
k_9	0.0	0.58957	0.059996	0.0	0.84789	0.040474
j_1	0.0031287	0.0	0.012717	0.014231	0.0027672	0.0063958
j_2	0.00035256	0.0043279	0.002858	0.0098	0.0	0.0012554
j_3	0.00058239	0.0	0.0	0.0096	0.0000058759	0.0019804
j_4	0.76569	0.96179	0.00004668	0.0	0.0049829	0.45731
j_5	0.0	0.036937	0.0	0.0	0.59054	0.038308
j_6	0.060907	0.59556	0.36591	0.79	0.19944	0.034774
j_7	0.21473	0.0012502	0.47997	0.53	0.0031376	0.36977
j_8	0.63668	1.0413	0.89987	0.95	0.38749	0.17982
j_9	0.19332	0.0014060	0.12999	0.17	0.27863	0.71893
Relative accuracy of the values	±8%	±4%	±0.05%	±0.01%	±8%	±0.6%
Error in the objective function	2×10^{-5}	5×10^{-7}	4×10^{-8}	5×10^{-7}	5×10^{-6}	4×10^{-5}

Source: Based on Midgley (1976), and used by permission of the Journal of Consumer Research.

then this would imply the presence of people with an unfavourable opinion of the product, and hence a less successful product launch.

The remainder of the constants, that is k_4 to k_9 and j_4 to j_9, relate to transfers between those who have already adopted k_4 to k_9 are measures of the effectiveness of the favourable or unfavourable opinions of individuals in persuading others to change states. By inference these are therefore measures of the perceived performance of the product, as indeed were k_1, k_2 and k_3. However, unlike j_1 to j_3, j_4 to j_9 relate to personal experience with the product, or other psychological factors such as boredom, rather than to the effects of advertising. Here again this means that these constants are also bound up with the consumers' perception of the product and its performance.

Table 5.3 reveals no great similarities between the respective values for the six products. This is as would be expected since the various products would produce different consumer reactions, together with the likely different effects of the distinct advertising strategies used in each of the six cases. However what is immensely interesting and encouraging is that in all but one case j_1 is greater than j_3 and in every case the combined effect of j_1 and j_2 is greater than j_3. Which means that advertising is always more effective in producing people in favour of, or neutral toward, the innovation than in producing those unfavourable toward it, and is normally more effective in producing favourables than rejectors — that is disregarding the passive category. In a sense we would have been somewhat perturbed if this had not been the case, but the fact that the special theory generates such realistic results is further evidence of its validity.

As to the rest of the figures then there are only a few discernible patterns, the most striking being that k_8 is *always* greater than k_9. Interpreted, this implies that unfavourable communicated experience is always more effective in making favourables neutral than is favourable communicated experience in making passives into favourables. This also coincides with the observation that in five out of six cases j_8 was greater than j_9, that is personal unfavourable experiences are more effective in making favourables neutral than the opposite internal transfer mechanism. It would therefore appear that unfavourable experience and influence can play a vital role in the process, and that an adverse trend against a product may occur because of a transfer of people from favourables to passives rather than a direct switch between favourables and rejectors.

However such conclusions remain tentative and many more products need to be studied before we can be emphatic. What the above does illustrate is the type of new behavioural insights which the theory gives on the process of new product adoption. Insights which have value in the management of innovation, and also suggest new avenues of research.

The next step which could be taken is to investigate the relation of the constant values to the products involved and the advertising employed. If it proves possible to link the parameters to the results of consumer surveys and/or the level and type of advertising used then it may also be possible to develop more effective media and product strategies.

We now turn from looking at the individual values of the various constants to compare the role of the two types of communication, interpersonal and the mass media. As previously mentioned this can only be achieved by a comparison of the resulting flows or transfers between states, and not by a direct inspection of the respective k and j constants. In other words by examining the numbers of people transferred by each mechanism.

Midgley (1975) reports the results of such an exercise based on a simple computer programme which printed out the values of each term in the equations, for example $k_1 AF$ or $j_5 R$, at each point in time, and over the periods of time considered. This was effectively the computation of the rate of change of each individual flow at a point in time rather than the numbers transferred over one week by that route. However the former provides an adequate index of the latter, and is much less difficult to compute.[17] By comparing the magnitudes of these individual rates of change we are able to obtain a very clear picture of the dynamic behaviour of the system, and the operation of the total state transfer mechanisms. Since for each state transfer mechanism there are as many such 'flows' as there are time periods we commence the comparisons by examining the peak or maximum values obtained for each mechanism. If we examine the first phase of the process, that is the creation of adopters, then quite naturally over the initial stages the advertising media are the most effective in persuading individuals to adopt. However, once and if there are a number of favourables or rejectors then interpersonal influence begins to affect the system. Comparing the maximum values of the rates of change leads to some interesting conclusions. Taking the total flows $k_1 AF + k_2 AF + k_3 AF$ and $j_1 A + j_2 A + j_3 A$ suggests that for two products interpersonal communication was more effective than the media, in one case the two effects were roughly equal, and for the remaining three products the media were more effective than interpersonal influence (respectively Products 3 and 5, Product 1, and Products 2, 4 and 6). However, a more subtle analysis, based on the effectiveness of communications in generating favourable adopters, reveals that the situation is a little more complex than this. Again using the peak rates of change as an index of effectiveness, it would appear that several situations are possible. For Product 1 interpersonal influence and advertising were almost equal in significance, both creating favourable adopters or passives. There was only a negligible amount of unfavourable influence generated and Product 1 was a success. On the other hand for Product 2 while the media were primarily creating passives, interpersonal influence was generating rejectors. This was also the case for Product 3 in that while the media were generating those in favour of, or neutral towards, the product, interpersonal influence resulted in passives and rejectors. In other words for both products the two mechanisms acted against each other and in the end neither were successes. Product 4 was a success, and one entirely initiated by advertising. For Product 5 adoption was primarily due to favourable communicated experience, with advertising playing a minor role. Lastly for Product 6 the combined effect of interpersonal influence and the media in creating favourables initially, at least, outweighed the creation of rejectors.

Nor is this the complete story; we have been discussing the peak effectiveness and these values can decline dramatically. Earlier we discussed Product 6 and advanced a rationale for why initial success turned into failure. This failure is illustrated by the flows in the system. At week 12 favourable interpersonal influence was at a high level, by week 35 it had declined to almost zero. The only people entering the system at that point in time were those influenced by the media, and this effect itself was declining — leading to a slowing down in the growth of market penetration.

Furthermore we have only discussed the six flows from aware to one of the three adopter states and it is just as necessary to examine the second phase of the process. Just as favourable or unfavourable influence is vitally important in transfers between the aware and the adopter states, so it is in transfers between adopter states themselves. A shift between favourables and rejectors can also produce a dramatic change in the behaviour of the system; indeed we can never really isolate this phase from the creation of adopters — both inter-relate in a complex and dynamic manner. Studying the flows between the three adopter states highlights the fact that people do change their minds, in that there is a very high level of transfer from one state to another.

Examining the peak rates of change reveals that, in terms of total effect, interpersonal influence was apparently always more 'effective' than the other psychological and product perception terms (that is summing all the 'k' terms and comparing them with the sum of all the 'j' terms). However this could be misleading if used in certain ways as a small proportion of people who have unfavourable experiences with the product may, over the process of time, generate this apparent predominance of interpersonal influence. Therefore the result should not be used to suggest that any individual j term is insignificant to the total system, indeed to the contrary, this term may have been the sole initial cause of the observed end result. What is demonstrated is the power of interpersonal communication in 'multiplying' the effect of individual product perceptions, whether good or bad.

It would also appear safe to say that after the initial stages of the product launch there are usually more people changing their adopter state, and hence their opinion on the product, at any one point in time than there are actually people adopting the product at that same point in time. Curiously enough this picture of a 'fickle consumer' has much in common with the basis of the recent theories of brand switching due to Ehrenberg (1972), Herniter (1973) and Bass (1974).[18] This commonality could conceivably be exploited in the future — to derive a model of the product life cycle.

Lastly, and in relation to the general form of the state transfer mechanism, Midgley (1974b) notes some limited evidence that the constant values obtained from differing amounts of data are themselves different. This is consistent with the general theory. If the k and j constants are the mean values of some varying quantity then we would expect averages taken over different periods of time to yield different estimates. Which suggests that the most fruitful line of development may not be to attempt directly to specify more realistic expressions for the state transfer mechanisms, but rather to seek some methodology which allows us to treat the above k's and j's as variables rather than constants. Given a dynamic picture of the behaviour of the reduced functions it may be possible to unravel their structure in a little more detail. The special theory provides an estimate of the magnitudes of these reduced functions but little more (in connection with the general theory that is). The benefits of greater knowledge in this area could perhaps be a linking of the system's behaviour to variables under management control, such as advertising and promotion, and thereby gain some assistance with strategic planning. The best approach would seem to be to relate the behaviour of measurable variables within the reduced functions to the behaviour of the functions themselves. For instance within f(I,AR,S) we can determine the behaviour pattern for AR. By comparing this to the behaviour pattern for f(I,AR,S) as a whole some facets of the latter's structure might be determined. Similarly the behaviour of f(I,M,S*) could be related to the known media campaign M(T). First, however, a method is needed for generating the dynamic histories of the reduced functions. Some thoughts on this topic will be given in Section 5.7.

In conclusion the results given in this section demonstrate that it is very largely meaningless to discuss one communication channel or state transfer mechanism in isolation from the other, or to stress one as more important than the other. It has been seen that interpersonal communication and mass media communication can work together or against each other, or in a more complex manner. Therefore it is argued here that any theory of new product adoption must incorporate and inter-relate both forms of communication within its basic framework. Further it is also suggested that the only possible method by which this can be achieved is via the application of mathematics. Any other method would be incapable of handling the dynamic complexities involved.

5.6 Conclusions on the Special Theory

It can now be seen that the special theory has performed reasonably, even surprisingly, well despite the limited assumptions on which it is based. These assumptions would therefore seem to have some justification, but more importantly the sum total of the results obtained provides substantial empirical support for the conceptual schema developed in this and earlier chapters. In particular confirmation for the dynamic picture of innovative behaviour has been found, and the adopter states proposed herein appear to have direct correspondence with reality. The special theory is consistent with the data and has a degree of predictive ability, both of which are desirable attributes for any theory. Furthermore the values obtained for the eighteen constants not only provide measurements of communication effectiveness, but in doing so highlight the complexity of the communication mechanisms. The social processes of the diffusion of innovations vary markedly from innovation to innovation, even for the cases cited — which were all low risk supermarket products.

Overall the strategy of using the general theory as a basis for deriving theories for special cases or types of innovation appears a viable one. This allows us to derive theories which can be empirically tested, thus increasing our knowledge, and which potentially, at least, are useful in the managerial sense. It must be stressed that the special theory can stand by itself as a model of the social processes involved in low risk innovations. It would appear to be an adequate conceptual framework for such situations, although of course one which can be developed further. Specifically the special theory could become a powerful forecasting tool, predicting as it does not only gross adoption but also the attitudes and opinions of the adopters (and hence by extrapolation the likelihood of repeat purchase). Much more research is needed before such potential is realised, although perhaps more in the nature of technical development than added conceptual sophistications. What is needed at this point in time is a more efficient methodology for employing the model, and one which lowers the costs of the data processing involved.

What this special theory obviously cannot achieve is a description of the social processes involved in the adoption of major consumer durables, or political ideologies, or so on. To achieve such ends we must return to the general theory and formulate a specific model appropriate to the situation in question. A model which might have similarities to the one discussed here, but which will also have important differences, which could not have been deduced by any other route. It seems probable that we will therefore always have this cyclical process of investigation in which the general theory is utilised to formulate simpler models for specific situations, and in which the results of testing these restricted simple models against empirical data are in turn utilised to modify and improve the general theory. By the very nature of its generality the general theory is unlikely to be directly testable in the forseeable future. However by developing more and more sophisticated variants for specific innovation situations we both hasten the day when this may be possible, and develop a series of powerful managerial and scientific tools. The crucial point is that such development must take place within the framework of a general theory, else it will be piecemeal, unrelated and unlikely to lead along fruitful avenues.

A Historical Note

To be historically accurate the special theory for low risk innovations occurred simultaneously with elements of the general theory. It was not until some time later that the general theory was coherently synthesised. However the order of presentation used here, general to special, is more logical particularly given that the general theory effectively explains some of the more unexpected results obtained from the special theory.

5.7 The Way Forward — Suggestions for Further Research

The general theory and the results of testing the special theory both indicate that a fruitful line of research is to seek a methodology whereby the k and j quantities may be treated as variables rather than constants. If feasible this would allow the behaviour of the reduced functions to be mapped out over time, and therefore hopefully reveal their general form. Subsequently and by comparison with data on other variables (media advertising, AR meetings, etc.), it may be possible to unravel the detailed structure of these functions.

For example, suppose it was possible to demonstrate that j_1 behaved as shown in Figure 5.8, this being the pattern which the general theory suggests.

Fig. 5.8: The Possible Behaviour of a Reduced Function

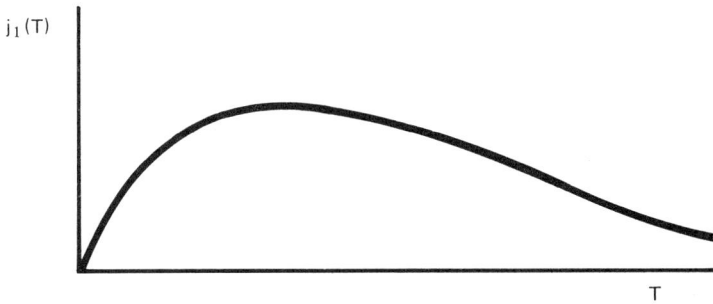

If the known pattern of media expenditure/exposure was then super-imposed, as in Figure 5.9, it becomes immediately possible to suggest that j_1 is a lagged function of media expenditure.

This is a simplistic example since theoretically there are also the effects of innovativeness I and the situational variable S^* to account for. The former presumably accounts for the change in the 'shape' of the function from M to j_1, while the latter, including as it does aggregate

Fig. 5.9: The Possible Behaviour of a Reduced Function Contrasted with the Behaviour of a Component Variable

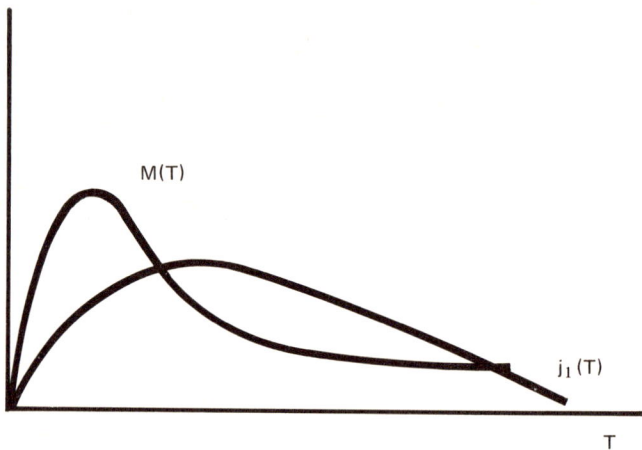

product perception, presumably accounts for the absolute magnitude of the function j_1. However this example does demonstrate how we might proceed given the appropriate methodology. Furthermore this approach seems intrinsically more viable than that of speculatively formulating mathematical expressions for the reduced functions and attempting, probably with considerable computational difficulty, to solve the equations for specific innovations.

Fortunately the requisite techniques for the proposed approach appear to exist, and lie in the area of optimal control theory.

The theorems and methods of optimal control theory were developed in the context of dynamic physical systems such as aircraft, rockets, generating plants, machine tools and so on — systems which have a close resemblance to that presented here. The basic notion is that all such systems have a trajectory of some kind, and this trajectory is dependent on how certain controls are manipulated. The trajectory may be the path between two points, power supplied to the national grid, metal removed from a casting, etc. The controls are things such as speed, steam pressure, cutting angle and so on — in other words, parts of the system which the operator may alter at will. It can be seen that normally a large number of possible trajectories exist and it is therefore desirable to select (by manipulation of the controls) the one which maximises or minimises what is called a performance index.

To use the example of a moon rocket there are obviously many paths between a point on the earth and a point on the moon. It is desired to determine which sequence of control values (the controls here being acceleration, direction, etc.), generates a trajectory between the two points which, say, minimises the amount of fuel used in the trip. By application of the Maximum Principle of Pontryagin and one of a variety of optimisation techniques such a sequence of control values may be computed. Good introductions to the subject are given by Kirk (1970) and Dixon (1972).

In the context of the simple theory the 'controls' are the k and j quantities (the reduced functions), the trajectory is the adoption curve and we wish to minimise the discrepancy between the theoretical adoption curve and what occurred in the real world. There would appear to be no insurmountable conceptual difficulties in applying optimal control theory to this task, though doubtless many computational problems will need to be mastered.[19] It should be noted, however, that the proposal is to use optimal control theory in a slightly different sense to the more normal application. Most of the k and j variables are not 'controls' as such, since we cannot easily manipulate them in the real world, but functions whose behaviour we wish to study. The rationale is therefore that this behaviour may be determined if we treat the social system as if it were a piece of electronic equipment or a missile, and seek the maximum agreement between the theory and real world events. What will be generated is the sequence of k and j values which produce such agreement — the behaviour we require to measure. To conclude, the point is really that in using such methods we will have a different perspective to that of the optimal control theorist.

A point which arises directly out of the above, but also has relevance to more straightforward applications of the special theory, is that of the data used to test the theory. To date, such tests have been achieved solely by reference to the adoption curve, and since the theory makes predictions of the corresponding curves for favourables, passives and rejectors it would seem desirable to test it against empirical data for these as well. This would certainly lend further credence to the theory.

Although some circumstantial evidence for this aspect was cited in Section 5.4, to contrast theoretical and actual time series for these adopter states would be a rigorous test of the conceptualisation.

Unfortunately as with most marketing research this could not be achieved by asking individuals whether they are favourables, passives or rejectors! To paraphrase Light (1975): 'If you want to know what people are don't ask them.' The adopter states as envisaged by this theory are highly situational, relating to the communication of experience between adopter and potential adopter. A direct questionnaire approach is unlikely to be a good indicator of such behaviour, *unless* it is carefully designed and developed in accordance with the precepts of the theory. A form of longitudinal method must be employed, a method which assesses perceptions of the new product at that point in time, whether an individual has discussed the product with anyone in the current time period, and if so what experience they communicated. All of which is no trivial survey exercise.

Next there is the problem of specifying special theories for other types of innovation. Here only a brief exposition will be given, indicating the lines along which such formulations might proceed and commencing with major consumer products.

Most new consumer durables have adoption curves of a much longer duration than those obtained for low risk products, taking years rather than months to be adopted by a sizeable proportion of the population. Furthermore it is probably true to say that in the early stages of the adoption process less advertising is done than for super-market products, and widespread distribution is not obtained as rapidly. Therefore awareness may be an important factor, if only in the first few months, and as such should be incorporated into a simpler theory for durable products. With this addition it would be possible to produce a special theory much like the one already presented, and test it in a similar manner. It appears that this would be the best way to proceed, particularly if the k and j parameters were treated as variables. While the general theory suggests some plausible explanations for the observed phenomena of durable innovations, it does not as yet indicate any quicker way of achieving the desired objectives. It may also be noted that it is desirable to collect data for the awareness curve as well as the adoption curve/s.

The 'plausible explanations' are that a major durable innovation quite obviously involves considerable financial and social risk to the individual concerned. Hence it is to be expected that in such situations individuals will give more credence to communicated experience, particularly unfavourable information, than in the low risk case, and require greater quantities of such information in reaching their decision. There are likely to be fewer individuals who will take the gamble solely on the basis of their own judgement and hence the form of the state transfer mechanisms suggests that the initial adoption rate will be relatively low. This will produce only a small number of early adopters and therefore a relatively small amount of communicated experience with which to persuade others. Given that these 'others' will be harder to persuade than in the low risk case then it can be readily appreciated that the state transfer rate will remain low, and hence adoption will only increase relatively slowly. The general theory also indicates that one of the chief components of the situational variables S, S^*, S^{**} will be price. It would be interesting to compare the behaviour of the reduced functions with the price fluctuations which are commonly encountered for major innovations, and for innovations involving different levels of cost to the consumer.

Interestingly enough it would appear likely that a special theory for some industrial innovations would have a similar form to that discussed above. Naturally the population would be the appropriate purchasing officers of the companies forming the market, and it might be expected that some reduced functions would depend on personal selling rather than the media, but otherwise the structure would be identical. Such a special theory could be applicable to industrial situations where the market was several hundred companies and the purchase decision rested with one or a few executives within each company. More atypical situations could not be handled in this manner.

Lastly the possibility of extending these or any other special theories to include repeat purchasing should not be overlooked. It can be hypothesised that the favourables and passives may be more likely to repeat their purchase of the product than the rejectors. Which feasibly forms the basis for a repeat purchase expression and for predictions of total sales as well as adoption or first purchase. In such an event, of course, the theories are no longer of innovative behaviour alone but of the product life cycle.

This completes the discussion of directions for further research. Should all or any of the outlined objectives be achieved then what can be expected to emerge in the future is a succession of increasingly powerful predictive tools for specific situations, together with an increasingly more realistic general theory of innovative behaviour.

5.8 Summary

On the basis of earlier chapters a general theory of innovative behaviour has been formulated. The starting point for this theory is a division of the population of a social system into five states; unaware, aware, favourable, passive and rejector. This provided the basis for the specification of a dynamic system in which individuals may change their state via any one of four state transfer mechanisms. These being those due to interpersonal communication of experience, mass media communication, other marketing activities, and individual experiences, the role of these mechanisms being derived from the behavioural background provided by Chapter 4. In particular only the favourables and rejectors were allowed to be influential in adoption decisions, the former persuading people to adopt, the latter persuading them against adoption. While the role of the favourables was quite easy to explain, it was only by recourse to an aggregate level and quasi-mathematical discussion of the state transfer mechanisms that the vital role of the rejectors could be satisfactorily explained. It was argued that most individuals need to receive a certain level of communicated experience before reaching a decision, and that some trade-off occurs between favourable and unfavourable information. It was therefore possible to express the interpersonal state transfer mechanisms at an aggregate level in terms of the innovativeness of groups of individuals, situational effects and the number of meetings between aware individuals and both favourables and rejectors. The role of the rejectors was therefore seen as depressing the rate of state transfer and slowing the rate of adoption. Appropriate functions were also developed for the other state transfer mechanisms, in terms of variables such as media advertising, promotions and individual experience.

With the aid of the various symbolic functions the general theory was presented as a system diagram, and the nature of this diagram explained. In particular it was indicated that the theory focused on the moment of persuasion and on information transfer in general. Most individuals were thought to adopt because they were persuaded to do so by fellow consumers. The role of the mass media was seen as creating awareness and stimulating the innovators to adopt. According then to the perceptions of the product held by these early adopters a wide variety of event sequences could occur, a variety and complexity which can only be handled mathematically. The general theory was therefore finally expressed as a set of non-linear simultaneous differential equations, an expression which describes the dynamic nature of the social processes involved in the diffusion of an innovation.

The key assumption of the general theory was seen as being that only those who had experience with the product may influence others.

It was then pointed out that it was not possible or desirable, at this point in time, to specify the exact mathematical form of the state transfer mechanisms. A more viable line of investigation was seen as specifying simple mathematical expressions, and only for certain types of innovation. In other words reducing the general theory to a special case. These special theories were seen as always being less difficult to handle and easier to test against reality than the general theory but, because of the necessary assumptions which need to be made, always less realistic and wide-ranging than the general theory. It was therefore argued that the procedure should be to develop such special theories which would not only be predictive tools for certain new product situations but also an assessment of whose performance (in explaining reality) would allow the general theory to be modified and improved.

The discussion then centred around one such special mathematical theory of innovative behaviour — for low risk innovations. The simplifying assumptions were outlined, and the resulting equations presented. The mathematical expressions used for the state transfer mechanisms in this case were then compared with the general theory and in particular the k and j parameters shown to be related to reduced functions of the general theory, and arbitrarily assumed to be constant. Methods for solving the equations were briefly touched on, and then the results of empirical tests detailed. The results obtained by reference to data for six new product launches proved of considerable significance. Not only was the special theory consistent with reality, and capable of yielding accurate predictions, but the dynamic behaviour of the adopter states appears to have strong links with real events. These results therefore gave strong support to the overall schema presented herein.

Then some space was devoted to a discussion of the actual values computed for the k and j parameters. As well as being related to the general theory these parameters were shown to provide measures of communication effectiveness. While some interesting conclusions were extracted the most important stems from an examination of the relative importance of the mass media as compared to interpersonal communication. It appears that it is meaningless to state that one form of communication is more important or effective than another. Sometimes the mass media were more effective and sometimes interpersonal communication, sometimes both worked in tandem and sometimes they worked against each other. What appears vital is to inter-relate the two in a conceptual framework such as the theory given here. What also appears crucial is an explicit recognition of the fact that it is consumer perceptions of the product which determine whether the communicated experience is favourable or unfavourable, and thereby the fate of the new product.

In drawing conclusions on the special theory it was stressed that this could stand by itself as a model of the social processes involved in low risk innovations, and as a forecasting technique. However it was pointed out that more development was needed on the latter aspect.

Finally suggestions were made for further research, and it was argued that the most promising line of advancement lay in applying the concepts and methods of optimal control theory. By allowing the k and j parameters of this or any other special theory to vary, it would be possible to contrast the behaviour of the reduced functions with other variables, such as media advertising, and thereby begin the task of unravelling the detailed structure of the general state transfer functions. Other suggestions were made as to data collection and special theories for consumer durables and industrial products.

In final conclusion, some empirical support has been found for the conceptual framework advanced in this text. We shall shortly utilise this framework to develop methods for the management of new products. It can be seen that this is no easy task; the dynamic processes involved in the diffusion of innovations are immensely complex and thus far we have only scratched the surface. The way forward appears to lie in the development of mathematical theories for special cases, but development within the context of a general theory. As these theories are tested and improved then we will not only gain powerful management techniques but also enrich our general theory of innovative behaviour.

Notes

1. Most comments will be made in the context of consumer products. However as will be indicated later the extension to industrial markets is relatively straightforward.
2. Negative since the number of people in state a is being decreased. As a comment on notation, and for non-mathematically inclined readers, the rate of change dA/dT may be best thought of as people per day, and at time T. The general notation for a function, that is $V = f[X, Y, Z]$ is a form of shorthand for the statement 'there is a mathematical relationship between X, Y and Z which equals V'. For instance this could be $V = aX^2 + YZ^{1/2}$. Note, however, that in the context here this relationship must make theoretical sense; any collection of terms will not do, and would certainly not generate the rate of change dA/dT

3. Note that for the moment the other state change mechanisms are being excluded from the discussion; these too will decrease the aware state.
4. Assuming homogeneous mixing of the population. This is not a great restriction at this level of generality. Any more complex clique structure could be expressed as a function of XY.
5. $A(T)$ is in the expression because the number of people left in the aware state determines how many may be affected by the media.
6. As in n.5. Here the number left determines the effectiveness of the promotion. Again the asterisks are used to indicate that the form of these functions is different to the other cases.
7. Setting aside the promotional mechanism as not being typical of most innovations.
8. Termed 'special' here to distinguish it from the general theory, and to indicate that it only applies to a restricted range of phenomena.
9. Based on United Kingdom experience for successful new product launches.
10. The notation for the variables is different to that in Midgley (1976).
11. The real situation is f $_T$ which we replace by j , where the area under the curve is equal. Hence $\int_0^T j\,dt = \int_0^T f\,dt$ but as j is a constant $jT = \int_0^T f\,dt$ and $j = \int_0^T f\,dt/T$ that is the mean value.
12. Magnitudes which are also indices of communication effectiveness.
13. This being the cumulative form of the adoption curve.
14. Comparisons based on the usual summation of squared errors.
15. A recent large scale study of the out-of-stock situation, carried out in the United Kingdom by A.C. Nielsen Ltd. (1975), indicates that in such situations 32 per cent of housewives buy a substitute product, 23 per cent postpone their purchase and the remainder attempt to purchase at another supermarket. In the case of Product 6 the quest of the latter group was unlikely to have been successful, and it may therefore be appreciated how frustration and annoyance can be built up.
16. There is no separate promotional state transfer mechanism in the special theory; these effects may be viewed as being subsumed into the media expression. However, as far as can be ascertained promotional campaigns were not a major feature of most, if not all, of the six new product launches discussed here.
17. To compute these numbers would require integration over each time period.
18. Also with the empirical evidence that the notion of brand loyal consumers is erroneous.
19. The only conceptual problem of any note would appear to be that the optimal controls are not necessarily unique. As in the area of multidimensional scaling the resolution of this problem lies in experiments with contrived data.

PART III THE MARKETING OF NEW PRODUCTS

An Overview of Part III

Part III is concerned with the development of a framework for successful new product management. That is, a systematic approach to the problem of new product introduction. But while there may be several possible alternative approaches to this problem the one presented here stems directly from the general theory of innovative behaviour proposed in Chapter 5.

Thus a comprehensive coverage of the many new product techniques has not been attempted. The methods and techniques discussed are those considered relevant to a particular line of argument, and their relative advantages or disadvantages are evaluated in the light of the general theory. If the general theory is accepted as a realistic model of market behaviour then certain consequences and conclusions as to new product management systems flow from this theory. These are what are presented in Part III.

Following this line of development Chapter 6 examines the familiar concept of the product life cycle, but now in relation to the general theory. This leads to a more realistic model of the life cycle, and a model which has certain implications for viable marketing strategies. Having established some optimum strategies the discussion naturally turns to how such objectives may be achieved, that is, to the central task of new product management. In reality this task appears to be composed of two main activities, although these are necessarily closely interrelated. One is the generation and development of product concepts, and the other the continuous prediction of an uncertain future market response.

Chapters 8 and 9 deal directly with these two activities. In Chapter 8 the various methods for generating and screening product concepts, conducting product tests and test markets, and devising marketing tactics are outlined. In Chapter 9 the problems of predicting eventual market response are explored in some depth. Throughout, close attention is paid to arguments derived from the general theory, and the reader could, perhaps, profitably refer back to Section 5.2 to clarify any points of doubt.

In some ways Chapter 7 could be viewed as a digression from the main theme of the text, since it is primarily concerned with the organisational problems of new product management. However the subject of designing organisational structures for effective new product management is a vital one, and obviously impinges on the aspects of managerial practice discussed in the remainder of the book. Thus Chapter 7 is included for completeness, and also in order to indicate the type of organisational structure which the author considers desirable. 'Desirable' that is, in the context of the procedures advocated in Part III.

Finally in Chapter 10 an attempt is made to draw some general conclusions from the text, and to suggest the way forward to better new product management and marketing.

6 INNOVATION, THE LIFE CYCLE AND NEW PRODUCT STRATEGY

6.1 Introduction

In this chapter we begin the task of devising a coherent framework for successful new product management, a framework which integrates the numerous specialised techniques and methods, but integrates them within the context and structure of the general theory of innovative behaviour proposed in Part II. The main element of this framework will be prediction, for the key question any manager must ask himself about a new product is 'how many will I sell'. The answers to this and more sophisticated questions are neither easy nor clear-cut. Nor can they be advanced with complete certainty; the launch of a new product involves uncertainty and risk. Indeed the theory developed earlier indicates that such risks will always exist to tax the skills of the new product manager. Without consumer trial in real world situations, and the consequent communication of experience, we remain unable to predict the dynamic behaviour of the social system – at least with any great degree of confidence. Yet it is often difficult to arrange for a reliable measure of the outcomes of such trials without launching the product onto the market. Clearly we cannot test an idea in this manner, or launch numerous prototype products onto the market, and we are therefore compelled to use certain surrogate measures in the hope that these will prove reliable indicators of future behaviour. This is particularly true in the early stages of development, when it would be neither economic nor relevant to ask consumer opinion.

It is vitally necessary to deploy the various tests and techniques in such a manner as to minimise the risks involved. Risk reduction lies at the heart of new product management. Furthermore the optimal way to reduce risks is to understand the phenomena concerned, that is, to have a working theory of innovative behaviour. Hence the emphasis on integrating techniques within a theoretical framework, and the reference to concepts developed earlier. Without such a theoretical framework or foundation all that would exist would be a set of unrelated techniques, the results of which would be impossible to interpret as there would be no way to connect these results to market behaviour. Such procedures, or more accurately lack of procedures, are a sure recipe for disaster. Gisser (1973) notes: 'Any one major decision made wrong can kill the product.' In the course of developing a new product from idea to manufacture there are a very great number of 'major decisions'. The need for a systematic and scientific approach to new product management is apparent. This will be discussed in more detail in Section 6.3.

The risks involved in new product management were mentioned in Chapter 1, but it is pertinent to refresh the reader's mind at this point. Gisser (1972) commences his book *Launching the New Industrial Product* with the following statement: 'Approximately 30,000 new products are introduced within the American economy in a given year. One year later, 24,000 of them will no longer be on the market.'

Booz, Allen and Hamilton (1968), report that only 1 in 3 of all introduced products are 'commercial successes'.[1] Many more embryo products of course never reached this stage, being abandoned in the development process. This study shows that, on average, it takes '58 ideas to yield one successful new product'. Furthermore Booz, Allen and Hamilton indicate that around 70 per cent of the dollar expenditure on new products is wasted on such uneconomic ideas. However while this is a depressing picture it is not a uniform one. It was noted that of 366 new products marketed by 54 prominent U.S. companies 67 per cent were successful — twice the overall success rate for all companies studied. The study suggests that the reason for this lies in the effectiveness and attitudes of the management of such companies, notably their acceptance of the 'principles of new product management'. It may also be noted that there was little difference between industries, the success rates for chemical companies being essentially similar to those for consumer product companies. In this as in many other areas there is no evidence to suggest that industrial and consumer marketing problems are different — both may benefit from the application of the same principles and techniques.

If launching a new product is such an expensive and hazardous exercise then the reader may ask why do companies run these risks, why not simply persist with the current market offerings. The simple answer is that they are forced to launch new products, forced by economic circumstances and market forces largely beyond their control.

Certainly if a company wishes to grow then it will find only limited opportunities to do so in its present markets and with its present product line. To enjoy sustained, profitable and relatively rapid growth it is necessary to develop and introduce new products successfully. Booz, Allen and Hamilton found that, of the growth in sales planned by companies in the USA between 1963 and 1967, 75 per cent was expected to come from new products.

Even if growth is not the objective, and it is increasingly being questioned, then eventually a company will find it necessary to replace its existing products in order to survive. 'A primary economic conclusion, derived from analysing the life cycles of numerous products, is that sooner or later every product is pre-empted by another or else degenerates into profitless price competition.'[2]

It is this concept of the finite product life cycle that will be examined shortly, in Section 6.2. There the validity and usefulness of the concept will be investigated, and related to the author's theory. By subsequently transforming sales curves into profit curves the discussion will be broadened to include considerations of new product strategy.

In Section 6.3 the need for a systematic approach to new product management will be explored in more detail, and this leads directly to Chapter 7 where, amongst other topics, the possible organisational structures for new product management will be discussed.

6.2 The Product Life Cycle: Implications for New Product Strategy

The first question to which an answer should be given is that of whether the product life cycle is a valid and useful concept. It is curious that, despite the fact that the life cycle is the central concept of a good many management strategy texts, relatively few empirical studies exist in this area. The handful which have been attempted to date have found some evidence in support of this model of product sales – fortunately because the various theories of innovative behaviour strongly suggest that such a cycle should exist, and it would be somewhat perplexing if the data had shown otherwise. As will be shown, such theories also indicate that a large variety of different cycles are possible, depending on the type of product and nature of the market. It is therefore not surprising that empirical support for the stylised life cycle displayed in most texts is yet to be found. This view of the life cycle, shown in Figure 6.1, may be applicable to some products but the majority have cycles of a very different form and pattern.

The stages 'introduction', 'growth', 'maturity' and 'decline' come from a somewhat nebulous biological analogy. According to the general theory of innovative behaviour developed earlier every innovation is an essentially unique sequence of events, and therefore it would be astonishing if every life cycle fitted neatly into the scheme displayed on the next page. What is in many ways surprising is that such a naive

Fig. 6.1: The 'Typical' Product Life Cycle

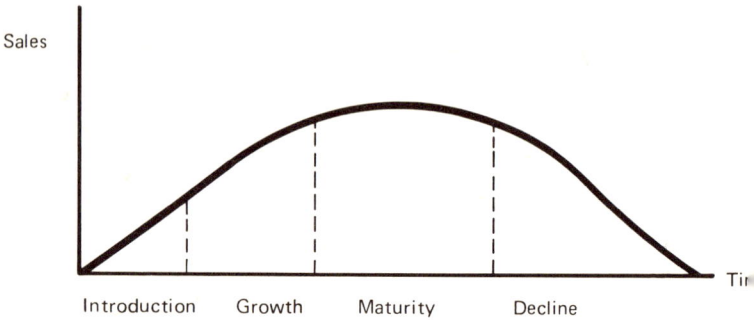

view of the sales cycle has persisted so long. Nor should this be thought of as a minor academic quibble; the fact that the life cycle has many different forms has considerable strategic importance. The shape of this cycle determines both the extent to which new products are required, and the time span over which they need to be developed.

The links between the general theory and the life cycle concept will be examined shortly; at this point the empirical evidence for the life cycle is presented. Cox (1967) studied over 200 ethical drug brands and found that over half could be described by a polynomial such as that shown in Figure 6.2.

In other words, for these products there was an initial cycle followed, after a distinct lapse of time, by a further 'recycle'. A further five unique patterns were needed to explain the rest of the drug brands.

On the other hand Buzzell and Nourse (1966) found that food products displayed patterns somewhat similar to the 'typical' life cycle, although they noted that the 'maturity' stage could be 'stable', 'growth' or 'innovative'. Unfortunately these conclusions were for product categories, and do not allow us to say anything about individual products.

Perhaps the most comprehensive study is that due to Polli and Cook (1969), although regrettably this concentrated solely on non-durable products, namely cigarettes, food items and health/personal care products. These three groups were termed product classes, within which the authors distinguished product forms (example, filter cigarettes) and within forms specific individual brands. Hence they examined the life cycle concept at three levels, class, form and brand, eventually testing it against 140 actual sales sequences. Regrettably again the only brand data was for cigarettes.

Fig. 6.2: The Cox Life Cycle

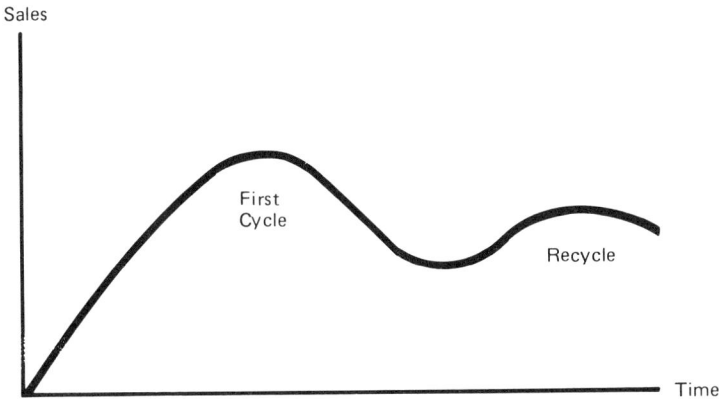

The actual statistical details of the tests conducted are too complex to discuss here except to note, by way of a digression, one interesting point. Polli and Cook defined the stages in the life cycle by the percentage changes in annual sales. For example in the food class 'growth' was an annual change greater than +5 per cent, 'sustained maturity' was a change in the band +5 per cent to 1 per cent, 'maturity' between +1 per cent and −1 per cent, 'declining maturity' between −1 per cent and −5 per cent, and 'decline' any change greater than −5 per cent. While these limits were derived from the overall distribution of all the food products in the class the interesting point is the use of such ranges to define a stage in the cycle. If this idea were applied to management practice then it could eliminate the common fallacy reported as follows. Some managers, no doubt brought up on the naive picture of the life cycle, regard any decline in sales as implying that their product is in the decline phase. In panic they deploy their resources to find a replacement and cut their losses by reducing expenditure on the existing one. Quite naturally it 'declines' still further, leading to more cut-backs, greater decline and its eventual extinction (King, 1973). Thus the manager's initial 'gut reaction' has become a self-fulfilling prophecy. It is obvious that some extension of the above idea would eliminate such 'disasters' — a point which will be taken up again.

Polli and Cook found considerable support for the life cycle concept, although more at the brand and product form level than at the product class level. At the latter they note that a decline may be followed by a long period of maturity. However of greater importance is their observation that at the form and brand level any decline (as defined by them) must be taken seriously by management, as it is likely to be irreversible. These authors also report that the growth stage is of a relatively short duration, while the maturity stage can be one of considerable length. Furthermore they indicate that maturity does not imply the stability of market shares — to the contrary, a stable product form is usually comprised of numerous brands, some in the growth stage, some in the mature stage and some declining.

The conclusion can be drawn from such results that a life cycle of some form or other exists at each level. For an example, if we were to take the class prepared pre-packed vegetables then this would have a cycle, but one of decades, if not centuries, duration. In 1976 it is probably still in the growth stage. Within this class we could distinguish such forms as canned vegetables, frozen vegetables, freeze dried vegetables and so on — each with their own cycle. It is interesting to speculate that at the moment canned vegetables have reached their mature stage while frozen vegetables may still be expanding their market share. Yet again within each form we can distinguish individual brands such as Heinz Baked Beans or Birds Eye Frozen Peas. Furthermore we may note that within either of these forms some brands have risen to prominence, while others have risen, declined and disappeared from the picture. It is to be expected that this process will continue.

This has been a concocted example and the definitions or boundaries may be argued. It does, however, serve to illustrate the point. Obviously the cycles in product classes and forms are more relevant to the long range planning function than they are of immediate importance to new product management. In the latter we will primarily be concerned with specific new products or new brands as King (1973) defines them.

Since Polli and Cook (1969) only examined brands of cigarettes some further evidence at this level should be presented. Davis (1973) reports the analysis of forty four test market operations involving the launches of supermarket products. He reaches the conclusion that the typical pattern of such sales is that depicted in Figure 6.3, where a high initial peak settled into a lower stable sales rate.

Fig. 6.3: Purchase of New Brands

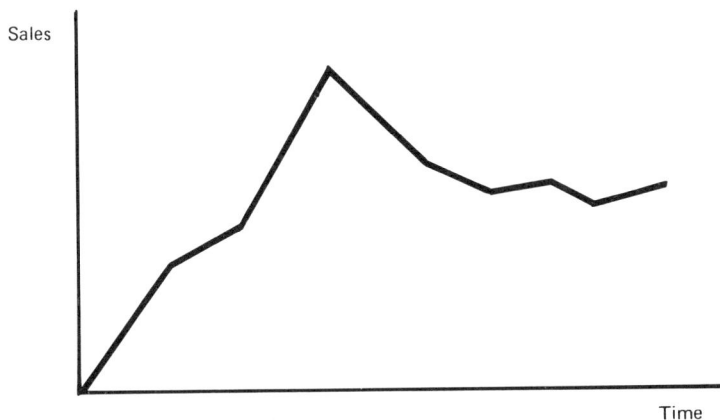

Source: Davis (1973), p.339, and used by permission of Crosby Lockwood Staples.

As these test markets were of limited duration this analysis was not continued for a sufficient time to complete the picture of the life cycle. Given earlier results we might expect, after a relatively long period, something similar to Figure 6.4, which provides a far better perspective than the 'typical' life cycle such as that shown in Figure 6.1.

With regard to durable products then, the evidence is less substantial. Brockhoff (1967) has investigated life cycles in the German automobile market, finding support for the concept and indicating the presence of complementary and substitutive effects between products of the same company. In another context Bass (1968) presents sales patterns for various classes of durables, patterns which broadly confirm the hypothesis. Otherwise little data exists and much more research is needed, particularly at the brand level.

King (1973) argues that the distinction between brand and product is a critical one, and it is worth taking some time to examine this topic.

Fig. 6.4: Life Cycle for a Supermarket Brand

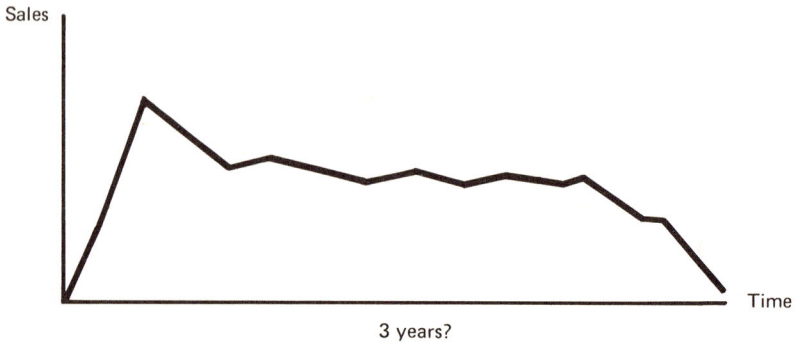

3 years?

The gist of King's discourse is that the brand is more than the physical product, it is the product plus a name which itself has psychological importance to the consumer. Thus a can of Heinz baked beans is distinct from a can of baked beans, and a Sony tape recorder from any tape recorder. While I would not disagree with this argument King then goes on to castigate new product texts and publications for using the term 'product' and for concentrating on the physical development of such new products. This is a little harsh as we use the term new product in the marketing literature as a synonym for innovation, and one conclusion from Part II of this text must be that an innovation is more than just a physical entity, especially when viewed through the eyes of a potential adopter. Nonetheless King is right to re-emphasise the concept of brand, lest we concentrate on the mechanics of development and forget that the end product is more of a total idea than something with merely physical attributes.

Where King may be mistaken is in suggesting that the concept of the life cycle does not apply to brands, his argument being that a 'brand' can have its 'product' changed to meet new circumstances and needs. In my opinion, this carries semantic differentiation too far. Quite apart from Polli and Cook's evidence it may be observed that brands exhibit the same diffusion process as major new product classes. For instance the six non-durable products used to test the special theory of innovative behaviour were all brands, some launched within existing product classes, yet they all display the characteristics of the classical diffusion process. However perhaps more convincing than a mere citing of evidence is an appeal to logic. We note, with Rogers and Shoemaker (1971) that an innovation is 'an idea, practice, or object perceived as new by an individual'.[3] Presumably when Brand ABC changes from product type X to product type Y then the consumers notice it.[4] Indeed they usually have no choice since the manufacturer hammers home the message 'new', 'different', 'improved', and so on. Thus the change is sometimes perceived by the consumers as a different and 'new' product, and the diffusion process recommences, or at least a diffusion process of some type occurs – 'sometimes', because it all rather depends on what the brand means to the consumer, what the product type is and what change is proposed. If the brand is in fact the manufacturer's name, say IBM, and the change is from computers to typewriters then, while no doubt the brand name will continue for some years to come, IBM typewriters are a new product and obviously their launch will be the diffusion of an innovation. However this is probably not what King had in mind, his comments being more directed to 'minor' changes in a brand whose product type stays essentially the same. For example the change from Maxwell House powdered instant coffee to Maxwell House freeze dried granulated instant coffee. In such cases if the consumers perceive this to be an innovation, then it would undergo the normal diffusion process and need to be handled with the same care and attention as the launch of the original product. If on the other hand the consumers perceive the change to be trivial, minute or frivolous then they are likely to reject it. In this case whether you view this process as the failure of the 'new' product or the decline of the old is merely semantic hairsplitting. The author would argue that all such brand/product modifications should be such as to cause the consumers to perceive them as an innovation, and their relaunch should be managed exactly as for a completely new product.[5] Any other course of action will either do little to alter the life cycle of the brand, or cause its earlier demise.

It is apparent that the discussion is now entering the realm of management strategy. However before proceeding any further it is necessary to demonstrate the link between the life cycle and the general theory of innovative behaviour, a demonstration which will hopefully show exactly where the usefulness of the life cycle concept lies.

In fact the link is quite simple. We remember that the theory of innovative behaviour describes adoption, that is first purchase of the new product, therefore all that is necessary to convert an adoption curve

to a product life cycle is to add in the repeat purchases of that product.
The adoption curve and the product life cycle are identical for a
product which is only bought once by any adopter — such as short-lived
fashions and fads, for example hula hoops. If the product is one which
is repurchased, a category most products fall into, then the shape of the
life cycle depends on the average interval between purchases. In
Figure 6.5 we have the 'typical' adoption curve presented in earlier
chapters.

Fig. 6.5: 'Typical' Adoption Curve

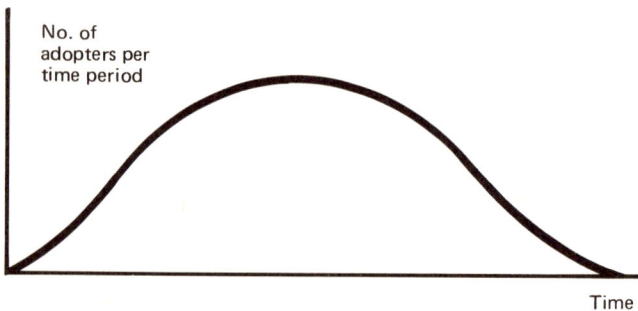

Suppose we have the type of product which the purchaser will not
replace for some length of time, and not in fact before most of the rest
of the population has adopted. In other words the average life of the
product is of the same order of duration as the adoption process itself.
Since these types of products are also only bought singly then the life
cycle would be something similar to that shown in Figure 6.6. The
obvious candidates for this pattern are products such as televisions,
refrigerators, etc., that is consumer durables whose consumption, as it
were, takes several years. Other similar products would be ethical drugs
since presumably most people would not repurchase until the need,
that is the same ailment, recurred. Hence Cox's (1967) 'recycle' is
perfectly explicable, and we might expect several such 'recycles'
before the product went into decline.

Fig. 6.6: Product Life Cycle for Durable and Semi-Durable Goods

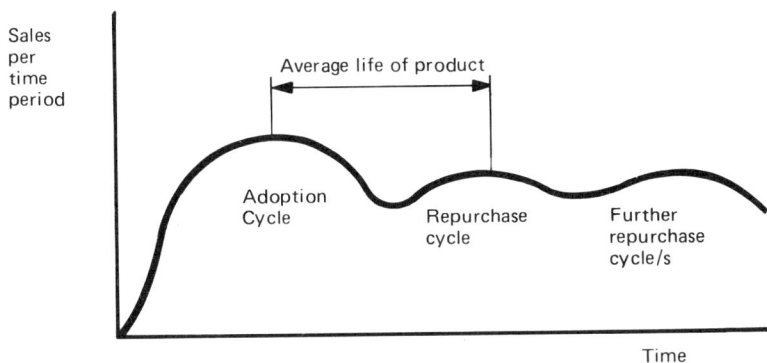

However in order to look any deeper into this phenomenon it is necessary to turn to the general theory, and in particular to note that it is unlikely that the rejectors will repeat their purchase. Thus we could hypothesise that for consumer durables where there was a high level of rejection then the peak of the 'recycle' would be lower than that of the adoption cycle. This might be interesting to test empirically, although it is of course possible for these rejectors later to change their minds, and hence their adopter state. If we now discuss products which are consumed fairly rapidly, and for which there is more life cycle evidence, then the general theory may be used to explain these observed cycles. Where the product has a life much shorter than the time between the introduction and the peak of the adoption curve, then a different shaped life cycle will be obtained — primarily because the favourable adopters will be repeating their purchase before other members of the population make their first purchase. The actual shape of the life cycle will be dependent on the behaviour of the three main adopter states,

Fig. 6.7: Relation between Adoption and Sales for a Successful Innovation

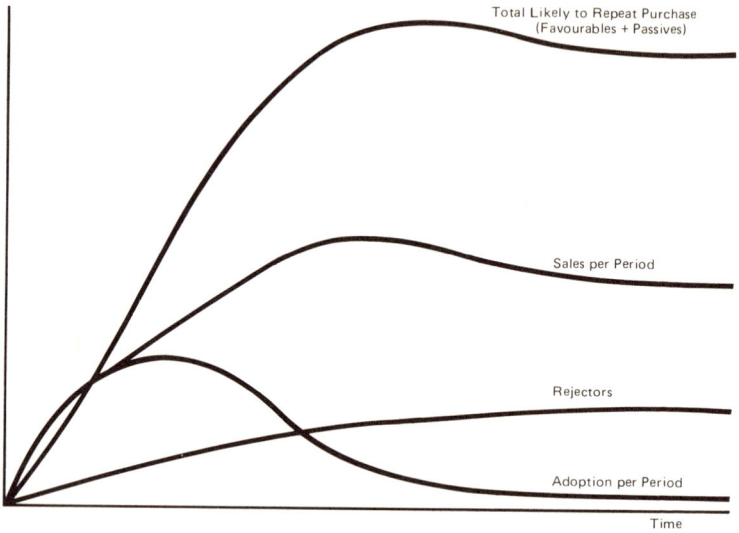

Total Likely to Repeat Purchase
(Favourables + Passives)

Sales per Period

Rejectors

Adoption per Period

Time

Fig. 6.8: Relation between Adoption and Sales for an Unsuccessful Innovation

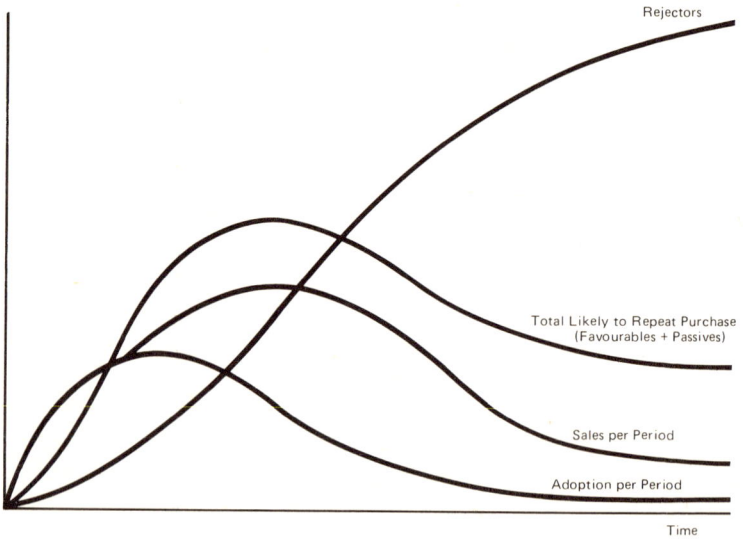

Rejectors

Total Likely to Repeat Purchase
(Favourables + Passives)

Sales per Period

Adoption per Period

Time

therefore in Figures 6.7 and 6.8 two 'typical' patterns are hypothesised, one for a successful innovation and one for an unsuccessful innovation. These figures are based on the general form of those empirically generated from the special theory in Chapter 5, and used here as illustrative examples. However since the special theory was devised for products such as those in question, which would mainly be low risk supermarket items, then it is thought these illustrations are reasonably realistic. The only relevant extra insight the general theory gives us is that the pattern of behaviour in these figures could subsequently change, dependent on individuals' later experiences with the product.

By way of explanation, the 'total likely to repeat purchase' is the sum of the numbers in the favourable and passive states at any point in time. The sales life cycle was computed using a hypothetical repeat purchase period, and making the appropriate transformation of the total likely to repeat purchase. Undoubtedly this is somewhat simplistic, and we really should apply a repeat purchase distribution and also allow for the passives and favourables to have different repeat purchase periods, but such sophistications would make the explanation unnecessarily complex.

For the successful innovation, Figure 6.7, the 'end' result (by the completion of the duration shown) is that most of the population either likes, or is neutral toward, the innovation. With these individuals regularly repeating their purchase it is therefore to be expected that the sales per period settle to a stable level. This level will always be lower than the peak sales magnitude because in the early stages there is adoption and repeat purchasing occurring simultaneously; when all the population has adopted (or at least when the rate of adoption has become very small), then there are only individuals repeating their purchase, and at distinct intervals. Furthermore this group of individuals is always likely to be less than the total number of adopters.[6]

For the unsuccessful innovation the process is almost exactly the same, the major difference being that since the number likely to repeat purchase is now small (relative to the total population), then the final level of sales is also low.

With either picture it is also necessary to explain the eventual decline and demise of the product. For the unsuccessful innovation presumably the manufacturer withdraws it, unless it is judged that modifications can be made and more individuals persuaded to alter their views. However as there is such a large body of unfavourable opinion established in the population this latter course is usually unlikely to succeed. Effectively it would require greater persuasion than the original adoption process. A better strategy would be to start again with a new solution to the consumers' problem.

For the successful innovation, then, this may continue in its maturity stage for some little while; normally it appears for a period of time much longer than the growth stage shown above. Eventually, however, one of two events may occur. Either the purchasers may become satiated with the product and change adopter state, or more likely another, newer, product will entice them away. Provided, of course, that this newer product is a better solution to the consumers' problem, and performs satisfactorily. Interestingly enough although the general and special theories were not specifically formulated to model this situation, they can do so quite adequately. For the competing product case it is only necessary to say that because of individual experiences — adoption of the competing product — there is a trend to the favourables and passives becoming rejectors, and hence to repeat sales declining. If these individuals adopt the newer product, and they find it satisfactory, then there is nothing inconsistent in this change of mind over the old product. What they will be saying (to themselves and others) is: 'I have used old ABC in the past and it was satisfactory, but new XYZ is much better and a definite improvement.' The information they would communicate is therefore unfavourable to product ABC, whence they are rejectors of this product. Note however they are favourables for product XYZ.

To conclude, the general and special theories of innovative behaviour provide theoretical support for the observed product life cycles. Further research is needed into aspects such as the relation between the adopter states and repeat purchasing, but at this stage there is certainly no inconsistency between the life cycle concept and the author's theories.

To digress a little here it can be seen that the general theory of innovative behaviour is in fact somewhat more than that. It also explains opinions about the product throughout that product's life cycle. Given a satisfactory explanation of the relation between adopter states and repeat purchasing then we would have a general theory of the product life cycle. Needless to say this is still some way off.

Since we have already buried the myth of the 'typical' product life cycle this also seems a good point at which to do the same for the adoption curve. It is obvious that the cumulative and per period adoption curves shown above, and based on the empirical patterns given in Chapter 5, bear only some resemblance of the S-shaped cumulative and bell-shaped per period curves discussed in earlier chapters. This is not because our examples are atypical of low risk products. As Pessemier (1966) and Polli and Cook (1969) note, an exponential curve is more appropriate to such products than the S-shaped logistic curve; nor are the per period curves invariably a normal distribution in the real world. It would seem that the regularities observed between diffusion processes are mainly that the cumulative curve increases, and that the per period curve has a peak! We now know that if data was collected for the adopter states then each innovation would be seen to be different. While this is probably overstating the case a little, the point which needs to be made is that the general theory can account for any observed adoption curve. The law-like regularities are in the structure and operation of the social system, not in the outcomes of such events — which are of infinite variety.

Returning to the life cycle then as far as strategic usefulness is concerned three conclusions can be stated.

1. After introduction, the sales curve will settle to a stable level, lower than the peak level experienced.[7]
2. As this stable level is primarily determined by consumer perceptions of the product's performance it is probable that the manufacturer will be unable to alter this level significantly, in the short term, by application of the marketing tools at his command. In short the system has considerable inertia.
3. Eventually a newer product will meet consumer needs in the area more satisfactorily, or the needs themselves will alter, and sales will decline.

The product life cycle concept is therefore useful in that it suggests that existing products should be continuously monitored — to detect those about to decline — and in that it indicates the broad parameters of a new product launch, and thus allows more realistic projections to be made. However in order to turn these ideas into workable strategies, it is necessary to examine the relation between the life cycle and corporate profits. Again this is a reasonably simple relationship. While a new product is undergoing development, costs are incurred without any compensating revenue. These costs usually increase the closer to product launch we get, because of tooling up, building inventory, etc. In the early stages of the launch costs still outrun revenue until an adequate sales level is reached and the new product begins to pay for itself.[8] Later sales and profits decline. Diagrammatically the profit/loss curve can be typically represented as in Figure 6.9.

Fig. 6.9: Profits over the Life Cycle

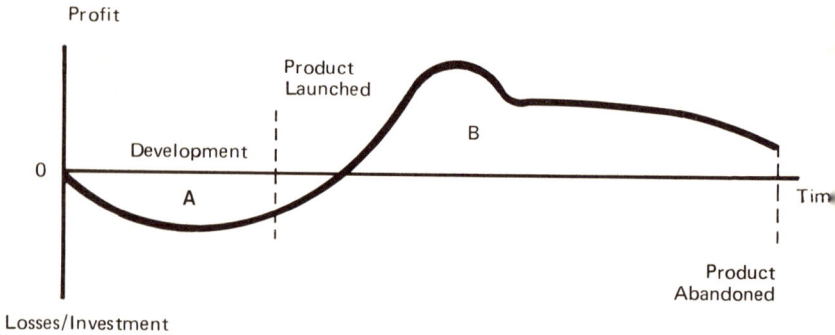

It is hoped that area B is greater than area A since this implies a positive return on investment. Effectively area A is the investment and area B the return on this investment, if both are discounted to present values at (t=0) then the rate of return may be computed. How great a return will be accrued obviously depends on a great many factors, but primarily on meeting the particular consumer need in a better fashion than any existing product — in other words, on securing a large share of the particular market. It would appear that possibly the best strategy for achieving this is to be the first to produce this improved product, that is to 'pioneer' as King (1973) terms it.

Note that here we are discussing the best possible strategy for the greater return on investment. It is perfectly possible to be second, third, fourth or even fifth onto the market with the improved product and still have a successful launch and a positive return on investment. However as Buzzell, Gale and Sultan (1975) have found in a study of fifty seven major American companies, the bigger the market share the bigger the return on investment. This is demonstrated in Table 6.1.

Table 6.1: Relationship between Market Share and Pretax ROI

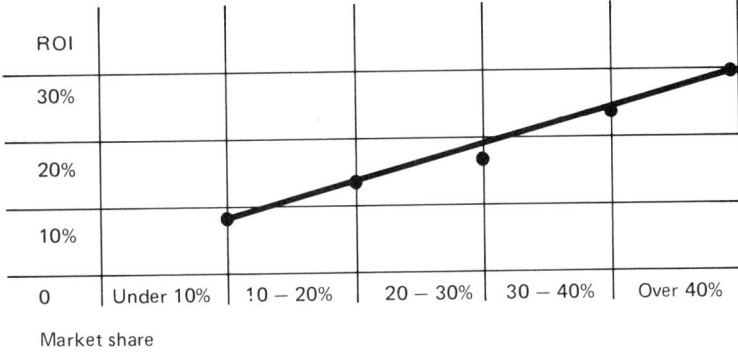

Market share

Source: Buzzell *et al,* (1975), p.98, and used by permission of the Harvard Business Review.

The reasons advanced for this relationship are: (i) that profit margins increase sharply with market share; (ii) the various economies of scale; (iii) the relative decline of per unit marketing costs with increased sales; and (iv) the 'unique competitive strategies' of market leaders. We have established that larger market shares mean higher profits; the last of the four reasons given provides the link between market share and being first on the market. Buzzell *et al.* (1975), note that market leaders spend significantly higher amounts on research and development, in fact 40 per cent more than the low share companies. This suggests that the leaders consider there is something to be gained by pioneering. Furthermore King (1969) cites Nielsen analyses to the effect that for twenty seven UK grocery product categories the first brand on the market sells twice as much as the second, and nearly four times as much as the third.

It is not hard to understand why the pioneer product should gain the dominant market share. Provided it is successful, that is provides a satisfactory and improved performance, then it alters the rules of the game. All the existing older brands are perceived as obsolete, and start to enter their decline phase. Any subsequent and similar product launched by a competitor is seen by the consumers as a copy, and also has to contend with an established image and distribution set-up. It is not surprising that most 'second' brands therefore find it immensely difficult to achieve the same success as the pioneer.

Indeed there would appear to be only two circumstances in which the second brand or product can prove more successful, that is obtain a greater market share. The first, and by far the most likely is that the pioneer failed to produce a satisfactory product. In this case the second company may learn from, and capitalise on, the experience of the first to produce the 'right' product and secure the dominant market position. Since most new products do encounter problems this is a viable strategy, although in the long run it may yield lower returns.[9]

The second circumstance is if the company following the pioneer onto the market can achieve a further technological breakthrough and therefore 'leap-frog' the pioneer. As most companies in most markets are in a similar state of technological development this is an unlikely event; it is certainly not a viable product strategy.

Any other strategy such as third onto the market, effectively a 'me too' philosophy, will yield comparatively lower returns since this product now has to struggle against two established predecessors. The chances of both the first and second products being failures would appear too slim to base a strategy on them.[10, 11]

To conclude the only viable strategies would appear to be first or second onto the market with the innovation. In fact given the long development times necessary for any such technological improvement or breakthrough, I would argue that all companies should aim to be pioneers, with the option of being second should a competitor be quicker to the market place. Which leads to the inescapable conclusion that a company must be continually striving to develop products which supersede its existing ones, even if these are highly successful themselves. It may see paradoxical to be involved in an all out effort to force one's own products into decline, but if the company does not do this itself then another will. In such an event the company must be in a position to be the next to launch, if not then it may find itself with declining sales and the option of a large investment which will, at best, result in a relatively small market share. The maxim for any company would seem to be 'strive to render obsolete everything you have done before'.

Thus far the comments have mainly been addressed to maintaining a company's profit position in its existing markets. This is perfectly logical as most innovations occur as a result of such activities, and are in the nature of continued improvements to the solution of existing consumer needs. Beyond this a company may set the objective of increasing profits in the future, and therefore seek to enter new markets, new that is to the company. In the normal course of events these will again be existing markets, that is satisfied by the products of other companies, and all the previous remarks stand. Very occasionally a company will make a 'major' breakthrough and create a totally new market. I do not wish to become embroiled in boundary definition, a peculiarly sterile field much beloved of systems theorists, and what constitutes a 'new' market is a particularly difficult and vague form of such activity. What will be said is that it appears that such 'major' breakthroughs, if they exist, are in fact the culmination of a long series of minor steps, often made by a great number of different agencies. That is individual inventors, government research laboratories, companies, etc. It is a progress of gradual improvements which often takes decades. Only towards the end of this process does the innovation become commercially interesting, and at that point the idea may be input into the company's new product development function to be evaluated as any other new product concept. Such breakthroughs are likely to involve greater risks to the company, since they involve educating the potential consumers to be aware of a new need, and its means of satisfaction, and this may take some considerable time. Such breakthroughs are very few and far between, and while it behoves any company to be aware of such developments, each is a unique event and warrants its own treatment. By far the greatest number of innovations are those which represent small improvements to the solution of an existing problem or need. Knight and Wind (1968) define an innovation as 'a new and better solution to a problem', the implication being that the problem is pre-existing. Whether we have always had the same set of problems/needs, or whether new ones are created at distinct points in time, or whether they evolve continually is an (existing) problem for philosophy not marketing.

6.3 The Central Management Task: Systematic Approaches to Predicting Return on Investment

If the preceding section has shown that a company should strive to pioneer new products, then it has also demonstrated that policies and procedures must be established to achieve such ends. No organisation can rely on chance inspiration alone for its new product ideas.

To maintain its present share of existing markets an organisation must constantly assess when individual items in its product line should be replaced, and continually be in the process of developing these replacements. It must also be monitoring its competitors' new product activities to ascertain whether some development programmes should be speeded up, so that the company is always in the position of being able to be first or second into the market with an innovation. Furthermore if the company wishes to grow beyond its existing business then it must consciously seek out and evaluate new markets and opportunities, according to a predetermined corporate plan.

All of which needs to be carried out systematically with well-defined objectives and well thought out procedures. It also requires a separate management team since it is too much to ask of those involved in the day-to-day management of existing products that they take charge of the organisation's future as well. The form and structure of the new product management function is discussed in depth in the next chapter; here an attempt is made to outline precisely what it is that this function must achieve, that is to define the nature of the management tasks related to new product development.

The ensuing discussion is based on certain assumptions about corporate objectives and although some of these have already been mentioned it is worth repeating them at this juncture. As was stated at the very beginning, the aim of this book is to discuss the procedures by which successful new products are developed. Thus a corporate plan is assumed to exist. However by plan is not meant a thousand page document detailing what the company will be doing in thirty years from now — such documents are usually not worth the paper they are written on. Rather all that is necessary in the context of new product development is a statement as to which of the company's existing markets are to be maintained, and which new markets appear appropriate to the organisation's future growth.[12] In essence a set of guidelines such that the new product management team knows 'where it is going'. Note however that by 'markets' is meant a distinct consumer need or set of needs, and not an arbitrary manufacturer-defined category. While not wishing to take this to Levittian extremes I would argue that the best definition of a market is arrived at from the views of the end users. Thus a company might decide to expand into markets such as 'means of in-home audio-visual entertainment' or 'additive products to assist in washing clothes', and so on. Definitions along these lines are wide enough to stimulate the imagination of the personnel involved, but not so wide as to lead to proposals having no conceivable relation to corporate strengths.[13]

Next it is assumed that the company is seeking to be a major force in its chosen markets, or is seeking to maintain an already established dominant position. It is therefore prepared to devote a major proportion of its resources to its future, that is to new product development. Hence there will be a long-term commitment to new product programmes and these will not, as far as is possible, be subject to short-term (and short-sighted) cut-backs. As Johnston (1972) observes, companies which sacrifice their research and development teams for the sake of the next balance sheet are unlikely to regain their former competitive position easily.

Given then that the company has the above objectives, and a new product management/development team of some form, then what is the nature of this team's major management task?[14] In fact, the first element in this task has little to do with new product management, at least directly. This is, of course, the continuous assessment of the company's existing products, an assessment made in the light of a knowledge of the product life cycle, and of possible new product launches by competitors. This assessment serves to delineate the scope and time scale for the development programmes, in that it indicates how many new products are needed and when. If the organisation wishes to pursue the best strategy (first or second onto the market) then timing is critical. Hence the emphasis on PERT/CPM techniques found in most new product texts. Programmes must run to schedule, and the scheduling/development procedures must be sufficiently flexible that completion dates can be advanced if necessary. Such techniques will be outlined in Chapter 8. It may also be noted that the above requirement for flexibility and quick response necessitates a very different organisation structure to that normally found in most companies, which is yet another reason for developing a separate new product function.

The next elements are those more directly concerned with the development of the new products. Pessemier (1966) lists six steps to the process:

1. *Search:* Studies designed to locate potentially profitable additions to a firm's product line or capabilities. Market studies, research and development work, and acquisition studies all qualify as part of a well-organized search program.

2. *Preliminary Economic Analysis:* Rapid, low-cost studies which eliminate weak proposals and informally weigh the relative desirability of promising proposals.

3. *Formal Economic Analysis:* Careful, detailed studies to clarify, improve and appraise the proposals that survive preliminary analyses. The end result of this activity is a recommendation to scrap the proposal, defer action, or proceed to develop a tangible product or capability.

4. *Development:* Transformation of the proposal into a tangible product and process.

5. *Product Testing:* Conduction of use and market tests to measure the reactions of resellers and final buyers to the product.

6. *Commercialization:* Involvement in full-scale production and marketing operations to establish the product in its desired place in the firm's product line.[15]

Booz, Allen and Hamilton (1968) present an essentially similar series of steps, as follows.

Exploration – the search for product ideas to meet company objectives.

Screening – a quick analysis to determine which ideas are pertinent and merit more detailed study.

Business Analysis – the expansion of the idea, through creative analysis, into a concrete business recommendation including product features and a program for the product.

Development – turning the idea-on-paper into a product-in-hand, demonstrable and producible.

Testing – the commercial experiments necessary to verify earlier business judgments.

Commercialization – launching the product in full-scale production and sale, committing the company's reputation and resources.[16]

While the appropriate techniques for each step will be discussed in Chapter 8 it is worthwhile at this point to examine these steps a little more closely, in the light of the theory of innovative behaviour advanced here.

This theory stresses that new product introduction, dependent as this is on consumer reaction, will always be a hazardous operation. We may reduce but not eliminate the risks involved. Therefore it is not enough to develop one idea in the hope this will prove a success, the idea must also be critically and objectively evaluated throughout the development process. The manager must continually question whether this idea will fulfil corporate objectives. Hence the emphasis on objective testing and not on management hunches or 'feel for the market'.

Since the odds are that most product ideas will prove to be uneconomic when analysed in greater depth then, as implied above, it is necessary to start the process by generating not one, but many, good ideas. In essence the whole of the development process is a screening process, but one which uses increasingly finer and more sophisticated 'nets' as the idea(s) approach actual production. As noted earlier, and according to Booz, Allen and Hamilton (1968), it takes about sixty ideas to eventually yield one successful new product. The generation of sufficient ideas does not appear to be a major problem, as will be discussed subsequently. Many methods are available for this, and relatively little cost is involved. It is only when the actual development of a physical product commences that the investment expenditure begins to rise sharply.

We therefore commence with as many ideas as possible and proceed to weed out all but the potential winners ('potential' as we may never be certain until after the launch). Most ideas are rejected because they fail to reach certain required standards of performance, standards which are explicitly laid down, and which are based on a thorough understanding of the company and the market. Therefore the systematic collection of relevant data is necessary, along with an explicit statement as to the company's assumptions about the behaviour of the market, and the selection of the appropriate evaluative or rejection criteria. In other words the dimensions along which the product ideas or concepts are to be evaluated, together with a judgement as to what constitutes the minimum acceptable performance along these dimensions.

That managers do not always proceed in such an objective logical manner is all too obvious. In an interesting experiment Cardozo, Ross and Rudelius (1972) discovered that marketing managers requested less information on consumer response than expected, and considerably less than a marketing research executive would in a similar situation. This experiment was conducted by programming a computer with all relevant data on an actual new product launch, allocating a 'cost' to

each item of information and a 'budget' to each participant. Some
thirty executives then individually acted out how they would launch
the product, by requesting the information they thought necessary to
reach their decision. Managers, as opposed to researchers, tended to
opt for basic market data and information on competitors. In some
ways they seemed to take a favourable consumer response for granted.
There would appear to be considerable room for improvement in the
area of decision making. The need for well-defined objectives and
procedures is certainly apparent.

However it must be admitted that the new product manager is in
somewhat of a dilemma with regard to consumer tests. The general
theory of innovative behaviour is based on the fact that the only
relevant criteria and performance standards are those perceived by the
final consumer. It is the consumers' evaluations of the product which,
as communicated experience, will decide whether or not the product
is to be a success. Furthermore these consumers only form their
judgements on using the product in actual situations. Thus in order to
in any way assess likely consumer reaction it is necessary to test the
finished product, or a reasonable approximation thereof, with a group
of consumers. Hence, and despite various subterfuges which will be
discussed in the next chapter, these consumer tests must come toward
the end of the development process. It is pointless to show consumers a
concept – they cannot use an idea, and therefore cannot express what
their eventual reaction might be. Certainly X per cent of them will tell
you they will purchase the finished product, but as many executives
have found to their cost the relation between such statements and actual
behaviour is, at best, tenuous. The dilemma is that most of the product
ideas will need to be screened out without any consumer tests, and that
one idea will be developed, at considerable cost, to the point where it
can be subjected to such tests. The reader may note that both Pessemier
and Booz, Allen and Hamilton recognise this unfortunate fact of life by
placing consumer tests as the penultimate step in their respective new
product development processes. To evaluate the product accurately we
must gauge consumer response; to gauge consumer response we must
invest large amounts of resources into product development.

Which is, of course, where the risks of new product introduction lie,
and why so many new products are allowed to enter the market and
fail. Having invested so much in development companies are often
loath to admit defeat at the testing stage, and press on regardless. This,
however, is not the way to develop new products. Even at the end of
several years costly endeavour the new product manager must be able

to take an an unbiased view of the situation, and abandon the project if necessary. Given that the process and phenomenon is as it is, then there will always be projects that will need to be abandoned at this late stage. What the manager must do is develop an understanding of the market and development processes, and a set of procedures whereby the number of such events may be minimised.

In the early stages of development it is therefore necessary to employ what are largely surrogate measures for likely consumer response (sales). These measures are such things as total market size, purchase frequencies, feasibility of manufacture and so on, the major techniques being check lists and rating scales, etc. (see Chapter 8). While crude, these techniques allow most unprofitable ideas to be eliminated, and resources concentrated on more likely prospects. As development proceeds and the final form of the product(s) becomes clearer then more reliable and accurate measures can be employed, leading to consumer tests.

Whatever the measures and techniques used they should all have one aim, that of predicting eventual consumer response. In many ways this is the central task of new product management, for all decisions must rest on a forecast of sales, and hence of return on investment. By contrasting the likely returns on investment from several ideas the best prospect may be selected. Return on investment is therefore the major criterion for evaluating new product concepts, and any assessment technique which cannot be immediately related to such a forecast is of little use. There are other criteria of course, such as feasibility of manufacture, compatibility with the distribution system, environmental and safety considerations, and so on. Theoretically all of these could be aggregated into the 'investment' part of the return on investment measure. However in the early stages of screening and development, where these other criteria are important and relevant, this would involve an unwarranted expenditure of effort on cost forecasts, quantifying qualitative considerations and the like. It is better therefore to keep such criteria separate; the checklist methods are adequate for these early judgements. Later in the process when all the remaining proposals will have passed these initial hurdles, and when it will be easier to make the necessary projections, then return on investment becomes the single over-riding consideration.

The central task of the new product manager is thus to generate, develop and evaluate new product proposals on the basis of their projected return on investment. Other important subsidiary tasks are monitoring competitive activity and maintaining close liaison with the technical staff responsible for research and development. Schematically the central task can be presented as somewhat similar to Figure 6.10, where all the stages of the process from market definition to product launch are shown. The vertical lines represent product review sessions — the outcomes of which are decisions to continue or abandon the development of particular concepts. For the sake of clarity only a few concepts are detailed, an actual development programme would be likely to involve a greater number of ideas.

Chapter 8 is devoted to a discussion of the various techniques for generating and screening new product concepts, and for refining and developing these concepts into actual products. Chapter 9 returns to the theme of this section and seeks to examine the means by which product performance may be predicted and hence decisions made.

It must be stressed that to perform the development process at all efficiently it is necessary to establish a formal, though flexible, system for carrying out the various tasks. Once established this system must itself be modified and developed as more is learnt about both the markets concerned and the development process. Subsequently recommendations will be made as to the various components of this system, here it is first necessary to discuss how the new product development function may be incorporated into the organisational structure, which is the main purpose of Chapter 7.

6.4 Summary

In this chapter we have begun to build a framework for new product development around the general theory of innovative behaviour. It has been noted that the main element of this framework is the prediction of an uncertain future, uncertain because the new product must be developed before consumer response can be assessed. New product management is therefore concerned with reducing the risk to the company, and it is argued that the only satisfactory course of action whereby this may be achieved is to understand the phenomena involved.

The extent of the risk involved has been stressed yet again. Most new products fail in some way or other, and most expenditure on new product development is wasted. Yet companies need new products and cannot afford to opt out of this activity. They need new products to grow, that is to develop market areas which are new to them, but the concept of the product life cycle indicates that they also need new products merely to maintain their existing markets — in fact to survive.

The theory of innovative behaviour suggests that the life cycle is a

Fig. 6.10: A Schematic Representation of the Central Aspects of the Development Process

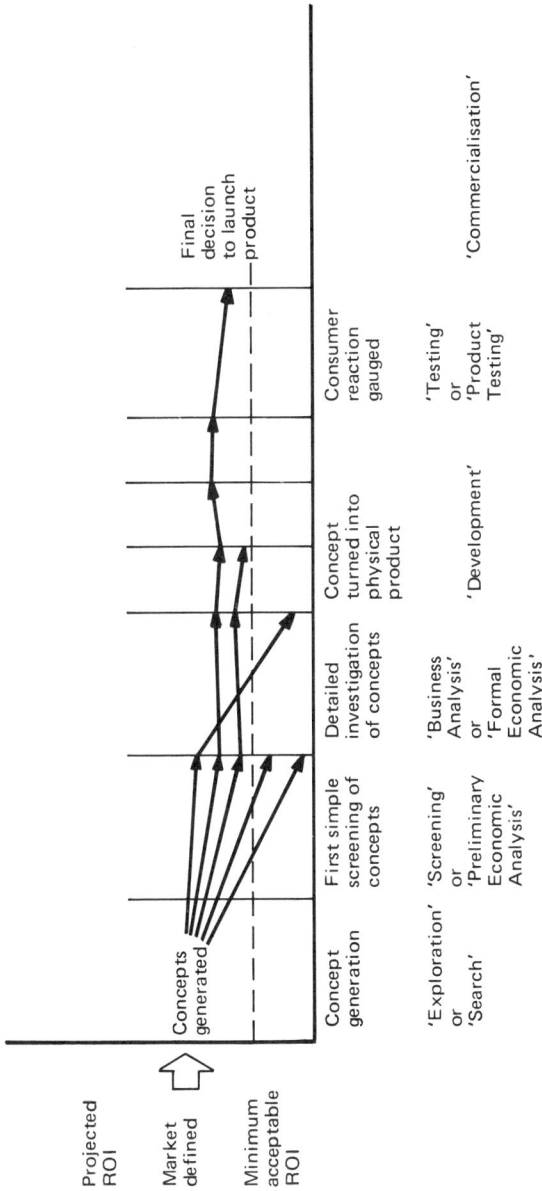

relevant and useful concept, and empirical support for these cycles was forthcoming. However the 'typical' and stylised life cycle often presented is misleading; as might be expected, reality is a little more complex than this. A naive view of the shape of the life cycle can lead managers into crucial mistakes. The evidence at the level of brand and product form confirmed the validity of the life cycle but indicated that while the growth phase was of relatively short duration, the maturity phase might last for a considerable period of time. The distinction between brand and product, though important, was seen to be in some respects merely semantic. Life cycles do exist at the brand level and are of vital concern to management. Success depends on the product performing well in the perception of the eventual consumers, that is it satisfies their needs. In the context of a change of product specification within the same brand name it was therefore argued that either this represented a satisfactory innovation to the consumer, in which case the diffusion process began anew, or if it did not then the product met with instant oblivion.

The link between the general theory of innovative behaviour and the life cycle was seen to be reasonably easy to attain. The theory describes adoption whereas the life cycle is a cycle of total sales, the link is therefore the rate of repeat purchase. If the product is only bought once then the adoption curve and the life cycle will be identical; if it is bought at infrequent intervals (longer than the duration of the adoption process) then an initial cycle followed by a sequence of 'recycles' will be observed. For frequently purchased products (e.g. non-durables), then initially we observe both adoption and repeat purchase occurring simultaneously, leading to an initial cycle of greater magnitude than that of the adoption curve. However when adoption is, or is almost, complete then the sales curve declines to a stable but lower level. How much lower depends on the number of rejectors at the end of the adoption process. Two illustrative examples were presented, one of a successful innovation, the other of a failure. It was seen that the final stable sales level is entirely dependent on the behaviour of the favourable, passive and rejector states of the general theory. By recalling that the general theory allowed for individuals subsequently to change their mind an explanation of the eventual demise of any product was obtained. Primarily it was considered that the advent of a satisfactory newer product caused individuals to view the older one unfavourably, that is to become rejectors. Another possibility was that the basic consumer need altered over time.

It was suggested that the general theory was in fact more than a theory of innovative behaviour, it also explained opinions about the product (perhaps more importantly changes of opinion) over a longer period of time. Significantly it was suggested that there was no need to retain a stylised picture of the adoption curve, and that the general theory was capable of explaining any observed adoption curve. The law-like regularities we should study are in the structure and operation of the social system, and not in the outcomes of this operation, which are infinitely varied. The S-shaped cumulative or bell-shaped per period adoption curves are theoretical crutches which are no longer necessary.

The conclusions drawn from this analysis of the life cycle were: (i) that the stable sales level would be lower than the peak sales experienced, often considerably lower; (ii) that this stable level, based on consumer perceptions, had considerable inertia; and (iii) that eventually sales will decline. The product life cycle is therefore an important concept since it not only indicates the extent to which new products are needed but the time scale to develop them. A vital part of new product management is therefore the monitoring of the life cycles of existing products.

The life cycle of product sales was then connected to a profit curve, and hence to return on investment. The size of the return was seen to be dependent on market share, and it was concluded that the best strategy is to be first onto the market with an innovation, that is to pioneer. Both theoretical and empirical support was provided for this conclusion. It was noted that the second brand could usually expect to gain a viable though lower share, and that it could gain a dominant share if the first brand was a failure. Any later entry onto the market was not viewed as a viable strategy. Given that a company should attempt to be first onto the market, and be in a position to be second if another company pre-empts them, then it was argued that a company should strive to render obsolete everything it had done before.

New product development therefore requires a set of well-defined objectives and laid-down procedures for translating ideas into successful products, procedures which could be separated into a sequence of stages such as exploration, screening, business analysis, development, testing and commercialisation. For the purposes of the text it was assumed that the company had a corporate plan (in the sense of a statement about which markets to investigate) and had a commitment to pioneering new products. Two essential elements of the management of new products were seen as the monitoring both of existing products and of competitive activity. Beyond that it was argued that risk can only be reduced not eliminated, and the way to reduce it was to make objective evaluations and to initiate the screening process with not one but many ideas. It was noted that expenditure increases dramatically as the product concept approaches commercialisation, and it was therefore necessary to screen out most ideas quite early in the process, and often before they took on a definite form.

This poses a dilemma since the theory of innovative behaviour indicates that the end result is dependent on consumer response, but consumer response in actual real-life situations. There is no way, short of giving consumers the finished product to try, that this response can be gauged. Therefore in the early stages of the development process the manager is forced to evaluate the product against surrogate measures or criteria. In fact all these measures should be surrogates for consumer response, that is sales, because this is what success or failure hinges on. Such predictions allow the computation of return on investment, which provides the objective measure through which the company may evaluate the product. The central task of the new product manager is thus to generate, develop and evaluate new product proposals on the basis of their projected return on investment. The only way by which this may be satisfactorily achieved is by understanding the phenomena involved, and by evolving systematic procedures around this understanding.

Notes

1. The difference between Booz, Allen and Hamilton's 1 in 3 and Gisser's 1 in 5 lies not so much in the actual phenomena but more in the definition of failure. Of the two, I prefer Gisser's withdrawn-from-market approach, since this is inherently more objective than asking company executives for their evaluation of 'success' or 'failure'.
2. Booz, Allen and Hamilton (1968), p.5.
3. Rogers and Shoemaker (1971), p.19.
4. Else why should the manufacturer bother to effect the change?
5. In the sense of development based on consumer tests. It is obvious that some aspects of technical development may not always need to be repeated.
6. It may also be noted that not all those likely to repeat purchase will eventually do so.
7. For durables there will be the recycle effect, but again at a lower level than the first cycle.
8. There is also the heavy introductory promotion to be taken into account.
9. Because sometimes another company will get it right first time.
10. There are, of course, exceptions to all these comments. Midgley and Wills (1975), for instance, demonstrate how the structure of the UK menswear industry effectively forces large retailers to adopt a 'me too' strategy.
11. Other strategies such as the segmentation approach are rightly demolished by King (1973). As he notes, attempting to fill a gap left by the pioneer involves considerable investment, and for what is inherently a smaller market. There is

also always the possibility that the pioneer, with greater experience and resources, will close the gap at a later stage.

12. It also presumably should include some statement as to which of the current activities are to be abandoned, and when. While not a new product activity and therefore beyond the scope of this text it should be noted that such decisions are not trivial, and that there is a growing literature on the topic. For example see Hamelman and Mazze (1972).

13. Thus as this author sees it the role of the corporate planner is to provide guidelines as to where these strengths lie. The role of the marketing executive, and the new product manager in particular, is to develop products which satisfy consumer needs. However there are an infinite number of such products and obviously someone in the organisation has to pick those areas on which to concentrate. The corporate planner, with a broader perspective into the organisation's overall strengths and weaknesses, is that person. Obviously marketing executives will provide some of the information on which such decisions are based, and hopefully also take part in these decisions. However the ultimate responsibility rests with those who have a wider view of the organisation's future.

14. By concentrating on the main aspects of new product procedures some other less central aspects will be excluded from this text. That is topics such as checking that the product conforms with safety regulations, consumer and environmental legislation, etc. It should not be thought that the omission implies that these topics are unimportant, indeed they form a vital part of new product management.

15. Pessemier (1966), p.11.

16. Booz, Allen and Hamilton (1968), pp.8-9.

7 NEW PRODUCT MANAGEMENT, THE ORGANISATION AND SOCIETY

7.1 Organisational Structures for Effective New Product Management

The purpose of this chapter is briefly to outline the various ways of organising for new product development, and the reasons behind recent trends in this area. We will also examine the impact of the resources crisis on future new product development.

The work as a whole is concerned with procedures for new product development, and there is insufficient space to do justice to the topic of organisational design. The procedures which are advanced here are those by which our knowledge of innovation and innovative behaviour may be put to good use in reducing risk. There is obviously another side or aspect to new product development, and this is the selection and motivation of the appropriate personnel for the job, an objective which may obviously be greatly influenced by the choice of organisational structure. However this aspect is more akin to the studies of industrial psychology and sociology than to innovation studies *per se*, and we will therefore only discuss those parts of it which relate to the procedural side. In other words how we may extract guidelines for organisational design from a knowledge of innovation. The other common problems of selection, motivation and communication are excluded from the discussion.

The folly of handling new product development within existing organisational structures has already been mentioned. New product development is a vitally important activity, yet one which is very different from day-to-day management tasks, because it requires a wider perspective and knowledge than more routine matters, knowledge which spans all the organisation's activities and functions. It is therefore normally handled by a team or group of individuals drawn from several departments rather than kept solely within either the marketing or research and development department. Certainly new product development should be based on consumer needs and therefore requires the constant attention of marketing personnel. More than this, however, it requires the expertise of people in the technical, finance and production functions. New product management also necessitates rapid and objective decision making, together with an alert and flexible approach to alternative futures. All of which are not the characteristics found in existing organisational structures, or displayed by executives in normal management roles. Hlavacek and Thompson (1973) point out that the nature of the process of new product innovation is diametrically opposed to the 'normal' processes and procedures of most organisations. First they note that it involves creativity, an activity which is often irregular, unpredictable and seemingly aimless, but which requires very highly trained specialist individuals, people working at the boundaries of their respective fields. The type of environment which is necessary for such individuals is very different to the one existing in the 'bureaucratic' organisation. Furthermore these authors note a fundamental difference between new product development and what is normally conceived as the efficient use of resources. Most organisations seek 'zero redundancy', that is the elimination of waste, duplicated effort and resources, etc. Hence the existence of management control systems which allocate each person a task and monitor their performance of this task.

New product development has an almost opposite strategy, since in the performance of such a development programme many ideas are generated, investigated and developed, and most are abandoned. Remember at least sixty ideas have to be developed to some stage, in order to achieve one final product. Thus in new product development there is a very high level of redundancy. Conceived in a limited sense it is an inefficient activity, and therefore poses great problems for any organisation. Unfortunately the fact that any other approach would be more inefficient (involving greater risk of failure) is not perceived by a great many executives in a very large number of organisations.

To digress a little, this is the primary reason why there is often hostility between new product executives and finance/cost control personnel. Viewed from the point of view of traditional financial management new products waste money, and large amounts of it. There would appear to be a great need for re-education and closer communication between disciplines in this area.

For all of these, and several more, reasons new product development programmes do not thrive in the hostile environment of an existing organisational structure. To some extent at least a separate structure or function must be created within the organisation, and charged with the responsibility of developing new products.

Historically the first step taken by many companies was to create an entirely separate new product department. Booz, Allen and Hamilton (1968) report that 86 per cent of the companies they surveyed had formal new product departments, quite a significant change from the 22 per cent obtained in their 1956 study. These departments were small (about five people), but in the main reported directly either to the top executive or a senior executive. Of the personnel, Booz, Allen and Hamilton found that this usually included a marketing man, a research and development specialist and an administrator.

While the new product department can give its personnel the freedom of action and absence of other commitments necessary to develop innovations, it would not appear to be the answer to the problem. Firstly it may suffer from exactly the same problems as it was hoped to avoid, that is it may degenerate into a bureaucratic organisation itself and cease to display the necessary innovativeness. Hlavacek and Thompson (1973) characterise this approach as the typical reaction of a firm to any problem — develop an organisation (with an associated budget) to tackle the problem. Which is precisely the wrong environment for new product development.

Secondly, this essentially staff department may become too isolated from the rest of the organisation. In this situation it may not be able to exert the necessary authority or influence over other departments. Whence it will not generate the necessary degree of commitment from other members of the organisation, and as a consequence its own personnel may cease to be sufficiently involved with the project. It is obvious that however structured no new product function can be completely isolated from the rest of the company. A new product department could not afford, for instance, to establish a production line without the co-operation and expertise of the production department. At some stage in its development a new product will require the attention, expertise and commitment of nearly every other department in the company. It will require the continuing involvement of the finance, marketing, research and development and production departments throughout its development. If the new product department is too isolated then it may not consider all the relevant factors, but more importantly it may create a product 'in limbo' as it were. At the commercialisation stage this product will be handed over to the rest of the organisation, and the individuals then responsible for its sales will not have been involved — they will therefore not be committed to its success. Similarly since the new product department itself hands over the product to others, prior to the product launch, then the new product personnel themselves may lose commitment. They at any rate have a perfect and ready made excuse should the product then fail. As King (1973) comments:

The new product staff man cannot really feel the deep commitment that comes from trying out the new brand in the market-place and discovering whether or not it is going to succeed. And the brand manager is taking over someone else's project: if it fails, it is hardly his fault. No amount of getting together and consultations can really get rid of this problem.[1]

Slocum (1972) considers that such departmental approaches lack 'the integration of thought, goals, objectives, and functions that is critical to successful new-product development'.[2] For similar reasons he also rejects other approaches such as 'task forces', 'committees', 'think' teams and 'support' teams. Another tactic which may also be disposed of at this point is the lone product manager, an individual assigned the task of developing the product by calling on the resources of other departments. Usually a staff not line position, it would appear that these individuals almost invariably meet opposition at every turn. Since other departments are not involved in the decision making it is often not in the career interest of individuals to co-operate in the requisite manner. It is also somewhat ambitious to expect one man to achieve such a task.

To overcome the defects of such approaches many organisations, and in particular the larger companies, have turned to what is known as venture management. This involves the formation of a small project group but solely for the duration of one project. In itself this latter constraint prevents the development of any bureaucratic tendencies, and by giving the team one task to tackle generates some degree of personal involvement. Further the personnel are taken from existing departments and on temporary assignments. By use of people from within departments many of the isolation problems are overcome, as such individuals have all the necessary personal contacts and if supported by senior management can exert sufficient influence to get things done. As the venture team members expect to return to their original departments when the project is completed then to some extent personal career considerations are less important and more objective decision making can occur. Since the groups are usually small (less than ten members) good working relations and team problem solving normally ensue. While there is nearly always a team leader, his leadership comes from his personal abilities rather than being imposed from outside. Nor is the team leader quite so weighed down by the threat of failure. If the project has to be abandoned then the leader returns to his old department, and with a useful fund of experience.[3]

However Slocum (1972) points out that there is no one fixed form of organisational structure for venture management, the basic concept must be adapted according to the needs of the company concerned. In his excellent text *New Venture Methodology* Slocum devotes some considerable space to a discussion of the advantages and disadvantages of various types of venture organisation. He also makes the important point that the venture team is not appropriate to all stages of the development process, advocating that the venture team leader should be appointed from the members of an 'exploration' group once the product concept is sufficiently clarified.

While it is considered that the venture methodology is the best approach to new product development currently available it must be recognised that problems still remain, and much can be done to improve practice in industry. Hlavacek (1974) has studied twenty one failed ventures and his conclusions are illuminating. Among the more important of these were that ventures were often abandoned because the sunk costs became too great, which Hlavacek rightly argues is due to insufficient attention and analysis in the early screening stages of development. Too many projects are continued too long.

In the middle of the development process ventures often encountered difficulties because of the inexperience of the personnel involved, or because of conflicts with top management. As King (1973) also notes, the problem of selecting the right individuals for a venture team is not an easy one to solve. Hlavacek considers that inexperienced personnel often fail to persuade top management because they do not take a broad enough perspective to their proposals. There is also the problem that top management may be biased against any new business which threatens the stability of existing operations. Hlavacek suggests that this may be overcome by allowing the venture team to seek support from more than one source in the company. This ensures the proposal gains a fair hearing, and also creates the desirable situation whereby different divisions compete to sponsor the project.

In the final stages of development ventures were often abandoned because of technical difficulties or because competitors had beaten the company to the market. The former could obviously have occurred for a great many reasons, some foreseeable and some not, but in my opinion the latter is always likely to eventuate at least to some degree. Given that the company has done its utmost to monitor competitive activity and that it is unable to be first or second onto the market, then the correct decision is, in all probability, to abandon the project. Resources should then be directed to being first with the next breakthrough.

In many ways these remaining problems are due to the inherent conflict in new product management. In order that the best possible product may be developed it is necessary to have a strong, multidisciplinary team of committed individuals who will thus be motivated to use their abilities to the full. The venture methodology provides the best available means of achieving such an aim.

However it is also necessary to take a dispassionate and objective view of the project, and subject it to a rigorous appraisal at every stage. Those so closely involved with the project are unlikely to be able to make such an appraisal, and this is where the conflict arises. Many organisations set up review committees, composed of senior management, but often this merely serves to replace one subjective appraisal by another. It can also lead straight back to the problems of bureaucracy and isolation that the venture method is intended to overcome.

The resolution of this conflict lies in the procedures for new product development which are outlined in the rest of this book. By understanding innovative behaviour, and by using this understanding to develop and test innovations, then more objective measures may be obtained, and better decisions made. Explicit objectives and performance standards must be established, and formal procedures laid down by which projections of likely returns from any new product may be computed. While it must be recognised that these projections will involve uncertainty, and that mistakes will still occasionally be made, once this is taken into account objective appraisals will be possible. Given a theory of innovative behaviour then these objective procedures can be developed and used to evaluate new product proposals. As mentioned before these proposals become hypotheses or theories which we set out to test in a scientific manner. In the words of King, new product development is a 'three-part process of theory, experiment and feedback'.[4]

Thus the relationship between the theme of this book, new product procedures and organisational structure is clear. It is first necessary to establish the requisite framework of procedures, and on the basis of a theory of innovative behaviour. This framework lays down objective measures of reaching decisions, and indicates how product concepts may be turned into successes. Within this framework we seek the organisational structure which yields the best developed products, and at present this is the venture method.

All of which suggests that the optimum organisational structure has the following form.

Firstly there is an obvious need for staff specialists to maintain, operate and develop this procedural framework. That is people well versed in the theories of innovative behaviour and in all the practical techniques used to develop new products. The basic role of these specialists will be to make projections and present assessments to senior management, and to advise venture teams. As will be seen shortly they will also need to be responsible for generating new product ideas, although of course in conjunction with line management. Note that nothing grandiose is being put forward; most companies will only need one or two such specialists.

Secondly that there should be a new product review committee or group composed of senior and middle management, the staff specialists mentioned above, individuals who are potential venture team leaders and existing venture team leaders. Again for most companies this would be a relatively small number of individuals. Indeed it should not become so unwieldy as to preclude all members meeting together; as envisaged such a structure has the advantage of facilitating a great deal of education by the transfer of experience between members. The purpose of this review body is just that, it sits to consider proposals from venture managers and staff specialists and form decisions as to respective projects. There will, however, be some differences in its deliberations according to what stage of development the products have reached.

In the early stages — 'exploration' and 'screening' — there will be no venture team associated with the product ideas, as this would clearly be impractical as well as undesirable. As the members of the review group will have other major roles in the company and may only meet once a quarter then it is therefore necessary for the staff specialists to be responsible for idea generation and the preparation of initial screening reports. Some ideas may originate from members of the review group, some from the specialists themselves, some from consumer research, or from outside sources. Whatever the origin the specialists collate these ideas and screen them according to an established procedure, and in the light of corporate objectives. The review group then studies the results of this screening, decides which ideas are worthy of further development and at this stage the venture approach is initiated.

However in the light of documented experience there will still be perhaps a quarter to a fifth of the original concepts left at this stage, and in most situations this will be too many to assign a venture team to each. The answer is of course that there is absolutely no reason for going straight to a full team at this stage — indeed there is every reason for not doing this. Remember the next necessary step is 'business analysis', that is the expansion of the idea into a concrete proposal with some statement of product features and development needs. Such a task can be handled by the prospective venture team leader in co-operation with the specialist, and on a part-time basis. Indeed it is probably possible and certainly more efficient to assign two or three, or even more ideas, to each leader who then follows them up in detail.[5, 6] They then submit their recommendations to the review body which decides which one, if any, of the concepts should be allowed to proceed to the development phase. Those prospective leaders whose assigned ideas have not shown any promise will remain on the review body and be first in line for another opportunity when a further set of ideas is processed. There will therefore be no reason for taking anything other than an objective viewpoint to each and every. idea.

The above procedure can also be extended to the early part of the development stage, until the point is reached at which a relatively small number of projects each require the full-time attention of the respective venture team leaders. These individuals then begin to form their teams, selecting personnel from existing departments as necessary and on a temporary basis.[7] Eventually by a continual process of review and development the position is reached where one full venture team moves into the testing stage, and perhaps then the commercialisation stage.

Now what has been described is a general scheme which must be adapted to the needs and resources of a specific company. A large company with many markets and a great pool of human and material resources on which to draw may decide to look for several new products in one or more new or existing markets simultaneously. It will therefore cast a very wide net at the exploration stage, thereby generating a large number of developable ideas at the screening stage and supporting several fully fledged venture teams in later stages of development. In the extreme such an organisation could conceivably have two venture teams competitively developing a product for the same market. However it would be naive to expect many companies, if any, to have this level of free resources. Indeed as King (1973) points out, most companies have the policy 'to produce the occasional major new brand'.[8] Such smaller organisations would therefore cast a smaller net.[9] Given resources that only permit one venture team and one development project at any moment in time then the scheme can be modified by postponing the point at which the venture team becomes fully operational. In other words the team leader would not begin to form his team until one partially developed concept had been selected for further investigation. For some companies and in certain situations this might necessitate extending the period of development in order to give all the generated ideas the appropriate consideration. It is necessary to be realistic in the application of the venture methodology — as originally developed and as often portrayed in the texts it appears to be for companies with large human and material resources to spare. However there is no reason why it cannot be successfuly applied to the great majority of companies, who can support fewer ventures. Hopefully by utilising the concept of a venture and the procedures of new product development such organisations can launch a greater proportion of successful new products, and thus generate the resources to expand their new product efforts.

Lastly it must be stressed that the need for empirically based and explicitly stated procedures is crucial. All those involved must understand the phenomenon they are managing and must evaluate their efforts according to the same ground rules. There is a vital requirement for education of the members of the review group and of the venture teams in all aspects of this topic. This should be the role of the staff specialist, and there is a good case for arguing that this specialist should be a member of the venture team(s).[10] Further, not only should he advise this team in the appropriate manner but he should also be charged with the responsibility of making the necessary projections, and in accordance with laid down procedures. The commitment of the specialist will be to the best (least error) projection possible, and his loyalty to the objective decision. As will now be discussed there will be increasing pressures on all organisations in the future to reduce the number of wasteful mistakes. The above is one way by which this ideal may be attained.

7.2 Innovation and Society: A Concept of Value

It could be that at some point in the near future, the dwindling supply of energy and raw materials will lead to a reduction in the number of products on the market and a curtailment of new product activity. The import of this is that new product management will be less vital and relevant to the company of the future.

However, I would take the contrary view and speculate that at least in the short and medium term there will be an increase in new product activity, and a virtual explosion in the number of innovations introduced onto the markets of the world. The nature and direction of all this activity will undoubtedly be different, the emphasis being on the efficient and non-polluting use of energy and on recyclable materials. There are signs that such innovations are already emerging; apart from obvious trends such as that to more efficient automobiles there are the recent commercial introductions of solar batteries and devices for turning refuse into methane gas. In the non-durable product categories there is, for one example, a noticeable trend to greater food value (efficiency) in convenience foods.

All of which has a certain historical progression to it. In the nineteenth century and the early part of the twentieth century manufacturers produced what they thought people should have. With lack of competition, unfulfilled and unsophisticated demand, these strategies were successful. However the very growth of the mass production and mass consumption society led to more affluent and sophisticated consumers, and thus to increased competition in the market place. A switch of emphasis became necessary – to producing what these consumers needed, or in other words to a marketing orientation.[11] Now we are likely to see another switch of orientation, and again one brought about by the steady growth of the consumer society. The new orientation will still stress the production of goods which satisfy consumer needs, but will also emphasise the optimal use of resources. As it were, a concept of resource-constrained marketing, but one which is at once different from the current marketing concept and from the economists' concept of the efficient allocation of scarce resources. Certainly the emphasis on the efficient allocation of these resources is there, but allocation according to consumer needs and not the whim of some distant decision maker.

This new change of orientation is likely to demand a higher level of technology than currently available, rather than a retreat to simpler forms of existence. It is interesting to note that by and large the trend has always been to greater efficiency – the television sets of 1976 consume less electricity and last longer than those of 1950, automobile engines last for tens of thousands of miles under stresses which those of the 1930s could not sustain for a fraction of this distance, and so on.[12] The resource crisis is because these innovations have diffused to so many individuals, not because they are inherently wasteful of resources themselves. What is necessary is to discover ways and means of solving such consumer problems at a new level of efficiency, and with due regard to the numerous constraints. Therefore rather than facing redundancy the new product manager faces an immense challenge, the challenge of making a radical change to his perspective of the world, and of introducing the required innovations. And the time span for this change is relatively short.

One way by which the new product manager may make an immediate impact on these problems is by becoming more efficient himself, that is less wasteful of corporate resources. By raising the 'success rate' for new products then society's resources will be allocated more effectively. In the author's opinion a new product failure represents a total waste of resources since it is obviously something which the consumers did not need, or which did not perform to their satisfaction. No such unsatisfactory products should ever reach the marketplace, and indeed a higher proportion should be abandoned much earlier in the development process than are at present.

If it is accepted that the way to raise the 'success rate' is by giving the consumers a voice in the development process then the policies and procedures discussed in this text represent a means by which this may be achieved. Consumers are given a voice not only in a theoretical and empirical recognition of how and why they behave as they do — that is, judge a product by its performance and communicate this experience to others — but also by the explicit and professional use of marketing research to assess these perceptions and opinions. In effect this is the conduct of the 'testing' stage in accordance with the theory of innovative behaviour.

The other side of the equation is the optimal allocation of resources, that is the economics of production, and the projections (made on the basis of the above tests) designed to assess whether the product is viable in corporate terms. New product marketing, and marketing in general, is the act of striking a balance between consumer needs and production economics. A viable new product therefore represents something which consumers need and which can be produced with an acceptable return on investment, that is it uses corporate resources efficiently. As by and large in the Western world corporations are entrusted with the utilisation of society's resources, then it follows that the above also represents an efficient use of these scarce resources. The partially complete equation is therefore: an efficient allocation of resources equals viable sales levels equals the satisfaction of consumer needs. This is the marketing concept.

If we then add the constraint or requirement that any future new product itself also utilises resources more efficiently than its predecessors then all the parties to the bargain should be satisfied, consumers, companies and even governments. We certainly cannot achieve more than this, and unless the advocated change of emphasis is made then we may well achieve far less. The dimension that has been added to the equation is that each new product uses less energy and material resources than before, or is capable of being recycled, while continuing to satisfy the relevant consumer need by performing as the consumer expects it should. This dimension was not in the marketing concept before, but it is crucial that it is there in the future.

Now this constraint may be imposed by governments or self-imposed by companies wishing to forestall government action or better husband their resources. Equally though it may be imposed by consumer demand, and this has already happened in some product fields, notably automobiles, home heating, etc. With increasing awareness of these problems in society as a whole this is a trend which can be expected to continue, and to affect wider areas of consumption. The consumers of the future will demand more resource-efficient solutions to their problems, and the successful new product managers will be the ones who develop innovations to match these rising expectations. The complete equation is therefore that the efficient allocation of resources is brought about by viable sales levels, which are dependent on the satisfaction of consumer needs by products which are as resource-efficient themselves as the current level of technology allows. The implication being that whether led by consumer demand or pushed by government decree, technology will evolve in a resource-efficient direction.

Given then that the consumers have the ultimate right to purchase the product or not, and that the company remains the means by which resources are allocated, then a successful new product has some intrinsic worth or value to society. By being 'successful' it represents an efficient use of resources, and its sales level or rather its return on investment (as we have to balance both sides of the equation), is a measure of this intrinsic value. A product which attains a major market share and hence a high return on investment in some ways therefore has a greater value to society than one with a minor share. Effectively it is satisfying a larger proportion of society and utilising a greater amount of resources in a more efficient way than the minor brand. However this can not be taken to the extremes of a monopoly; indeed it requires the competitive stimulus of a market structure whereby several firms are vying to make the next innovative breakthrough in order to maintain society's desired level of corporate efficiency. Nor does it imply that the minor brand has zero value and should be withdrawn; there obviously are minority consumer need segments and therefore minor as well as major brands. Some consumers view the minor brand as perfectly satisfactory and provided that the associated sales level is a viable one then these consumers are entitled to their belief. Only products which fail to make an acceptable return on investment, or returns losses, have a zero or negative value to society – these products represent waste.

By representing such losses as negative returns on investment – losses on investment might be a better term – we can establish some concept of perceived intrinsic value to society. 'Perceived' because success or failure, and hence value, primarily rests on the perceptions of consumers. One additional point is necessary here. Society requires companies to make a certain level of positive return on investment – in order to sustain share prices, satisfy creditors, maintain levels of capital investment and a host of other reasons. Therefore zero intrinsic value equates to a positive return on investment, although of what magnitude it is only possible to speculate. We therefore take an arbitrary point – 10 per cent. Diagrammatically this concept of value can be represented as in Figure 7.1[13]

It is perhaps of interest in itself as a way of conceptualising value, but it can also be made more relevant and meaningful to this discussion by considering the following.

Let us suppose we may obtain a suitably representative sample of recent new product launches, measure returns on investment, and thus compute the distribution of intrinsic value. We may speculate that this distribution looks somewhat akin to Figure 7.2.

The only grounds for displaying this particular shape for the distribution is that most new products are unsuccessful, and as a consequence some 70 per cent of new product expenditure is wasted (see p.164). Hence most current new product introductions are also 'wasteful' in the terms defined above.

The task for the new product managers of the future is to alter this picture, in effect to skew the distribution to the right. In this future most new products must represent positive value to society; certainly the area to the left of the zero must be reduced and that to the right increased. While risk and uncertainty may not be eliminated they certainly can be reduced. The way in which this may be achieved is clear. More objective and theoretically sound new product development procedures must be applied in order to increase the 'success rate', and hence value to society.[14] Since this implies a more accurate reflection of consumer needs, and as social trends are to more resource-efficient products, then these procedures will almost automatically result in such products. In the future the product with a high perceived value

Fig. 7.1: A Concept of Value to Society

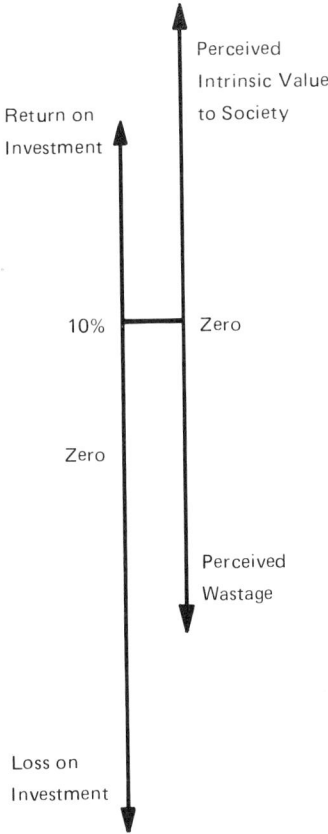

will be one which itself represents an efficient use of resources.

What has been said here is speculation based entirely on my reading of the literature and interpretation of trends. However, it must surely be admitted that the alternatives to the above are less socially desirable, representing either a retreat to lower standards of living and all that entails, or the authoritarian allocation of resources. Either way the consumer is the loser, and every member of society is a consumer. Thus the penalties of failure in this task are great, effectively the dislocation of society as we know it. Equally the rewards of success will be immense

Fig. 7.2: Speculative Current Distribution of Value to Society

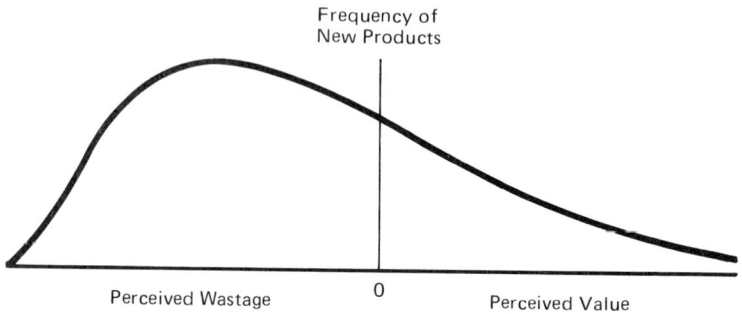

when measured in terms of the more affluent and rational society which would result. The next few decades will decide whether the Western free enterprise system will meet these challenges, and make the transition to a more enduring form of economic organisation. To a great extent success or failure rests on the skill and expertise which the present and next generation of managers bring to bear on new product development and marketing.

7.3 Summary

In this chapter the discussion has centred around those aspects of organisational structure which are determined by the new product procedures advocated in this book, that is, by the general theory of innovative behaviour. It has been demonstrated that new product development cannot be handled within the existing organisational structure and with traditional management methods. Most organisations are bureaucratic, that is they seek zero redundancy, whilst new product management involves high redundancy and apparent 'inefficiency'. It is therefore necessary to establish a separate team of individuals with the requisite expertise in marketing, technical development, finance and so on, who operate within their own organisational structure.

The first approach tried by most companies was to establish a new product department. However while in some ways a step forward such departments quite often become isolated from the rest of the company, and this has a detrimental effect on new product development. At some stage in the process nearly every dpeartment in the company will be involved with the new product, and in the associated decision making.

To achieve the necessary liaison and co-ordination of effort many companies have turned to the ideas of venture management, a venture team being a temporary group of individuals selected from existing departments solely for the duration of the project. There is no fixed format for a venture organisation, as this depends on the company concerned, nor can a venture team handle all stages of the development process. There are also many practical problems of implementation still to be overcome. Nonetheless the concepts of venture management represent the best method currently available for structuring new product development organisations.

However it was noted that both venture management, and any other form of new product management, involved an inherent conflict between the need for motivated and committed individuals, and the need for objective evaluation of the product concept. Hence the existence of new product review committees, but as was seen these do not always resolve the problem. Here it was stressed that the resolution of the conflict lies in established procedures and standards of performance which remove as much subjectivity as possible, and which are based on the theories of innovative behaviour.

An organisational structure was suggested along these lines, the main elements being staff specialists, a new product review group (composed of specialists, senior managerment and venture leaders) and the venture teams themselves, together with a manual of procedures. Illustrations were provided to show how this general scheme might be adapted to individual company circumstances. The role of the staff specialists was seen as vital since they provide both the expertise and understanding of the phenomena, and a commitment to objective evaluation and decision making.

The last topic addressed in this chapter was the possible impact of the resource crisis and whether this would have an effect on new product activities in the future. It was argued that it would, but to increase rather than decrease the rate of technological change. In order to move society forward to a more resource-efficient technology, more extensive and effective new product development programmes are needed. It was suggested that the way to achieve this goal rested on an application of sound evaluative procedures, and on a change in managerial philisophy, that is a reorientation of the marketing concept. This new conception stresses that the 'efficient allocation of resources is brought about by viable sales levels, which are dependent on the satisfaction of consumer needs by products which are as resource-efficient as the current level of technology allows.'

Furthermore it was then argued that every product has some value to society, and a measurable concept of this perceived intrinsic value was developed. The future of the free enterprise society depends on how effective new product managers are in increasing the total perceived intrinsic value, by their successful introduction of resource-efficient innovations.

Notes

1. King (1973), p.43.
2. Slocum (1972), p.36.
3. Hlavacek (1974) however notes that some individuals, especially young MBA's, promptly moved on to better positions with another company!
4. King (1973), p.33.
5. At this stage the job could be handled by the staff specialist alone. However it is vitally necessary to involve the venture team leader in order that he is committed to whatever concept is finally selected. This should present no problems as the workload at this point is a relatively light part-time one.
6. As the ideas will still be fairly vague the comparison between them is a necessary part of the screening mechanism.
7. Membership of a venture team might be a necessary qualification for later selection as a team leader. In this way current experience and expertise could be used to train the next generation of leaders.
8. King (1973), p.45.
9. It could be argued that the control should be the level of performance a product has to reach to pass initial screening. In other words that the larger company could pass a higher percentage of the ideas. However this would be bending the rules for the purpose of matching ideas to available resources, and should be avoided at all costs. Having established objective standards the company should only consider the ideas which meet these standards. If too many pass the initial screening, then some may be shelved until resources are available; if too few, then resources may be deployed to rectify the situation in the future. In this context the 'net' is really the number of markets considered (consumer needs/problems) and the larger company will axiomatically have a wider perspective, as a consequence of its absolute size.

10. One specialist can, and probably should, be a part-time member of several venture teams.
11. For the purposes of this discussion we ignore the transition stage of sales orientation.
12. Incidentally, modern engines are also more efficient in their use of fuel and oil.
13. Note also that investment includes not only those costs directly associated with the developed idea, but also those associated with ideas which were abandoned in the process of the development programme. It may also include some apportionment of any previous development programme which completely failed to generate a launchable product. These are all necessary expenditures in developing the product which is eventually launched.
14. By providing more reliable assessments such procedures would also lead to greater efficiency within the development programme itself.

8 THE TECHNIQUES OF NEW PRODUCT DEVELOPMENT

8.1 New Products and Marketing Research

The purpose of this chapter is to provide a selection of those techniques thought appropriate to each stage of the development process – a selection made according to the author's views and from a particular theoretical stance. Of necessity only a few of the many possible techniques will be outlined, primarily the latest advances, and the reader is referred to the cited publications for further guidance, and more detailed expositions.

As the central task of new product management is to generate, develop and evaluate new product proposals on the basis of their projected return on investment, the techniques presented will be mainly those directly connected to this task, that is those that assist in estimating consumer response and/or in modifying the product. Other topics, such as the development of the marketing 'mix', while undoubtedly important, will be mentioned only briefly.[1]

In essence we would really like to know what the potential innovators would think and feel about the product, and what they would say about it to others. This would enable us to predict the likely adoption and repeat purchase rates, and hence to compute the probable return on investment, the latter being essentially consumer response in corporate terms. However unless we conduct at least a small-scale experimental diffusion process, it is extremely difficult to assess this reponse, and to conduct this experiment requires a finished product. Clearly this is impossible to achieve until the final phase of the product's development, and therefore in earlier phases we use surrogates for this eventual response, that is indicators of possible return on investment. Semantically *succedanea* (that which one falls back on in default of another) would be more precise than surrogate. However, surrogate is the more common term. This is primarily in the hope that such measures may eliminate the worst of the original product ideas, and ensures that the finished product has as few deficiencies as possible.

In the earlier stages of development, the ways in which the above are achieved are necessarily divorced from consumer opinion, there being no product as such to show them. The techniques appropriate to these stages are therefore rough and ready, the aim being to eliminate fifty bad ideas quickly, and concentrate resources on the ten ideas which may have potential. Once these remaining ideas begin to take on more meaningful form then consumer testing can begin, small-scale at first, but becoming more extensive and sophisticated as development proceeds. While all these tests will perforce be in atypical situations (for the consumer), they hopefully provide valuable insights into eventual market response. However until an experimental diffusion process (test market or pilot launch) is conducted, there will be no great certainty about the outcome.

The fact that these techniques are so fraught with difficulty should not be disguised. There are problems enough in conducting marketing research in more real consumer behaviour situations, let alone in conducting research in an atypical or unreal situation and then trying to relate the results to future purchase behaviour.[2] More than this, it will be claimed that the present applications of marketing research to new product development are often ill-conceived and badly executed, and that much can be done by way of improvement. On reason for the above is that such marketing research studies are usually conducted with little understanding of the phenomenon, and as a consequence, often on the wrong sample of consumers. The other main reason for this unhappy situation is a failure to recognise that the measures are only surrogates for eventual consumer response.

A dramatic improvement could be made by explicitly performing these tests on the more innovative members of the target market.[3] As mentioned several times before, it seems pointless to ask less innovative individuals about the new product — they cannot give a reliable answer as they themselves do not know what this answer will be until they have received the requisite amount of communicated experience. Of course such a reorientation of marketing research methods poses considerable technical difficulties, and a great deal of research in this area is still necessary, but any move in this direction is likely to bring benefits as it would be theoretically more sound.

However, it must be admitted that the above would provide only part of the solution to these vital problems. Even asking the potential innovators what they might do with respect to an as yet non-existent product is still only an indicator (albeit a more accurate one) of their actual behaviour when the product is launched onto the market, and says little about the experiences they will communicate. The other major improvement to be made is to conduct research into the relationship between these surrogate measures and eventual consumer response, thus providing more realistic assessments. One way this might be achieved is by the use of systematic new product development procedures, and it is hoped to show this both here and in Chapter 10.

The various techniques for each stage of the development process will be specifically outlined, but for the sake of convenience, they will be grouped under three, not six, headings, namely concept generation and screening; concept development and evaluation; and consumer response; (corresponding to exploration and screening, business analysis and development, and testing and commercialisation respectively — see p.184). There is nothing sacrosanct about the six stage model, and it is worth nothing that both the stages obviously overlap to some extent, and that every product concept does not necessarily follow the same neat path from concept generation to commercialisation. At any point it may be deferred, to be returned to at some future date, or it may remain in a particular stage for extra development and modification. The process should be flexible and adaptive to at least this extent. Therefore at each meeting of the review group several decisions are possible. These may roughly be characterised as: (i) abandon the concept; (ii) continue development at the level appropriate to the particular stage; (iii) allow the project to pass to the next stage and continue development there; and (iv) postpone further development of the concept and re-evaluate in the future. Towards the end of the development process, that is in the 'testing' stage, we also have the possibility of a fifth course of action — to launch the product. Some authors suggest that it is feasible to consider the launch decision at an earlier stage, given that the forecasts are sufficiently risk free at that point (see Christopher, 1973). Here it is argued that these projections will never be sufficiently risk free at such a point in the development process. Consumer response (in real life situations) must be ascertained before proceeding to full commercialisation.

We now turn to an examination of the first two stages, that is how concepts are generated, and then how they are screened.

8.2 Concept Generation and Screening

First it should be remembered that an appropriate market should have been indicated in the corporate plan (and more likely several such markets), either as an existing market to be maintained, or as a new market to be investigated. Hence the new product group commences to look for ideas in a specific area rather than at random. Having thus specified the needs the company wishes to satisfy, how are the necessary ideas to be generated?

In fact there are two main sources for these ideas — externally from consumers and/or internally from the company's own personnel. Both have advantages and disadvantages, but as they are only required to generate ideas which are then input to the development and evaluation process, then either can be perfectly adequate to the company's needs. Of course a combination of both sources may be employed if this is thought desirable. The generation of ideas is actually a relatively easy task, and certainly not as difficult as is often made out. Translating the idea into a viable product is the problem, not forming the concept in the first place.[4]

Taking the first source, the consumers themselves, then there are several ways in which individual members of the public may be used to produce new product concepts. Sampson (1970) describes one such approach, based on the synectics technique of Gordon (1961). In essence this involves getting together a group of individuals from diverse backgrounds for the purpose of solving a problem, and then employing various devices to arrive at the solution in a creative rather than routine manner. As Sampson points out, some individuals are more creative than others, and the company would do well to recruit the former. He describes the tests thought appropriate to the selection of such individuals. Nor could the company rely on one such group, as sometimes the interpersonal dynamics are not conducive to idea generation. Sampson argues that the main advantage of the synectic approach is that the ideas generated can break away from being mere modifications to existing products, and that therefore it is a more valuable method for those problems which require 'inventiveness'.

On the other hand the approach advocated by Tauber (1975) centres on getting consumers to discuss the problems they experience with existing products. His rationale is that consumers can discuss such problems fairly easily, and he goes on to develop a survey methodology for achieving a quantitative assessment of consumer 'problems'. This general approach is also suggested by Light (1975). The end result being problem statements such as 'cereal packets are too big' or 'sauces don't pour easily' and so on. Apart from the possible disadvantage of being based on existing products, and therefore not generating radically new ideas ('possible' because this depends on both the market concerned and corporate objectives), there are other difficulties with this method. For one thing it requires someone to translate the problem into a solution (product concept), and for another, it requires some assessment to be made as to whether the problem is actually important to the consumer. That is, is it a factor in their purchasing behaviour. For these reasons Tauber suggests that his method be employed to generate 'clues' which are then used as the starting point for creative group techniques such as the synectic approach above, or more conventional 'brainstorming' sessions.

Of the techniques based on existing products perhaps the most well-known is that termed 'gap analysis'.[5] Broadly speaking this group of techniques rests on the assumption that it is possible to construct a multi-dimensional representation of how a consumer perceives a particular market. A simple, and hypothetical, example of such a perceptual map is shown in Figure 8.1.

Fig. 8.1: A Perceptual Map

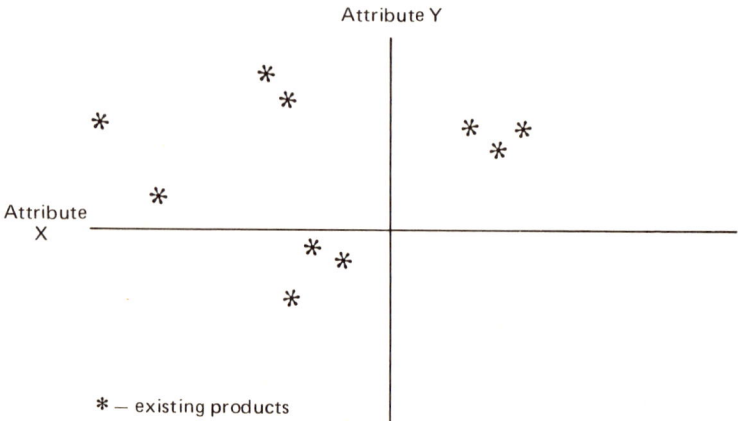

The dimensions are assumed to represent the attributes (characteristics) of the various products as perceived by the consumer. Given then that the existing products in a market can be so mapped, the proponents of these techniques argue that gaps can be identified, that is areas where no product exists at present but where a new product might be positioned in the future. In the figure, there is 'obviously' a gap in the lower right-hand quadrant. However as King (1973) rather unkindly observes 'gaps' often exist because nobody wants a product with those characteristics.[6] Certainly the existence of a gap in no way ensures a viable new product.

More sophisticated versions of the above techniques use the notion of an ideal point, that is what the consumer perceives of as the ideal product. The actual construction of such perceptual maps and the subsequent location of an ideal point is the realm of the non-metric multi-dimensional scaling techniques, and joint space analysis, topics which lie outside the scope of this book.[7] These techniques are of comparatively recent origin, and many theoretical and practical difficulties remain to be overcome. At the time of writing perhaps the most thorough and well thought out approach to generating ideas by these means is that described by Shocker and Srinivasan (1974). There is only space to highlight the main features of their method here, and the original article is well worth further study. There are four stages to the method as follows:

1. Identification of the product market, by ascertaining which products the consumers perceive as having the same uses.
2. Representation of these products in a multi-dimensional space with 'actionable' dimensions or attributes, that is attributes which can be connected to product characteristics, and are therefore useful in product development.
3. Construction of a model of consumer choice between existing products. This involves relating the distance between products in the attribute space to individual preferences. This relationship or model may then be used to predict how an individual would react to a new product concept.
4. Using the model to search for viable new product ideas.

The core of the method is in stage 3, effectively an individual choice model which allows us to predict how this one person would react to any arbitrarily located new product. In stage 4 an arbitrary location is selected and all the individual 'choices' aggregated. The overall 'market share' (as it is) can be evaluated, and an optimisation algorithm used to iteratively move the location until we find a point corresponding to a large market share.

Thus the major advantage of Shocker and Srinivasan's approach is that it does not just produce a 'gap' but the location (or locations) which are best preferred by the sample of respondents.[8] The ideas generated by this method therefore have a certain degree of viability already associated with them.[9] The obvious disadvantage is that the ideas are only modifications of existing products; there is no room for radical changes in this scheme. However for the majority of situations this method would appear to be a step forward, especially if it is remembered that the sole purpose is to generate ideas.

Of course it is not necessary, nor perhaps usual, for ideas to be generated from the eventual consumers of these ideas, it is merely desirable in certain circumstances. The requirement is that the idea, or rather the resulting product, satisfies their needs in the particular area, and a perfectly viable concept may come from within the company.

One method for creating ideas by utilising internal company resources has already been mentioned, that is the synectics technique. Indeed the method appears to have been invented for in-company purposes, where the group would be formed from various executives — in our context a sub-group of the review body, including the prospective venture manager perhaps. Suitable references to this method are Gordon (1961) and Prince (1970).

Another useful procedure is again due to Tauber (1972), who questions the validity of group techniques such as synectics, and cites evidence to the effect that individuals working alone are more creative. He derives an appropriate method termed the 'heuristic ideation technique', which relies on 'decomposing' the products associated with, say, one industry into a large list of factors. That is factors such as product form, technology, packaging, ingredients and so on. Every combination of these factors is then examined using a series of heuristics to reduce the vast number of possible combinations to a much smaller number of interesting possibilities. Again this has the disadvantage of requiring an interesting combination of factors to be translated into a product concept; there is also the difficulty of specifying the factors in the first place. The advantages are that the technique is simple to use, and generates a wide range of possibilities.

Of the other internal methods worth mentioning are technological forecasting either by pooling expert opinion as in the Delphi method, or by extrapolating trends in various product characteristics (e.g. size of basic electronic components, etc.).[10] In themselves neither of these immediately produce ideas; they serve mainly as a starting point for creative thinking, and as means of indicating what it might be feasible to manufacture in the future. For a technologically based concern it is obviously worthwhile combining these methods with something along the lines of the synectics technique, or even simply 'lateral thinking'.[11] The nature of technological development often precludes the use of the consumer based methods, since the product concepts are often far removed from existing products.

However I do not propose to draw conclusions as to which of the above approaches is best. Each has its merits, and must be selected according to the specific situation. Indeed it would appear that a combination of several methods would often be preferable to one alone. Companies should also entertain the notion of making idea generation an on-going and continuous activity, rather than in response to the need for a particular new product. This would enable them to build up a bank of ideas on which to draw at the appropriate moment, and obviate the need for sudden panic driven attempts to produce product concepts — which are practically always guaranteed to stifle any creativity in the organisation.

Having obtained a sufficient number of product concepts the next task is to assess which of these concepts are worth developing further, that is to screen the concepts with the aim of isolating the ones with higher profit potential, this screening being achieved by observing how each concept performs on a series of evaluative criteria. These criteria are essentially surrogates for return on investment, which we cannot compute directly at this point as all we have is a short description of each concept. We therefore use criteria such as 'effects of sales on present products' and 'raw materials availability' in the hope that products scoring well on the various criteria will generate a higher return on investment than those scoring poorly. However not only do we have to score each concept on each criteria, but we obviously have to decide which criteria are more important than others in order to arrive at a considered evaluation of each concept. It is also necessary to establish some level of performance above which development will be continued and below which the concept will be rejected as likely to generate a poor return on investment. I will use the term rejection level, following the analogy to hypothesis testing. It also implies that most concepts are rejected, and this is what should happen in practice. The important questions at this point are whether we apply a rejection level to each criterion, or to the overall score for the concept, and how we go about computing this/these rejection levels.

O'Meara (1961) presents the first well-known variant of these scoring methods, as well as a list of possible criteria or 'factors' as he terms them. He postulates four major factors — marketability, durability, productive ability and growth potential — and these are each separated into a list of sub-factors. Examples of the latter, and from each major factor, are 'relation to present distribution channels', 'resistance to cyclical fluctuations', 'production knowledge and personnel necessary', and 'expected competitive situation'. As can be seen they all relate either to return or to investment. Within each major factor the decision maker(s) have to decide how important each sub-factor is; that is what weight should be given to it, and similarly what weight should be given to each major factor. A scale from 'very good' to 'very poor' is then applied to every sub-factor with the decision maker being asked to evaluate the probability of the concept being very good, good, average and so on. These probabilities are then multiplied by the score for each scale position (very good = 10, very poor = 2), to produce an expected value, and this value multiplied by the appropriate weight to give a final score for the sub-factor. By repeating the process for all the sub-factors a total score can be computed for each factor, weighted and aggregated to form a grand total for the concept.

This procedure represents an important step forward in that it is systematic and more objective than previous methods, yet it is in essence very simple to employ. In fact just the type of procedure which we would wish to use at the screening stage, where it is desirable that several individuals evaluate all the concepts — but without any great expenditure of effort and resources. Unfortunately the method has several important deficiencies, and could not be recommended as best current practice. Firstly it can be stated that there are very grave theoretical doubts as to whether the arbitrary numbers we have invented can be manipulated in such a manner. The units of measurement for each sub-factor are probably different, and even if they were standardised (an immensely difficult task in itself), we might still have qualms about the various arithmetical operations. Secondly the sub-factors are not independent of each other; indeed as indicators of the same final outcome — return on investment — they could not be. An overall score therefore contains some interaction effects and is difficult to interpret. Lastly, we have no guidance as to what the total score represents; that is, does a score of, say, 71 indicate a good or a bad product.

Thankfully Freimer and Simon (1967) have gone some way to overcoming the last two of the three problems mentioned above, and Roberto and Pinson (1972) have resolved the first.

Freimer and Simon argue that the correct description of the concept is provided by the set of individual scores on each sub-factor, rather than a total score. That is that the profile is what should be evaluated.

While this is not a new suggestion, their advance was to demonstrate how probability distributions of the individual scores from past products could be used to interpret the chances of success or failure. From these distributions they compute an average total score for past products, which can be compared with the score for the concept under evaluation, and an index of how likely it is that this concept will be successful. However their method is somewhat complex, and does not overcome the problem of measurement and arithmetical manipulation.

Therefore Roberto and Pinson (1972) have combined both the above approaches with a modification of their own which appears to eliminate all these difficulties. Basically, instead of applying weights to the sub-factors, management is asked to rank them in order of importance, that is 'long-term profitability' as most important, 'availability of raw materials' as next most important, and so on. Each member of the new product review group then scores every concept along all the various criteria, using a scale similar to O'Meara's. These scores are then aggregated and an average score on each criteria produced. Next the average scores for the most important criteria are compared with the predetermined rejection level (obtained from an analysis of past products), and concepts with too low a score rejected. Those which 'pass' the first criteria are then evaluated on the second in an identical fashion, and so on. The end result is that only some concepts pass all criteria, and these authors describe procedures whereby these may be ranked in order of performance.

As each criteria has been examined separately there are no problems of measurement or aggregation, and the required level of performance has been specified at each point, a far easier task than specifying one for a total score. This method also has the advantage of being similar to the way most people make decisions, and is therefore easily grasped by those involved. Above all, and although it sounds somewhat tortuous verbally, in practice it is very simple to use.

To conclude this section there are important implications for new product development in the above screening technique. Firstly there is a great need for such techniques, as otherwise evaluations tend to be made subjectively, and with different decision makers reaching conclusions on the basis of different criteria. The very act of deciding on what criteria to use can be a useful learning exercise for the company, and the process of evaluating concepts on these dimensions serves to clarify individuals' thinking to a considerable degree. However the method must be simple as several people have to use it to evaluate a large number of ideas, without spending too much time on

any. Which is why the technique of Roberto and Pinson (1972) appears
to be one of the better ones available. Second, and more importantly,
the form of these techniques requires the establishment of formal
systematic procedures, and the collection and recording of information.
The first time a company employs one of these screening techniques
there will be no past histories to ascertain whether a particular score on
a specific criteria represents a good or bad prospect. The rejection
levels will therefore be set mainly on the basis of managerial judgement,
perhaps coupled with some retrospective analysis of past products
(how would we have scored brand x). Only when the company has
processed a fair number of new products will the necessary experience
be gained, and more realistic levels established. To do this requires both
formal procedures and the recording of the relevant information. [12]
Thus these techniques are unlikely to make an immediate and dramatic
impact; like the product concepts they are designed to evaluate, they
require some investment before any return is seen, the return being in
the form of an empirical relationship between the surrogate measures
and eventual consumer response.

8.3 Concept Development and Evaluation

By this stage in the development process the large number of initial
ideas will have been reduced to those thought worthy of further
development. As a first step the remaining concepts will be subjected
to deeper forms of analysis than were warranted at the screening stage.
The venture leader, together with the staff specialist, will collect all the
existing information that can be found, and supplement this with the
opinion of various experts within the company. Thus they will prepare
a report detailing the estimated size and historical trends of the market,
product usage rates, surveys of buyer behaviour and so on. They may
also commission reports from the research and development department
– on the feasibility of development, likely problems and costs, estimates
of product unit costs, etc. In fact all the relevant data and expertise
within the company will be collated and analysed, and, as noted in
Chapter 7, depending on corporate resources, any one venture leader
may assess several ideas at this stage, and in the above manner.

Using the analysed information as a base the leader and specialist
will make the first 'guesstimate' of likely return on investment and this,
together with fully detailed estimates of costs, returns, cash flows, etc.,
will be submitted to the review group. Naturally, at this point, the
forecasts will be somewhat speculative and involve wide margins of
error but this is not to say that such forecasts should not be made, or

that attempts should not also be made to ascribe likely error limits to the predictions.[13] It should certainly be possible to estimate the magnitude of the resources required and returns possible, and to suggest whether the return on investment will be 10 per cent or 100 per cent. These business analyses will effectively have drawn boundaries around what it is possible to achieve with the particular concept — provided of course that the eventual product proves satisfactory to its purchasers. Therefore to some extent the projections made at this point assume that a satisfactory product will eventually be developed.

At the next review session the various reports will be discussed and the appropriate rejection level applied — by this time the rejection level will be the minimum return on investment acceptable to the company.[14] At this meeting some concepts will be rejected, some allowed to be developed further and perhaps some referred back for further analysis. It seems probable that the latter will be those where the estimated returns on investment are sufficiently close to the rejection level that it is uncertain, given the error limits, whether or not they would be acceptable. Or those concepts where there is insufficient information within the company to make an estimate at that point in time. By referring these back more information could be collected, by way of basic market research surveys, the opinions of consulting engineers and so on. However the ultimate decision rests with the review group, and will obviously depend on their assessment of the various concepts, and in particular how many are acceptable (for development) without further study at this elementary level.

Assuming that some concepts pass this first hurdle then what does their development entail? The first point to note is that it entails aspects which will not be covered in this book, that is the technical development of the concept first to the prototype stage, and then on to a finished product. This requires the co-operation of the research and development and production departments, and it is the function of the appropriate venture team members both to ensure this co-operation and to guide the technical personnel in their efforts. Efforts which form the major part of the development stage, and which absorb most of the financial resources that are available to the particular project.

In achieving the gradual progression from concept to finished product the next step after the business analysis stage is often to elicit the responses of consumers to a dummy or mock-up product. The aim here is to establish some rough guidelines for the development of the product, and the techniques used are termed concept tests.

Unfortunately these concept tests are also often used to get consumers to predict their future purchasing behaviour and thereby assist in the evaluation of the concepts. As has already been indicated, this is an area fraught with difficulties, and it is very largely impossible to determine purchase behaviour by these methods, at least as they are currently applied and in the present state of knowledge. Which is not to say that such methods do not have a role in the development process, or that this role might not become more central in the future.

The proponents of concept testing, amongst whom Clemens and Thornton (1968) are prominent, argue that the techniques used to identify possible concepts (gap analysis) can also be employed to construct a profile of the desired characteristics for these concepts. The argument is by no means controversial; the method of Shocker and Srinivasan (1974), for instance, leads to ideas expressed in terms of the possession of a certain degree of each product characteristic. What is open to doubt is the next step, as follows.

The profiles are translated into verbal and visual descriptions which may be presented to a group of consumers in a theatre, together with similar descriptions of existing and competitive products. Apart from a wealth of demographic and psychological data, Clemens and Thornton advocate the use of a 'prize draw' tactic to determine purchase intentions, which, they argue, can then form the basis for decisions relating to the further development of the tested concepts. King (1973) however doubts such claims, stating:

> 'nor is there any case for trying to make decisions by *testing* these new brand concepts. It is not completely pointless to try out verbal descriptions of new brands on potential consumers; there is always some value in finding out people's responses to a relevant stimulus. But the idea of using such tests to make decisions between concepts or to make go/no-go decisions is very dangerous indeed. The fact is a concept and a finished brand are two very different things.[15]

Tauber (1975) goes further, commencing his discourse with the bald statement 'concept tests and product tests do not work'. One reason he puts forward is also one of those suggested here, that marketing researchers have failed to recognise the surrogate nature of these tests, and therefore have not attempted to link them to a useful measure – predicted return on investment. His other reason, the failure of purchase intention scales to predict behaviour in any way, he reaches from empirical considerations. Here it can be noted that since most

applications of concept tests appear to be with a 'representative' sample
of the target market, then this lack of predictability is not at all
surprising. It is really only worth demonstrating the concept to likely
innovators, and even then these individuals cannot as yet indicate the
type of messages they will transmit to the rest of society. It could well
be that, should a manufacturer be foolish enough to rely on a concept
test alone, the innovators might express satisfaction with the concept
but find the performance of the finished product unsatisfactory. In
that case they would probably be the only purchasers and then only on
one occasion! Therefore while the use of potential innovators as
respondents for concept tests would be a distinct improvement, this
would still only be a partial solution, and such tests *must* be coupled
with product performance measures at a later stage in the development
programme. We will discuss how to locate these potential innovators
in the next section.

Other improvements can also be suggested. Iuso (1975) observes that
anyone who applies simple rating scales is asking for problems. To give
one of the instances he cites, while a respondent may rate the concept
highly, they may have no *need* for the eventual product, an argument
similar to that of Tauber (1973). Iuso advocates the conduct of
'lengthy conversations with appropriate consumers' by means of semi-
structured and open-ended questions. It is then the researcher's job to
assign scale values, using an explicitly defined procedure to avoid
subjectivity, and to arrivè at a measure of 'concept acceptance'. Tauber
also provides a technique to overcome this interest/need problem.
Lastly Wind (1973), presents a complex integrated set of procedures for
evaluating concepts, based on a systematic application of multi-
dimensional scaling and conjoint measurement.

However, while all the above are improvements, none of them
addresses the basic problem. Even if we use potential innovators, and
even if we employ sensible techniques, we will not be able to predict
the value direction of interpersonal influence, and are therefore unable
to forecast directly the return on investment. That is, as things stand at
present. What, then, can the role of concept testing be, both now and
in the future.

First, it can be used to ensure that the developed product meets the
expectations of the potential innovators. In other words a dummy
product can be used as a starting point for group discussions, or
individual interviews, on the theme of what the respondents expect or
anticipate the product should do. If conducted with care, such exercises
can provide very useful guidelines to further development. In certain

circumstances they also provide an indirect assessment of return on investment; the author is thinking, here, of cases where the discussions highlight the fact that there is a gulf between expectations and what can be achieved technologically with limited resources. This might cause us drastically to revise the predicted return on investment (downwards — since it implies increased investment for similar returns).

Second, the fact that the use of the concept test as a developmental guide can sometimes lead to a reappraisal of forecasted return on investment suggests that much might be done so that it may *always* be used in this manner in the future. Thereby becoming an evaluative as well as a developmental tool. The way this may be achieved is clear; as with earlier comments, it requires the recording of test results, a procedure for generating a predicted return on investment from these results, and an eventual examination of this procedure in the light of actual market response. The new link in the chain — the procedure for generating a predicted rate of return — could be the same form of exercise as the business analysis. However it will shortly be argued that it is more efficient to use an interactive forecasting model. Naturally the link between concept test and model will improve as more development programmes are brought to fruition.

Hence while the current role of concept testing is solely in guiding development, there is no doubt that it could become an important method of evaluating concepts as well. The benefits are obvious, for at the dummy product stage little cost has been incurred.

The penultimate outcome of the development stage is a prototype product which can be shown to, and used by, a sample of consumers, and thereby more accurate evaluations made. It is on the basis of these consumer tests that the company completes the development of a finished product, and begins to plan eventual full-scale production. However before discussing these tests it is first necessary at least to mention two other aspects of the process.

It should be fairly apparent that a physical product is not all that needs to be developed. Any product needs some marketing communications, that is advertising, promotional material, pack designs and so on, and these must be developed as carefully as the product itself. Not because these are important to the long-term profitability of the product — that is dependent on its quality and performance — but because they are vital to the initial adoption process, and especially its earlier phases. The general theory of innovative behaviour indicates that advertising should be used to generate awareness, and that it also has a crucial role in persuading the innovators to adopt. By analogy in this latter role, advertising serves as a priming mechanism. If we can persuade the innovators to adopt, and if the product satisfactorily meets a need, then favourable experiences will be communicated, and the social processes will take over the task of convincing individuals to try the innovation.

The company therefore needs to begin the formulation of its communication strategy, and the development of the necessary materials, during this phase of the new product programme. Then the prototype product and the prototype communications mix can both be tested and refined simultaneously, an aim which is not merely desirable but vital. Both elements go together to form the complete entity that is a successful new product. King (1973) devotes considerable space to the methods of developing communications for consumer products, while Gisser (1972) touches on these matters as they affect industrial products.

The venture team should also begin to make more realistic appraisals of the return on investment, in the light of the likely media expenditure. Glaister (1974) using a model of innovative behaviour based on the general epidemic theory (see Bailey, 1957), shows that the optimal advertising policy is heavy expenditure in the growth phase, followed by a gradual reduction to zero as the product reaches complete adoption. There is evidence that elements of such policies are followed in practice. The implication is that losses may well be incurred during the early stages of the product's launch, and these must be taken into consideration when evaluating proposals and formulating plans.

Lastly the nature of new product development, involving as it does a large number of costly and interdependent activities, requires formal planning methods. These can be incorporated into the overall system of new product procedures and are likely to be of the PERT type.[16] The need for such techniques becomes apparent at the point where the concept is sufficiently clear and viable that a development plan can be formulated, and this need becomes more pressing as commercialisation is approached.[17] The full development of a new product requires numerous activities to be completed, and in a definite sequence if the project is to be brought to fruition smoothly and efficiently. Thus the construction of an activity network and an investigation of critical paths forms an integral part of new product management, whether it is done by simple wall charts or by the use of sophisticated computerised techniques. Such analyses also indicate where resources are being expended, and where extra resources might speed up the programme. The latter is of some importance; as has already been mentioned, it may be necessary to accelerate development to match or surpass the activities of competitors. This requires the planning technique to be flexible and easy to use, and this is the prime advantage of many of the computer-based methods.[18] In a matter of minutes the whole new product schedule can be revised and updated and the cost consequences appraised. It is normally possible to issue copies of the new deadlines to all the relevant parties with very little effort, and since the (small) venture team will be responsible for such activities, this is yet another reason for adopting a computerised method. Pessemier (1966) discusses the application of PERT to new product development; an introduction to these techniques themselves is provided by Lockyer (1967). Recently Bellas and Samli (1973) have proposed the application of a more powerful method, GERTS, to new product development, and this appears to overcome some of the limitations of earlier methods. However, there is no doubt that, whichever of the specific techniques is chosen, they all provide a means by which the venture team may control and co-ordinate the organisation's new product activities.

8.4 Consumer Response

When the point is reached at which a usable prototype product can be made, then the company will begin to assess consumer response on a wider basis, and in more realistic situations. It is probable, and desirable, that in fact several prototypes will exist during the early phases of consumer testing, although these are likely to be more in the nature of variations on a theme than radically different products.[19] This is desirable because in the absence of detailed records (on how surrogate measures relate to actual behaviour) the comparisons may be useful. Naturally the form these prototypes take will be dependent on the market — it is far easier to prepare six variants of a new cake mix than it is two alternative car designs. The type of product will therefore determine how much latitude the manufacturer has to experiment with different formulations.[20]

At this stage the company should also have prepared several 'prototype' media and promotional campaigns so that it may begin the important task of integrating the product and its communications mix. The finished product must not only match expectations, but project the image that it matches these expectations.

In testing the prototypes, it has already been argued that the only sensible procedure is to elicit responses that are indicative of future behaviour from potential innovators. The attitudes, opinions and expectations of the rest of the population will largely be formed by the reactions of these innovators to the product's performance, and in actual usage, not laboratory conditions. Which is why it was important in earlier stages of development to determine just what the potential innovators expected of the product concept, and to design the product around these expectations. Now, at this later point in the process, it is just as important to allow the potential innovators to try the various prototypes in their own homes (or factories, offices, etc., for industrial products) and assess their perceptions of the performance of the different formulations. These tests will still only provide surrogate measures — that is predictions of possible future behaviour — but measures which are likely to be more reliable and accurate than those generated by any other procedure. The current market research practice of using a 'representative' sample, where what constitutes 'representative' is arrived at in ignorance of the precepts of innovation theory, is likely to be of little use in predicting future behaviour. For every sample of 100 respondents, 25 may well be potential innovators, but the other 75 will not, and the responses from the latter will obscure any meaningful patterns in the data.

Of course it must be admitted that the isolation of these potential innovators is not an easy task. As was shown in Chapters 3 and 4, all that can be done at present is to identify the characteristics of a pool of possible innovators. Furthermore, these characteristics appear to vary considerably with the type of innovation (major, minor, fashion, etc.). No attempt will be made to reiterate this earlier material, and readers may like to refresh their memory at this point by referring to Sections 3.4 and 4.5. Dependent then on the product category the pool of potential innovators may be 10, 20, 30 or perhaps even 40 per cent of the total population. But even in the latter case, it is surely worth isolating a sample of this 40 per cent rather than one of the total population. The fact that only a proportion of these potential innovators will *actualise* their innovativeness when the product is launched in no way invalidates these claims. The noise in the data from potential innovators who do not actualise their potential is certainly likely to be less of a problem than that generated by those who take their attitudes from others, that is the less innovative members of society.

The difference between the proposed methodology and current practice is primarily one of degree and perspective. In some market situations it may be dangerous to rely solely upon tests conducted on potential innovators. For instance, the company might possibly develop a product which satisfied the needs of the innovators perfectly, and therefore received favourable recommendations, but did not fulfil the need of other segments of the population. While this product might be *adopted* by nearly all the market, only the innovators would repeat their initial purchase. Therefore in certain circumstances and for certain products it may be necessary to run checks on the rest of the target population, to assess how divergent their needs are from those of the innovators. These checks could take the form of group discussions or depth interviews, built around the topic of the individuals' problems or needs in the particular product area. Note that the aim is to ascertain whether there will be any difficulties with the level of repeat purchase, rather than with adoption. The latter is in a way almost guaranteed, provided, that is, that the product satisfactorily meets the needs of the potential innovators.

While there is no evidence on this matter, it can be speculated that these checks will probably be redundant in the majority of markets. If we were to take the whole area of low risk products then it would appear that in most cases the needs of innovators and later adopters are remarkably similar. It is only for more esoteric or radical innovations that these needs sometimes diverge, and unfortunately it is for such products that the checks may also be impracticable; that is, where the innovators are totally or partially responsible for creating the new need, as well as recommending a product to satisfy this need. Therefore while probably a necessary reassurance for management, checks on the less innovative are only rough and ready instruments, and should not be viewed in anything other than this supplementary/ confirmatory perspective.

The main instrument both for assessing whether the product performs satisfactorily and for projecting likely response remains the various tests performed on potential innovators. However before discussing the format of these tests, some comments should be made as to how the company might identify potential innovators.

One approach which might be feasible is to determine the characteristics of the innovators of previous new products, in a manner similar to the various studies discussed in Chapter 3. When the relevant characteristics had been isolated, then it would be a reasonably easy task to use them to recruit respondents for the consumer tests. However while studies such as those cited are of considerable theoretical importance, this would appear to be a somewhat clumsy and inefficient technique to employ in new product development. At the very least, considerable improvements are needed. The main difficulty is that there has been relatively little work done on these characteristics as they affect new product introductions, and it would therefore be unwise for a company to rely on the characteristics listed in the literature without any empirical confirmation. This then raises the problem that although the company can use the literature as a starting point and thus eliminate some effort, it will still take several major surveys before any confidence can be placed in the results. In common with many of the methods discussed previously, there will be no immediate impact on the new product programmes.

It is for these reasons that the second approach discussed in Chapter 3 (Ostlund 1974), appears to hold greater promise. All that is required with this method is an assessment of how a representative sample of the target population perceives the innovation along the dimensions of relative advantage, compatibility, complexity, trialability, observability and perceived risk. According to these perceptions it should be possible to classify an individual as a potential innovator or later adopter. The technique is described in more detail on pp.66-70.

What is impressive about Ostlund's work is that on two occasions he effectively managed to predict behaviour on the basis of measurements made some months before this behaviour occurred. And on the second occasion the method correctly classified 77 per cent of the innovators.[21] Now two studies do not constitute validation of the method, and Ostlund did not employ the perceived innovation attribute technique in quite the same role as is envisaged for it here.[22] One difficulty is that to use the technique to select respondents for product tests it is necessary to assign cut-off points along each dimension, defining those above as potential innovators and those below as potential later adopters. The first time this is done the levels will be somewhat arbitrary; it is only after observing behaviour that a more accurate assignment may be made.[23] However despite all this, it can still be seen that the method makes much more immediate impact on the development programme than the more traditional approach, where it would take several studies to arrive at what is effectively the starting point for the perceived attribute approach. The latter has the advantage that it may be applied immediately, and also to a market in which the company has no previous experience.

The choice between the two approaches rests in the hands of the managers concerned, and needs to be made on the basis of a careful consideration of the type of markets and products in which the company is interested. One practical compromise solution might be to use the perceived attribute approach in the early stages of the company's involvement with a particular market, and at the same time to collect a wide range of information on the characteristics of those selected. Should it eventually prove possible to use these characteristics to select potential innovators in a less costly manner than it is feasible for the company to do so.

Having identified and recruited a group of likely innovators of the particular product the next step would be to perform a variety of tests using these respondents. First and foremost, the company must ascertain whether the product performs satisfactorily — in the perception of the innovators — and this needs to be done in as realistic a fashion as possible. If the product is merely handed out to a hundred individuals with an exhortation to 'try it out' or 'give it a good test' then these respondents may well behave in an atypical manner, rendering the results of the test difficult to interpret. A better procedure would seem to be to allow the respondents to view advertising and promotional material on the various new product formulations, and existing products if any. At the end of this exercise, having perhaps evaluated the products and the advertising, they would be given the choice of a gift, either one of the new products or their usual brand.[24] The proportion who choose a particular new product obviously gives some indication of the likelihood of the innovators purchasing the product, and these individuals can be contacted again after a suitable period.[25] In the follow-up interview respondents would be asked questions on their usage of the product (when and how), and on whether they regard it as satisfactory. Rather than ask a direct question on the latter, it would be better to ask about problems experienced in use, and so on.

If the innovators had been recruited using the perceived innovation attribute approach then the same measures used there could be re-employed, with the aim of detecting any shifts in their perception of the product. These individuals would also be asked whether they had discussed the product with anyone, and if so what they had said, and if someone was to ask for advice about the product what recommendation they would make. Despite the (apparent) cost, the interviews should be primarily based on semi-structured open-ended questions, administered by a competent interviewer. In this way meaningful dialogues may be held between company and prospective consumers.

The end results of these product tests are *indicators* of (i) how likely the innovators are to actualise their innovativeness (from the 'gift choice'); (ii) whether a genuine need exists (from the usage questions); (iii) whether the product satisfies this need (from the performance questions); and (iv) whether favourable experience would be communicated. On the basis of these indicators and cost/revenue information, a projection of the probable return on investment can be made for each of the product variations. Hopefully at this point, one will stand out as the candidate for final development. If not, then further tests may be necessary, along lines suggested by these first measurements.[26]

This represents merely the framework for these consumer tests and many other measurements would be built around this. It would be necessary to test the various media campaigns to assess whether they communicated the correct message as to what the product could do. As previously mentioned, such advertising tests could easily be incorporated into the first stage of the product test. There is also the question of what price to charge for the product, a vital consideration in determining an accurate estimate of return on investment. The price should be fixed, not on any naive 'cost plus' basis, but according to what the consumers are prepared to pay. Gabor and Granger (1965), demonstrate that most individuals have a price *range* in mind when about to purchase an item. The upper limit represents the most they are prepared to pay, while the lower represents the price at which they begin to suspect the quality of the product. These authors present an elegant method for determining the price the majority of individuals would pay, based on simple questions which could easily be incorporated within the above procedure.[27]

To conclude thus far whatever the various modifications and embellishments may be the basic elements of the product test should be the selection of likely innovators, the conduct of a variety of measurements in a 'laboratory' situation, providing some individuals the opportunity to try the product in a realistic in-home situation, and follow-up interviews on these individuals.[28] By this means, I would argue that more accurate and reliable projections of eventual market response will be obtained.

However the measures discussed above are still surrogate ones, merely providing more accurate qualitative and quantitative information than was possible in earlier stages of development. Nor do these measures in themselves easily yield a forecast of return on investment. The results of the product test are couched in terms such as the 'proportion likely to adopt', the 'proportion likely to repeat their purchase' and the 'proportion likely to give favourable information'. All of which are static measures and ones from which there is no simple means of extracting a sales forecast. What is required is a detailed model of innovative behaviour whose components or parameters can be more directly related to these measures. Using this model then allows the manager to translate the static measures into dynamic consequences – a forecasted return on investment. These models will be discussed in more detail in the next section, but for the moment it is assumed that one will be employed in conjunction with the above and all other tests and evaluations.

It must be admitted that the costs of all this product testing are likely to be high, and certainly greater than more traditional market research exercises. Effectively since the form of test envisaged requires different samples for different prototypes, and different samples for different media experiments, then it may be necessary to use several hundred respondents in order to obtain large enough sub-samples. There is also the cost of producing the required number of prototypes to distribute. However, unfortunate as this may be, if the company wishes to improve its success rate, then the expenditure must be made – the 'cheaper' methods simply do not work. In the future there will be no room for the elastic perception of expense prevalent amongst many managers, the idea that it is not 'expensive' to commit the company to a multi-million pound product launch, but it is 'expensive' to spend £50,000 on establishing whether the launch is justified. Companies must invest in product testing just as they invest in capital equipment.

Once a prototype has performed satisfactorily in these product tests, then it is passed over to the production department who, in conjunction with the appropriate venture team member, translate this prototype into a producible item. Here we will gloss over what is in fact quite an involved process, for there is a considerable difference between manufacturing a few prototypes and regularly manufacturing thousands of finished products. The only point which needs to be made is that while adjustments and modifications to the product may be necessary, to cut costs or assist in quality control, the performance to the consumer must remain as tested. No major changes of this nature can be allowed, or a product which tested satisfactorily may prove to be a failure on introduction to the market. As the product reaches the stage where it can be reliably mass produced then the venture team have to face up to the thorny question of whether or not to test market.

In fact it will be clear from the arguments advanced so far that there is no such choice, and that some form of test market, or rather experimental diffusion process, is necessary. To this point in the development programme, all the measures made have been surrogates, and while the venture team will be confident that the surviving, and now fully developed, product concept is viable, they cannot be certain. None of these earlier experiments and tests have simulated the dynamic social processes of adoption, and it is vitally important to gain some further insight into these processes before proceeding to commercialise the product. The question is therefore not whether to hold a test market, but how to conduct this test market.

The original conception of a test market was that of a small geographical area, considered to be representative of the total market, into which the product was launched for a short period, the objective being to gauge consumer response, and possibly also to sort out any problems before national introduction. Having evaluated the product, and providing this evaluation proved satisfactory, then the company could proceed to gear up for a full-scale national launch.[29]

However as both King (1973) and Hayhurst (1971) observe there are two factors which may possibly militate against the usefulness of the traditional test market. First, it is difficult to identify a region which is representative of the total market, and this makes attempts to scale up the results to a national forecast difficult, and second the situation may change between the test market and the national launch. More specifically if the manufacturer makes his capital investment and production decisions after the test market then considerable time may be lost, time in which the now alerted competitors can react.

The first of these factors raises the question of the precise purpose of the test market. Is it so that national results can be estimated, or because the manufacturer wishes to experiment with various factors of the marketing mix? Davis (1970) terms these approaches 'projectable test launch' and 'pilot launch' respectively, while Hayhurst (1971) refers to them as the 'static' and 'dynamic' schools of thought, the essential difference being in the objectives, either to forecast national sales or to optimise the product mix. Here it is pertinent to question whether these objectives are mutually exclusive.

Some authors have reported difficulties in forecasting national market shares or sales from test market data, difficulties bound up with the unrepresentative nature of the test market region.[30] However, it would be fair to say that many such studies were done some years ago when forecasting methods were relatively simplistic and error prone, and this may have much to do with the unsatisfactory results. To forecast the adoption of a new product requires a model of the social processes, and it is only in comparatively recent times that these models have been available. Certainly as will be seen in the next chapter, both Urban (1970) and Assmus (1975) appear to have had little difficulty in forecasting national results from test market and/or pre-test market data. Lack of projectability can no longer be a fundamental objection to test marketing, although there is obviously a need for improvements in current practice.

It can also be noted that, provided the company has carried out the previous tests and procedures effectively, then there are relatively few aspects of the product mix that can be altered during the test market. By the time of the test market, the company's original ideas have been reduced to one variant of one basic concept, and this then developed to the point where sufficient quantities can be produced to hold the test market. The scope for altering the formulation of the product during the test market is minimal. Similarly both the content of the communications campaign and the price the innovators will pay has been established in previous experiments. The only quantities which can be varied to any extent are the amount of advertising and promotion, incentives to retailers, and possibly the price to later adopters.[31] The test market therefore only allows scope for 'fine tuning' and not major changes.[32]

To my mind, the fact that predictive models can be devised, and that the room for experimentation is anyway somewhat restricted, resolves the question posed above. The twin objectives of prediction and optimisation are not mutually exclusive. While in the past it was difficult to assess, say, a 10 per cent increase in advertising half way through the test market the advent of detailed market models makes this feasible, especially as the changes possible are so relatively minor. Obviously the diffusion process in the test market has its own momentum and it is impractical to restart the process every time a change in the marketing mix is made. However, provided sufficient data is collected, the type of model envisaged allows the venture team to assess how adoption would have progressed if this variation had been present from the start.[33]

A more valid criticism of test marketing rests in the second factor mentioned, that it may alert competition. The solution to this problem is by no means as easy as that of the first, involving as it does the nature of the product and of possible competition. Each company will have to make its own assessment of every situation, and the conclusions drawn will be dependent on the individual circumstances.

A primary consideration would appear to be the relative magnitude of the capital investment needed for the test market, as opposed to that required for a national launch. While the test market is conducted in a 'small' region, 'small' often means several hundred thousand potential customers, and as the test must run for several months (in order to assess the results) then a sizeable investment of manufacturing capacity and finance is normally required solely to conduct the test market. If however this amount is much less than that required for a national launch, then the company may be wise to make a final decision about capital investment after the test market. This will, of course, be dependent on the probability of a competitor launching a product during the delay which must inevitably result from postponing the investment decision in this manner.

The need for monitoring the activities of competitors has already been discussed, and it would be the task of this marketing intelligence function to assess the probability of a competitor making such an introduction. As well as the more obvious analysis of the life cycles of existing products, there are many other legitimate means of obtaining the necessary information. These are discussed by Kelly (1968). If the delay might prove detrimental, or if the difference between the investment required for a test market and that for a national launch is not so marked, then the venture team may consider another alternative.

Since the test market is normally conducted in one of the company's sales regions, then a popular expedient is the so-called 'rolling', 'sequential' or 'phased' launch. Here the test market or pilot launch is treated as the first stage of the national introduction. If the product performs satisfactorily, it is introduced into another sales region, and then yet another, and so on until the total market is covered. In this way the necessary investment is spread over a longer period of time, and the competition is given no warning of the launch and consequently little time to react. Another advantage is that if difficulties are encountered at any point in time, then the product may be abandoned with smaller losses than would be incurred with an unsuccessful national launch. On the other hand, if the venture team and the review group feel sufficiently confident, then they may move directly from the pilot launch to a full national introduction.

Of course the pilot launch involves a slightly larger initial investment than the traditional test market. If the product performs well, then the company is committed to sustaining sales in the pilot region rather than suspending them after three or six months. For this reason while the pilot or phased launch method would appear to have considerable advantages over the traditional conception of a test market, it is not possible to make a categorical recommendation for every situation. The venture team involved will have to make a considered decision as to which route to take with their particular product.[34]

Whatever is decided, the test market or pilot launch is really an experimental diffusion process where the venture team seeks to 'fine tune' the product and its communication mix, and to project an accurate national return on investment with a model of the social processes involved. To make a reliable projection, a great deal of information is required from the experiment, and it is appropriate to give some indication of the nature of this information.

Using the general theory of innovation as a basic model, then it can be seen that we would like to know the rate of growth of awareness and adoption, the extent of satisfaction or dissatisfaction with the product, and the consequent quantity of favourable or unfavourable information. More than this, it will be required to measure how well the distribution system is functioning, and since this is the first time the product has been manufactured in any quantity, it will also be necessary to calculate revised and more accurate production costs.

All of which can be obtained from a combination of: (i) periodic awareness and attitude surveys (to measure the effects of marketing communications); (ii) group discussions or rather qualitative research (to check that the correct marketing 'message' is being transmitted); (iii) a consumer panel (to measure adoption and repeat purchase and hence indirectly satisfaction); (iv) periodic surveys linked either to (i) and/or (iii) for the purpose of estimating the proportion of favourables, passives and rejectors (to determine type and extent of communicated experience); (v) retail and wholesale audits (to measure gross sales and the efficiency of the distribution channel); (vi) periodic surveys on retailer and wholesaler attitudes and behaviour (to detect the reasons behind any problems in the distribution channel); and (v) detailed audits of production costs.[35] The reasons for most of the above are by now fairly self-explanatory, but perhaps those relating to distribution should be discussed, albeit briefly.

There is no doubt that attaining a high level of distribution is of crucial importance to the success or failure of a new product. We have seen one example of this earlier in the case of Product 6 in Section 5.3. Put simply, low distribution levels yield low sales. There is also considerable evidence that the buying decisions of retailers are complex, and numerous factors are taken into consideration by these individuals. Among the more prominent factors are the reputation of the company (has it been successful in the past), the newness of the product (how different is it from its competitors) and the level of advertising and promotional support it will receive. Montgomery (1975) discusses some of the research in this area. The rather obvious conclusions are that if the company has a poor reputation, or launches a 'me too' product, or fails to provide adequate advertising support, then its chances of getting the product accepted by the retailers are minimal. However, even assuming that the company concerned has an average or high reputation and is launching a pioneering product, then success is not automatically guaranteed by a high advertising budget. Parsons (1974) has shown that while this will increase acceptance by the retailers, this is often at the expense of one of the company's existing brands. He concludes:

> Due to the shelf-space squeeze, the retailer. . .often forces the
> manufacturer to trade-off facings of its weakest brand
> in order to achieve a position for the new brand. If the new
> brand ultimately indicates that it is not a better product
> fulfilling an honest consumer need, the retailer will show little
> compunction and promptly remove it from the shelf.
> The effect is probably a net loss of facings to the
> manufacturer.

The company must obviously consider the possible damage to its other products when reaching any decision about the new one.

The fact that this type of problem can arise within the distribution channel underlines the need for the detailed research suggested earlier as part of the test market. Indeed, it is desirable to conduct some studies on these aspects *prior* to this test market. For instance at the product test stage, samples could be shown to retailers and their attitudes probed. By these means, the manufacturer will eliminate the danger of insufficient retail outlets stocking his new product.

To return to the main theme of the discussion, it can be seen that the various comments have effectively blurred the distinction between the 'testing' and the 'commercialisation' stage in the development process. With a phased launch, the venture team may be still 'testing' as the product enters its last sales region. It is for this and many other reasons that it appears desirable for the venture team and the review group to retain responsibility for the product throughout the introduction, and until the product approaches the mature stage of its life cycle. At the point of market introduction, the venture team will have acquired considerable expertise and knowledge relating to the specific product and will therefore be able to diagnose and rectify problems accurately and speedily. Some management tasks will be increasingly taken over by the departments from which the venture team members were drawn, and the venture team should perhaps take charge of training the individuals who will manage the mature product.[37] However a national launch is an immensely complex operation requiring careful planning and co-ordination, and full-time experienced managers. It is also the type of operation where numerous things can go wrong, any one of which may destroy the product's prospects.

Hence the need for the continuous collection of data similar to that provided in the test market, and the systematic monitoring of performance against objectives or targets. Crawford (1966) describes a useful technique in this context which is based on the idea of trajectories. The venture team must decide on the relevant dimensions of the product's performance (variables such as awareness, adoption, repeat purchase, distribution, percentage for or against the product and so on) and determine how these variables should behave over time if the product is to be a success. These trajectories may best be represented graphically and Figure 8.2 illustrates some of Crawford's examples. By contrasting actual performance with the target for that point in time the venture team can obtain early warning of problems. Furthermore the problem area is identified rather than having to be extrapolated from poor sales. In the figure, the problems of awareness and trial experienced by a dental product are clearly visible.

However, while this simple technique highlights problems requiring action, it does not suggest what the consequences of the problem or the remedial steps might be. Again there is a need for a predictive model of innovative behaviour which would use the available data to compute the likely variation in profit and return on investment. Furthermore, it would allow the venture team to explore alternative courses of action. In Crawford's example, the venture team could have assessed whether an increase in advertising would rectify the situation, and if so, what effect this would have on the projected return on investment. If it appeared likely that the return would be too low, or if the problem lay in the product itself, then the company concerned would have to consider abandoning this product.

Which brings us to the end of the new product development process. Hopefully, by diligently applying all the various techniques which have been described here, and by retaining an objective frame of mind throughout, the venture team will be able to hand over a successful market leader, thereby ensuring the company's future in this particular market for at least some period of time. Management must then begin

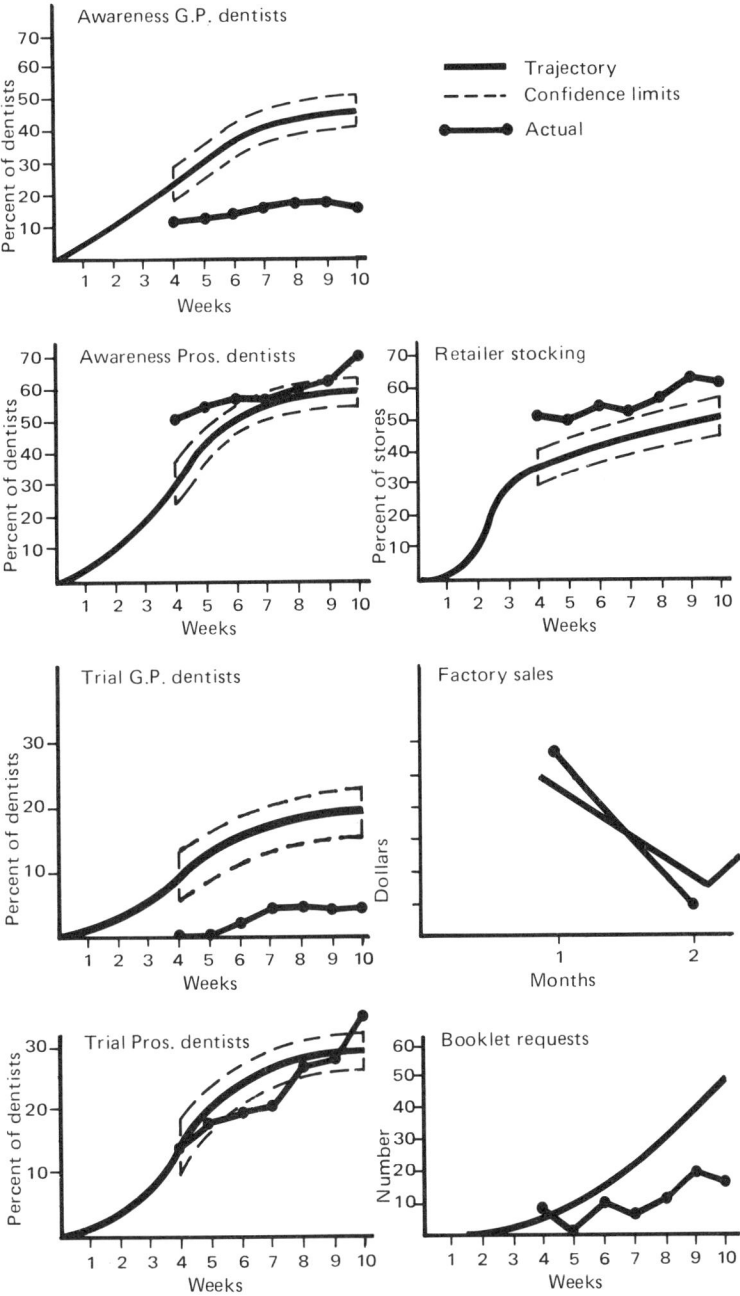

Fig. 8.2: Product Trajectories

Source: Crawford (1966), p.120, and used by permission of the American Marketing Association.

the cycle anew, seeking to develop a new and better replacement for this product.

8.5 The Need for Predictive Models of New Product Performance

In this chapter we have discussed some of the techniques which can be used to assist the development of a new product. More specifically, an examination has been made of the methods for evaluating the concept in terms of the return on investment it might generate. These methods being broadly classed as concept screening, business analysis, concept testing, product testing and the experimental diffusion process. It was noted that all the methods were only surrogates for eventual market response.[38] Furthermore, with the exception of the experimental diffusion process, they were all static measures along a variety of dimensions of the social processes of the diffusion of an innovation.

The reader may perhaps have wondered how it is that a manager can convert such measurements into a sales forecast, let alone an accurate estimate of return on investment. For instance, the results of a group discussion about the concept are merely what people said about it, or the results of a product test are couched in terms like x per cent of respondents did not like the taste, and so on. Quantities which have no direct relation to actual or likely sales in the future.

The answer is quite simply that in the past, the executives concerned had no option but to make a highly subjective guess as to what certain test results meant in terms of eventual sales, producing an estimate arrived at by implicit and intuitive thought processes, and often based on a very poor understanding of innovative behaviour. It is also true that even at present the vast majority of forecasts are made in this manner. It could be argued that it is not possible for the human brain to inter-relate all the various pieces of information in the requisite manner, and that it is unlikely that such guesses would ever result in an accurate sales forecast, even when made in conjunction with naive forecasting models such as those of the growth curve type.

What is needed is an explicit model of innovative behaviour and repeat purchasing, that is of the life cycle, and one whose parameters bear a close relation to the surrogate measures. With such a model, the manager is able to examine the test results and set the parameters accordingly. The model then reproduces the dynamic complexity of a new product introduction and computes the expected consequences of these results. The application of a cost model will then generate the estimated return on investment. The manager may also explore the consequences of changes in advertising, promotion, price and so on.

This type of model is a very important tool in the development of new products, providing as it does the necessary link between that which can be measured and that which can meaningfully be evaluated in corporate terms. It is therefore unfortunate that so few companies utilise these models. After ignorance of the basic phenomenon itself, the failure of companies and agencies to devise predictive models must rank as a major deficiency in current practice.

By employing one of these models, the company can also achieve more than just the efficient development of one product. For if detailed records are kept over several new product programmes then the model will assist in evolving more reliable connections between the surrogate measures and eventual market response. Effectively a predictive model can become an immensely powerful learning device for the company as it transcends both subjective and intuitive decision making processes. However, before this topic can be discussed, it is necessary to describe the essential features of such models.

8.6 Summary

At the outset of the chapter, it was stated that the venture team would really like to know how the potential innovators would react to the product in real life. As this is not possible prior to an experimental diffusion process, then all the techniques described subsequently were surrogates for eventual market response. It was noted that this posed considerable difficulties, not the least of which was the failure of practitioners to recognise the nature of the techniques employed.

The first group of techniques was discussed under the heading concept generation and screening. It was seen that there were two ways of generating product ideas, either from within the company or from consumers. Among the methods discussed were synectics, multi-dimensional scaling and the heuristic ideation technique. No conclusions were drawn as to the relative worth of these methods, each having advantages in specific situations. However, it was suggested that idea generation should be an on-going corporate activity.

Having generated sufficient ideas, the next task was to screen them and thereby identify those worthy of further development. The various techniques being classed as scoring methods since they involve rating or scoring the product concepts on a number of evaluative criteria, those concepts which failed to meet the required standard of performance being rejected. The possible criteria and ways of scoring were discussed, and the deficiencies of some methods highlighted. The method due to Roberto and Pinson (1972) was recommended because it raised no

244 Innovation and New Product Marketing

mathematical problems, was relatively simple to use and closely followed the way most executives make decisions of this nature. In particular, it was argued that the first time a company uses such a method the rejection levels must necessarily be somewhat arbitrary. If, however, detailed records are kept over the course of several development programmes it will be possible to evolve more realistic and objective levels. This was the first time the idea of empirically linking the surrogate measure to market response was met in any detail. The argument being here, as well as subsequently, that it was only by such an investment that the company would improve its new product procedures.

Next came concept development and evaluation, starting with detailed desk research — the business analysis. The result of this analysis being concepts which now had a definite form, and which could be considered for technical development. As a possible guide to the technologists, the various techniques known as concept tests were discussed in some detail, the basic method being to elicit the responses of a group of consumers to verbal and visual descriptions of the concepts. It was argued that current practice could be improved if concept tests were conducted on the innovators alone, but even given this improvement, that such tests only had a limited role at present. Specifically, it was stated that they should be used as a developmental tool to discover what expectations consumers hold of the product. In the future, if a link can be established between the surrogate (concept test) and market response, then they may also become an evaluative technique. Two other related topics were discussed within concept development — the need to develop the marketing communications and the need for formal planning procedures of the PERT type.

At this point, we turned to perhaps the most crucial stage of the development process, the measurement of consumer response. Again, it was noted that the only sensible procedure was to gauge the response of the likely innovators, and suggestions were made as to how these individuals might be identified. Of the two main ways this might be achieved, it was concluded that the perceived innovation attribute method, exemplified by Ostlund (1974), had distinct advantages.

The first tests to be conducted at this stage were in-home product tests where potential innovators were allowed to try various prototypes in as realistic a manner as possible, the end results being indicators of likely adoption, the genuineness of the need, extent of satisfaction and whether favourable information would be communicated to later adopters. While still a surrogate measure, the product test allows the venture team to make an objective appraisal of the various prototypes. One of these is then singled out to be further developed to the point where it may be mass produced.

The next question addressed was that of whether or not to test market the product. It was argued strongly that such an experimental diffusion process should be carried out and that the real question was how to conduct the test. On this topic, it was concluded that lack of projectability was no longer a problem, but the possibility of alerting the company's competitors was. For this reason, it was suggested that while each company should consider its own situation, the best strategy appeared to be that of a sequential launch, the first stage of which was the test market or pilot launch, the role of this pilot launch being both to optimise the product mix and predict the return on investment from a national launch.

The general theory of innovative behaviour was then utilised to determine the type of research which must be conducted during the test market. Comments were also made on distribution problems and the necessity of controlling the product launch closely.

Finally, it was stressed that all of the many measures taken were static, and further that each only determined some aspects of the social processes involved. In order to compute a return on investment, a predictive model of the life cycle is needed, and the employment of such a model would produce a marked improvement in new product success rates.

To conclude, three important points have been made in this chapter, and, at the risk of belabouring them, they are: (i) in the main it is only meaningful to measure the response of likely innovators; (ii) all such measurements are only *surrogates* for eventual market response; (iii) a predictive model is needed to translate these surrogate measurements into likely return on investment.

Notes

1. The 'mix' being communications, pricing and distribution.
2. A large proportion of marketing research is concerned with asking respondents why they currently purchase an existing brand. Here we are effectively asking them whether they would buy a product whose characteristics and performance are largely unknown to them, and not now but in the future.
3. Using 'innovative' and 'innovator' in the sense defined in Chapter 3, that is as a pool of those individuals more likely to innovate.
4. An interesting exercise is to pick a product field and try to think up some new ideas for an hour or so. Individuals vary but most people should be capable of coming up with something in this period.

5. Clemens and Thornton (1968).
6. King (1973), p.95.
7. See Green and Tull (1974); Shepard and Romney and Nerlove (1972). Multi-dimensional scaling requires the collection of 'similarities' data, while the computation of ideal points obviously requires the addition of preference data. Interestingly Stefflre (1969), observes that there is considerable homogeneity amongst individuals as to which brands are similar, it is only when discussing preference for one or other brand that the differences between people appear.
8. It is also feasible to constrain the optimisation to regions where it is possible to manufacture a product.
9. Interestingly enough these authors suggest extending the method to compute revenue/costs and therefore a return on investment associated with any location. The location with the highest return on investment could therefore be computed.
10. For a discussion of these methods see Wills (1973).
11. De Bono (1967).
12. Neither is it necessary for these procedures to remain fixed and inviolable; they may evolve as the company learns from its experiences, the recorded information serving as a repository of these experiences, and thus guiding the evolution of the system.
13. A simple way of assigning these error limits is the well-known expedient of asking the decision maker for likely, optimistic and pessimistic estimates.
14. Remembering that we are primarily discussing the evaluation of concepts for a specific market. Thus other factors such as size of investment, cash flows, costs and so on will be roughly of the same magnitude, and return on investment therefore the best sole criterion. Only when the company is deciding how to allocate resources between two very different markets, and therefore evaluating very disparate concepts, need considerable attention be given to the magnitude of these other factors.
15. King (1973), p.109.
16. Programme Evaluation and Review Technique – a generic term for a wide variety of techniques.
17. There is a good argument for applying PERT type methods to the whole of the new product process, as long as those involved do not become obsessed with the method itself – to the detriment of the development programme.
18. Control Data Corporation PERT Manual.
19. Remembering that we are discussing the efforts of one venture team toward one market. There may well be other venture teams within the organisation and with totally different kinds of products, but these will be aimed at other markets.
20. Which is often the reason why manufacturers of major durable products only half-heartedly embrace the marketing concept. Having invested large amounts of money in producing one prototype product formulation, the managers involved are sometimes very reluctant to make any changes to this at the testing stage. In situations where it is simply impossible to produce several prototypes the solution would appear to lie in better procedures in the concept generation, screening and evaluation stages.
21. It may be surmised that some of the 23 per cent not correctly classified were potential later adopters who because of situational variables and/or receipt of communicated experience decided to be more adventurous on this occasion. See Section 4.5.
22. To develop a discriminant function requires some behaviour to occur. The function obtained may then be used for subsequent new products in the same field.

23. Nonetheless this would still be more valid than current practice. If the levels were set too high, then some potential innovators would be excluded, if too low then some potential later adopters would be included. In either event the sample would be more accurate than one selected without due account of innovativeness.

24. Or perhaps cash if no other products exist.

25. Note that if the perceived innovation attribute approach was being used these exercises might be conducted on the total sample, but only the innovators followed up.

26. If the company has too many possible prototypes to go directly to this type of test, a less sophisticated version might be used as a first step. This would involved identical selection and measures but no prototypes would be given out for in-home trials. Needless to say this would also be less accurate and reliable.

27. At this point the author could have discussed those two favourites of new product texts, 'skimming' prices and 'penetration' prices. However Glaister (1974) has shown, by theoretical considerations and under certain assumptions, that the 'penetration' strategy is optimal. In other words the company starts with a cheap introductory price, and one less than unit cost, and then progressively raises the price as demand increases. To the author this seems a little naive; in the days of governmental price control the scope for raising prices is strictly limited. Gabor and Granger's method used in the way suggested means that a price is chosen that most innovators will pay. As adoption increases then their method can be used to reassess price levels for a wider section of the population.

28. Other forms of laboratory situation might be equally feasible. For instance the mini-test discussed by Pymont (1969). This needs further investigation.

29. By national is implied the next stage from a test market. In many countries and with many products there are intermediate stages between test market and complete market coverage.

30. Notably Gold (1964).

31. And even the scope for varying these quantities is limited. There is obviously an upper limit to advertising above which was impractical on a national scale, a price below which no return would be made, etc.

32. If major deficiencies are found in the product or its associated communications then it will either be abandoned, or the problems rectified and a further test market conducted.

33. The model due to Urban (1970) even allowed a correction to be made for competitive sabotage during the test market.

34. The method of Bayesian analysis may be useful in this context. For examples of applications to test marketing see Wills (1971), and Beattie (1969).

35. Conducting this amount of research will undoubtedly be expensive, but again it is stressed that these costs are minimal compared with the costs of a national failure.

36. Parsons (1974), p.946.

37. Some of whom could be drawn from within the venture team.

38. Even a test market is in some ways only a surrogate for eventual market response.

9 PREDICTING PRODUCT PERFORMANCE

9.1 Simple Forecasting Approaches

In the search for a predictive model of the life cycle it is tempting to turn first to simple forecasting approaches. That is, to models which have a simple and understandable structure, and which are easily implemented by the company, the majority of these models being of the so-called growth curve type and characteristically possessing only a few variables (normally adoption and time) and a small number of parameters to be estimated. Unfortunately the very simplicity of such models is their greatest weakness, and the apparent benefits to be gained by using them are in practice illusory. With this simple structure the parameters are necessarily at a high level of abstraction and aggregation, and are certainly a long way removed from anything which may be measured in a concept or product test. While this is of no great importance in the traditional curve fitting exercise based on actual data, it effectively renders these forecasting methods useless prior to a test market. Some further explanation is needed here.

In applying any model of adoption, or sales, or whatever, there are two basic philosophies we may take for assigning values to the parameters of the model.

The first may be defined as the *direct* empirical approach, which requires sales to have occurred, and data to be available. The parameter values are then computed by the traditional curve fitting exercise such as that employed to fit the special theory of innovative behaviour to data (see Section 5.2.). Obviously the earliest this can be employed is during the test market (when the first sales, as such, occur). Thus it cannot be used during the major portion of the development programme.

The second philosophy will be called the *a priori* assignment approach, which in itself is almost self-explanatory. Here the parameter values are assigned prior to any sales, and used to generate a forecast of the probable sales curve. This approach has the advantage that a forecast may be made at any point where we can assign the parameter values, and the disadvantage that these values have to be determined ahead of the phenomena they purport to describe. In a perfect world these values could be measured in some form of product test, input into the model, and an accurate forecast produced.

248

Unfortunately this is nearly always impossible as the parameters of most models do not correspond to anything which can be thus measured. Which is where the simple forecasting models are so obviously deficient and why it is better to have a more complex, but also more realistic, model. The narrower the gap between the nature of the parameter and that of the surrogate measure the easier it is for the manager to assign a parameter value. Eventually it may even prove possible to derive an empirical relationship between the measure and the parameter, and therefore remove the remaining element of subjectivity. However in the initial phase of evolving the new product procedures some subjective managerial judgements will be necessary, simply because the venture team must have predictions of product performance in these stages, and ahead of any test market exercise.[7] As was seen in the preceding chapter the test market or pilot launch only allows the company to make adjustments to the product and its market communications. If the product has major defects and does not perform satisfactorily then at best it will have to be taken out of the test market and redeveloped. By the time the requisite improvements have been made it is likely that the company's competitors will have caught up in the new product race. Bad products should never reach the pilot launch stage.

In actual fact it will subsequently be recommended that both the approaches above should be used to complement each other in the evolution of a company's new product procedures. At this point though, it is worthwhile examining the simple forecasting approaches because they are quite widely used in industry, and this will serve to clarify the argument.

Perhaps one of the most common growth models is the Gompertz curve, which has the property of resembling the cumulative adoption curve.[2] The Gompertz curve has the form:

$$\log_e Y = \log_e U - m \exp(-rt)$$

where Y is the number of adopters up to time t, U is the ultimate number of adopters, m and r are constants. If actual adoption data exists then it is a trivial matter to estimate the three parameters (U, m and r). However here we are more interested in *a priori* assignment and in this case Hendry(1972) notes the parameters are determined if the manager can estimate the initial adoption, the ultimate adoption U and the likely lifetime of the adoption process. He also observes that if the average (replacement) life of the product can be estimated then a forecast of the sales curve may be made. In some ways this study represents an attempt to link the parameter values to meaningful quantities, but one that does not really succeed. Exactly how is the manager to estimate the four derived quantities? It may be possible to guess 'initial adoption' and the 'average life' of individual products, but 'ultimate adoption' and the 'lifetime' of the process are another matter. Diffusion processes vary so tremendously in different markets, even for the same innovation, let alone between different innovations, that past experience will be unable to provide guidance. Nor is there any way of devising a consumer test to estimate these quantities; they are at too high a level of abstraction. In the context of durable products attempts have been made to link the parameters of the Gompertz curve to economic factors, but without any great success.[3]

We may also observe that the formulation of the above has no connection with what is known about innovative behaviour. In an attempt to overcome this problem Bass (1968) has used some facets of the theory to arrive at a growth model. Specifically he divides the population into innovators and imitators and makes the basic assumption as follows: 'The probability that an initial purchase will be made at T given that no purchase has yet been made is a linear function of the number of previous buyers.'[4] This bears some relation to this author's conception of interpersonal influence, and results in a simple quadratic expression for adoption, which again works well in curve fitting exercises. Equally however Bass's parameters, the 'coefficients of innovation and imitation', are at a high level of abstraction and cannot be related to consumer tests. Nor does this model take account of unfavourable influence or even marketing communications. While undoubtedly an advance over earlier growth models this particular formulation does not suit the purpose envisaged here.[5]

For low risk products one of the most well-known techniques is that due to Parfitt and Collins (1968), also reported in Parfitt (1968). Their model has some basis in diffusion theory, and is also derived from observed regularities in consumer panel data. In particular they noted that the repeat purchase rate for a new brand tends to decline from an initial level to a lower but stable plateau, and that purchasers of some new brands buy greater or smaller quantities than the market average. The predicted market share is given by the multiplication of estimated penetration (cumulative adoption), repeat purchase rate and the buying rate index. Thus far, Parfitt and Collins' approach is much closer to our idealised model, because both repeat purchase rate and the buying rate index could be estimated from the product tests by appropriate questions on the usage and satisfaction. However the major problem is with forecasting the penetration, which was achieved in the study by a simple model, namely:

$$dy/dt = r(U-y)$$

which may be solved to give the penetration or adoption y as:

$$y = U(1-\exp(-rt))$$

U being ultimate penetration, r a growth parameter and t time. Yet again this model works effectively if data on the diffusion process is available, but it is almost impossible to assign *a priori* values to U and r. Eskin (1973) has extended this type of model.

As Nakanishi (1973) notes these simple approaches also have another defect — they neglect to make any explicit allowance for the effects of marketing variables.[6] If the venture team wish to discover the answer to questions such as 'what will happen if we increase advertising by 10 per cent', these models will not provide any answers. The need for models which will provide answers to these tactical issues is vital, especially during the development stage and prior to test market.

The simple forecasting models are therefore of little use to the new product executive; they require actual sales data to be on hand before predictions can be made, and by that time it will be too late for effective decision making. However this discussion has clarified what the attributes of a useful predictive model of new product performance should be, and these fall into three main areas.

First, the model should be firmly based on a theory of innovative behaviour, or else its predictive powers may be limited and its reliability suspect. The model must therefore incorporate the dynamic effects of communicated experience and marketing communications.

Second, the parameters must be at a sufficiently low level of abstraction that values may be assigned to them without reference to actual sales of the innovation. In other words it is possible to estimate these values from the results of consumer surveys or experiments, as well as from experience with previous new product introductions.[7] This will allow forecasts to be made quite early in the development programme.

Third, it should be possible for the new product executive to experiment with variations in the marketing tools at his disposal, and thereby assess the likely consequences of these variations. Unless the executive can determine the possible effect of changes in advertising, distribution, price or other such factors the model has little value as an aid to decision making.

We will now examine the models which possess some, if not all, of these desirable qualities.

9.2 Predictive Models of New Product Performance

Having established the qualities of an ideal predictive model it is proposed to discuss here only those models which appear to approach this ideal, rather than all the available predictive models of new product performance. For this reason some well-known models have been omitted.[8]

To the best of my knowledge there are at present only five models worthy of inclusion, and indeed none of these completely satisfies all of the three criteria specified at the end of the last section. Nonetheless they represent a considerable advance on the simple forecasting approaches, and the majority of them have performed well in a variety of circumstances.

Chronologically the oldest of these models is DEMON (for Decision Mapping Via Optimum GO-ON Networks) which is described in Charnes *et al.* (1966, 1968a and 1968b). Strictly speaking, as the title suggests, DEMON is more of a network and decision making model than a forecasting tool *per se*. It has much in common with the PERT networks discussed earlier, although a network oriented to consumer testing activities and managerial evaluation rather than the totality of product development. DEMON represents a point of view on new product development/evaluation closely allied to the one given here. In particular Charnes *et al.* observe that many of the possible tests are alternative routes to the same end — a reliable prediction of future demand. Each activity may improve on the currently available forecasts, but each will also involve a cost. The decision maker must weigh the alternatives carefully and plot the best path through the network. Furthermore all the various estimates involve uncertainty, and the probabilistic nature of the task must be taken into consideration. The aim of DEMON is to find the path through this chance constrained network which optimises the expected profit. It is interesting to note that the path chosen is seen as generating a cumulative body of evidence on the product, with each activity adding an increment to the total, as opposed to a series of independent 'hurdles' which the product has to pass.

However to make such decisions requires some form of forecasting, and it is Charnes *et al.*'s suggestions in this area that are relevant to the discussion here. Within DEMON it is recognised that the end result of any testing activity is an estimate of likely national demand, calculated from a surrogate measure and forming a probability distribution about the unknown national demand. This distribution and the relationships between the surrogates and the demand estimates lie at the heart of the model. Unfortunately it is assumed that the organisation has predetermined these relationships, and has a 'model' of the market in some form or another. In many ways DEMON takes for granted the fact that a solution to this critical problem exists, and offers no real advice as to how such a solution might be obtained. DEMON tends also to assume that only marketing stimuli (advertising, price, promotion, etc.) are the cause of adoption and sales, and thus ignores the evidence provided in earlier chapters which suggests otherwise. It can also be observed that the computational problems involved in implementing this model are formidable, and that no actual implementations appear to have been reported. DEMON's value lies primarily in indicating what might be achieved once a valid predictive model has been evolved, and links established between this model and the surrogate measures.

Another early model is NEWS (for New Product Early Warning System). This was developed by an advertising agency in 1968, and has since been used quite extensively.[9] Of particular importance is the fact that it has been employed *prior* to test markets, and has yielded fairly accurate predictions of subsequent market response.

This model focuses on the central sequence of the diffusion process, that is awareness, adoption and repeat purchase, and seeks to relate these states both to measurable parameters and marketing mix variables. It was specifically developed for low risk products, and the growth phase of the life cycle. The structure of the model is inherently very simple, being designed to describe the number of individuals who are only aware of the product, or who have adopted it, or who are continuing to repeat their initial purchase. From the proportion of the population in the last two states at any point in time, the market share of the new brand may be estimated.

The number of individuals in these three main states are computed by a series of generating equations, all of which are simple mathematical functions of various parameters. It is the latter which are of relevance here because they are all quantities to which a manager might easily assign a value on the basis of his interpretation of a product or advertising test. That is they are quantities such as the length of time between purchases, retention of advertising messages, the rate of conversion from awareness to adoption, and so on. Also incorporated are marketing variables such as the total advertising effort, promotional effort, etc. There are five such generating equations and twelve basic parameters and variables.

According to its developers, NEWS was intended to forecast national sales on the basis of test market results, a task in which it is reported as having been successful on seventeen occasions. It has also demonstrated considerable power as a diagnostic tool, allowing the management concerned to correct deficiencies the model identified from the test market results. Perhaps understandably, given the form of the model, these deficiencies were in the effectiveness of the advertising and promotion rather than the product itself. However this model is also reported as having been used to *predict* test market results, and in this role as having been correct in six out of nine forecasts. Here the managers of the various products subjectively assigned the parameter values on the basis of the limited information available to them from pre-test market surveys and experiments. These results clearly demonstrate that executives can assign parameter values, and that these values can result in reasonable predictions of future market response. That is, always provided these parameters mean something to the executive concerned.

The major drawback apparent in NEWS is that it is not explicitly based on any theory of innovative behaviour. In particular the mathematical formulations used in this model do not incorporate any expression for interpersonal communication. Undoubtedly elements of the results of interpersonal influence are subsumed into some of the model's parameters. For instance the conversion factor from awareness to adoption which is either measured empirically from a test market or assigned subjectively (although perhaps on the basis of a buying intentions study) effectively represents the net effect of mass media messages and favourable interpersonal communication, which is perhaps why this model is still able to produce realistic forecasts. However if interpersonal communication had been given an explicit role we might expect that the predictions would be improved, and the diagnostic power of the model strengthened. Specifically its ability to explain product defects (as opposed to those of the marketing communications) might be heightened.[10] It is also unfortunate that the authors of this model do not subject its forecasts to any rigorous test, preferring instead to compare the predicted and actual market share on an average basis over the forecast period. This could mask considerable discrepancies between the forecast and actual events, and makes it somewhat difficult to evaluate just how accurate the model is — although it appears to be highly accurate. For a new product introduction we need to be able to predict the trajectory of the market share as well as its average order of magnitude. Despite these reservations, the NEWS model illustrates what can be achieved in the area of new product forecasting for a comparatively modest investment of effort.

In historical sequence the next topic is the work of Claycamp and Liddy (1969) who produced what is known as the AYER model (after the name of the advertising agency involved in its development). The AYER model represents a significant contribution in that Claycamp and Liddy set out to devise a method which would predict new product performance solely on the basis of the type of data available before the launch or test market. In other words information from product usage tests, media tests and so on, in conjunction with assessments of likely levels of distribution, price, etc.

The model was specified after discussions with practitioners and is composed of three interconnected sub-models. This can be seen from Figure 9.1, where it will also be noticed that only product and advertising parameters and marketing variables are listed, no consideration being given to interpersonal communication of any form.

In actual fact only two of the sub-models have been applied to data and discussed in the literature — those for advertising recall and initial purchase — and these were formulated as the following two equations:

$$AR = a_1 + b_{11} (PP) + b_{12} (\sqrt{AHI*CE}) + b_{13}(CP^*)$$
$$+ b_{14} (CI) + e_1$$

$$IP = a_2 + b_{21}(AR) + b_{22}(DN^*PK) + b_{23}(FB)$$
$$+ b_{24}(CP) + b_{25}(PS^*) + b_{26} (CU) + e_2$$

The first equation serves both to predict advertising recall after launch, and to provide the advertising input (AR) to the second equation. The second equation predicts initial purchase, that is trial or adoption. The parameters of the model are those mentioned previously but with the addition of the a and b quantities above. That is everything in the

Fig. 9.1: The Ayer New Product Model

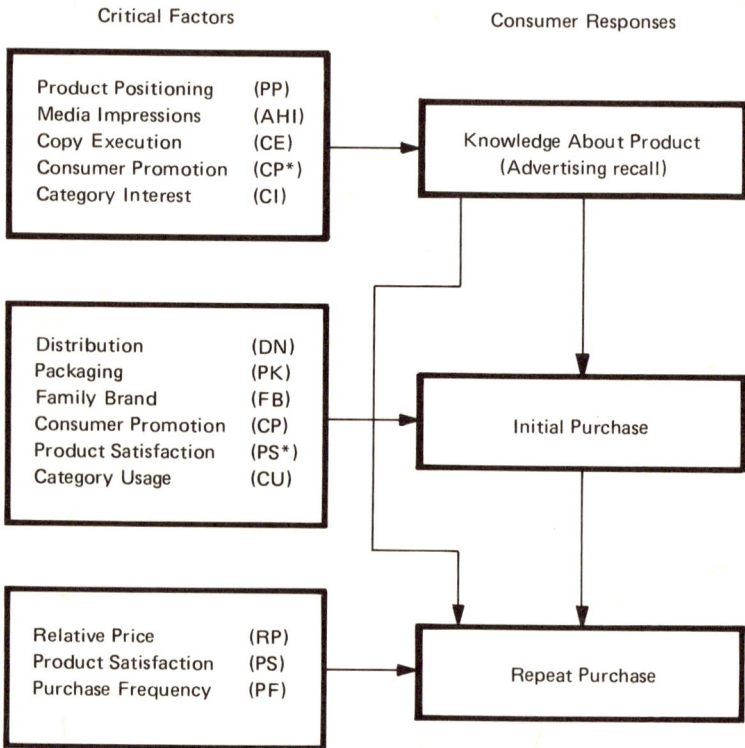

Source: Claycamp and Liddy (1969), p.415, and used by permission of the American Marketing Association.

equations — with variables (MI, CP^*, DN, CP).[11] These parameters were estimated in the following manner.

A sample of 35 new product introductions was monitored and for each at the end of 13 weeks on the market a number of surveys and store audits were conducted. These studies determined variables such as advertising recall, trial rates, product satisfaction, distribution levels and so on. Those parameters which could not be measured this way, that is copy execution, package quality and so on, were assessed by having executives rate them on predetermined scales. The advertising recall sub-model was then fitted to this wealth of empirical and subjective data by a straightforward regression technique. Once the parameters of this equation had been established then it was a simple task to generate the AR values for the second equation, and then fit the latter to the data in the same manner. The two sub-models and the associated parameter estimates were then checked by reference to an independent sample of a further 23 existing products. The findings were that the initial purchase equation predicted reasonably well but the advertising recall equation was less satisfactory.

However the sternest test of the AYER model was provided by applying it to the type of situation it was designed for. Pre-launch information was collected for 8 new products, and used to predict initial purchase 13 weeks into the launch, at which point actual levels of adoption were established by survey. The results were remarkably successful, to quote the authors:

> ... in five of the eight cases the predicted value of initial purchases is within ±5 percentage points of actual trial levels obtained in the consumer surveys and only one prediction is off by as much as ten percentage points.[12]

Hence by using a combination of empirical and subjective pre-launch information Claycamp and Liddy produced accurate forecasts of the future adoption levels, using a model primarily derived from an empirical analysis of past new product introductions, although this exercise too had subjective elements. This is precisely the type of procedure which is being advocated here, and the fact that such a technique has succeeded in real life provides added strength to the arguments. Subsequently a more sophisticated approach along these lines will be outlined, this being the model due to Assmus (1975).

However at this point it should be stressed that the AYER model also has definite shortcomings, the chief being that it is not based on any theory of innovative behaviour. Indeed the AYER model does not possess a theoretical foundation of any kind, being essentially a weighted index of all the parameters and variables thought relevant to adoption. Albeit an index which has been constructed by reference to the performance of previous products, and is therefore capable of predicting future events *of a similar nature*. The manner in which this index was developed, by reference to the results of past diffusion processes, means that, whether or not the authors admit it, this model takes some implicit account of the effects of communicated experience. This suggests that while it may be a reasonable predictive tool it will perform poorly in a diagnostic or strategic role. The same argument was raised in respect of the NEWS model, and will be expanded subsequently.

Another difficulty inherent in the AYER model is that it only provides a static forecast of trial at one point in time, the point being fixed by the time period when the original developmental data was generated. For evaluation of the product we require a dynamic period by period forecast, and one which predicts repeat purchase as well as adoption. While it is conceivable that the AYER model could be extended to provide such a prediction it is likely that the estimation procedures would prove cumbersome. To conclude, Claycamp and Liddy's work demonstrates that the type of procedure envisaged here is feasible, but it seems likely that the route to more effective predictive *and* diagnostic models lies in other directions.

Perhaps the most ambitious and realistic predictive model is that due to Urban (1970) and called SPRINTER (for Specification of Profits with Interdependencies). This model is immensely complex (containing five hundred equations) and it would be impossible to do it justice in the space available here. Instead only a relatively brief outline will be attempted.

SPRINTER has one over-riding virtue which is that it is one of the few new product models, and the only one discussed here, with a basis in the theories of innovative behaviour.[13] This on the one hand accounts for the complexity but on the other gives the model some considerable strength. The basic philosophy of the model is defined by Urban as the 'behavioural-process macromodel'. Rather as with the general theory of innovative behaviour, individuals are viewed as changing states on receipt of some stimuli or other. As with the general theory, Urban too concentrates on the flows of people between states and seeks to model these by his equations. Here the parallels end because SPRINTER is much more complex than the general theory, dividing individuals first into five overall states of awareness, intent, search, choice and post-purchase behaviour. Each of these overall states is then subdivided into states such as 'brand- and ad-aware' and 'loyalty I class'. Each of these is yet again separated until eventually we have groups of individuals such as 'shop in a store not carrying our brand' or 'number with intent to repeat and redeem coupon'. As an example Figure 9.2 represents the potential-trial class, that is those individuals who may adopt.

Fig. 9.2: Part of the SPRINTER model

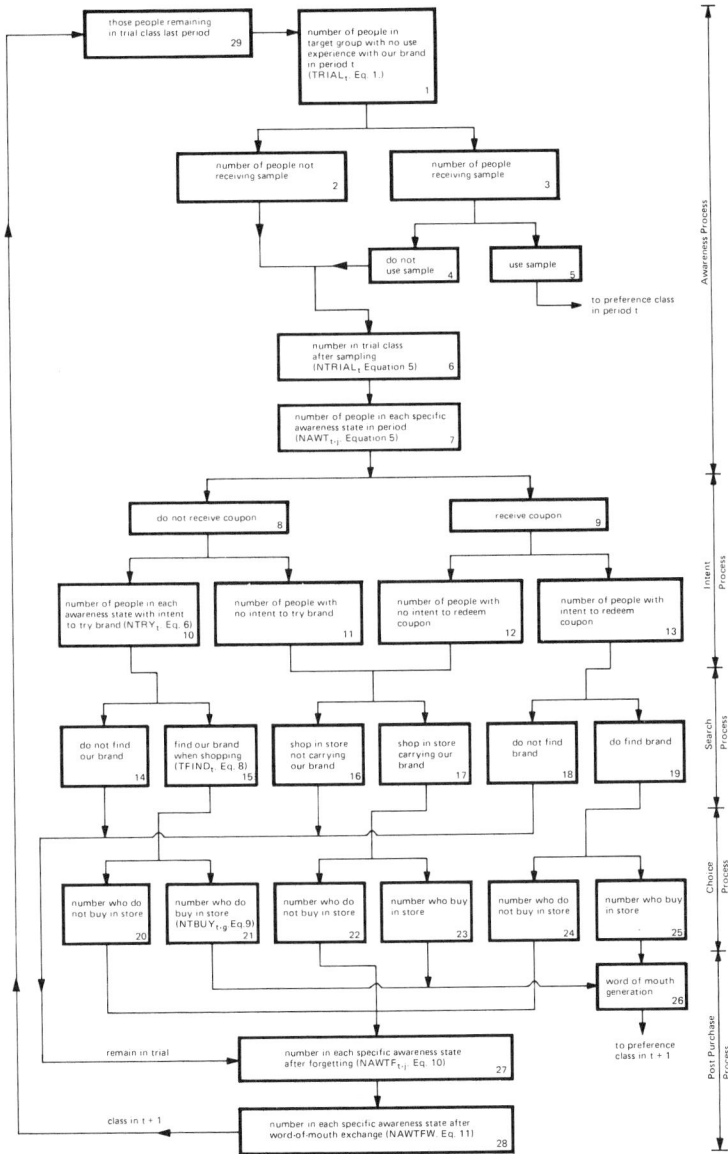

Box	Text
29	those people remaining in trial class last period
1	number of people in target group with no use experience with our brand in period t ($TRIAL_t$, Eq. 1.)
2	number of people not receiving sample
3	number of people receiving sample
4	do not use sample
5	use sample → to preference class in period t
6	number in trial class after sampling ($INTRIAL_t$ Equation 5)
7	number of people in each specific awareness state in period ($NAWT_{t-j}$, Equation 5)
8	do not receive coupon
9	receive coupon
10	number of people in each awareness state with intent to try brand ($NTRY_t$, Eq. 6)
11	number of people with no intent to try brand
12	number of people with no intent to redeem coupon
13	number of people with intent to redeem coupon
14	do not find our brand
15	find our brand when shopping ($TFIND_t$, Eq. 8)
16	shop in store not carrying our brand
17	shop in store carrying our brand
18	do not find brand
19	do find brand
20	number who do not buy in store
21	number who do buy in store ($NTBUY_{t-g}$ Eq.9)
22	number who do not buy in store
23	number who buy in store
24	number who do not buy in store
25	number who buy in store
26	word of mouth generation → to preference class in t + 1
27	number in each specific awareness state after forgetting ($NAWTF_{t-j}$, Eq. 10) — remain in trial
28	number in each specific awareness state after word-of-mouth exchange ($NAWTFW$, Eq. 11) — class in t + 1

Process labels (right margin): Awareness Process, Intent Process, Search Process, Choice Process, Post Purchase Process

Source: Urban (1970).

Source: Urban (1970), p.812, and used by permission of Operations Research.

The level of complexity of SPRINTER therefore approaches that of a microanalytic simulation model, but rather than go the simulation route Urban chooses to specify equations for the fraction of each group or class of individuals which transfers to another class on receipt of a stimulus.[14] To this extent the equations for these transfers are aggregative, but the net effect is certainly not as aggregative as the equations of DEMON, NEWS or for that matter the general theory of innovative behaviour presented here. The advantage of the macromodel approach over simulation is that only one computer run is needed to produce results, rather than the numerous (and at this level of complexity) expensive repetitions needed by Monte Carlo methods.

The equations used to determine the number of people moving from one class to another during one time period are fairly straightforward combinations of the number of individuals in the first class and a response function. There are variants of the latter for advertising, price, distribution, sampling and word-of-mouth communications. All these response functions and a variety of other parameters have to be estimated from data, SPRINTER then proceeds to compute the consequences in terms of market share in an iterative manner, and for each time period after launch.

Various cost, profit and risk sub-models are then brought into play to determine expected profits and return on investment. An interesting sophistication is that SPRINTER has a facility for computing the probability of achieving a predetermined target rate of return on investment.[15] According to Urban the company's rejection level would not be a certain return on investment but the probability of achieving that specified return with any particular product.

One of the most important advantages of SPRINTER is that the manager may interact with the computer model in order to find the best introductory strategy for the product. While this process could be mechanised too, Urban rightly argues that the judgement of the manager can be put to good use. In this mode the executive specifies initial values for the various parameters, together with a range of feasible variations from these values. SPRINTER then investigates all possible combinations of the input values and reports the one generating the highest return. By repetitively interacting with the model in this way the manager can gain confidence that he has the best marketing strategy for the product. He may then evaluate whether it is worth developing this product any further. SPRINTER can also take account of possible competitive reaction. Incidentally, this facility for exploring possible strategies is also a strength of the NEWS model.

On paper SPRINTER would seem to be an immensely powerful tool for new product management, and I would certainly not dispute this. However it is unfortunate that this model was designed for the purpose of forecasting national sales on the basis of test market results, and for monitoring potential problems during the national launch. It was *not* designed, nor indeed has it been used, to predict test market results from earlier surveys and experiments. Which is regrettable because as noted before a forecast of likely performance is needed *prior* to the test market so that bad products can be abandoned without great waste of resources. The role of the pilot launch is to refine a basically satisfactory product so that the national launch will proceed smoothly. Hence while SPRINTER fulfils two of the criteria, perhaps more adequately than any other model discussed here, it fails on the third. On the other hand there would appear to be no inherent barrier to using SPRINTER, or a similar model, in the required fashion and at this juncture it is therefore worthwhile examining precisely what SPRINTER has achieved.

The first test of this model was in replicating the market share obtained during a test market. As the model's parameters were estimated from data collecting during the test market this was not a particularly strong test, a fact Urban acknowledges. However it should be noted that this was not a curve fitting exercise, the parameters being calculated from a mass of survey and audit data and then used to predict market shares. Thus the fact that the predicted and actual market shares were essentially similar lends considerable support to the model. As often happens in test markets a competitor tried to sabotage the results by doubling his advertising and increasing his use of free samples. By use of the appropriate sub-routine in the model the effects of this competitive move were adequately accounted for. At the conclusion of the test market further SPRINTER analyses were produced, which revealed that the marketing strategy could be improved if: (i) a price cut was made and; (ii) more effective advertising was produced. In the absence of these improvements it was concluded that the product should not be introduced.

However the company was already committed to a national launch so SPRINTER could then be tested in its monitoring role. To achieve this the parameters were subjectively modified, to account for the difference between the test market situation and that likely to be experienced at a national level.[16] Further awareness and usage surveys were also conducted during the introduction and the parameters adjusted as a consequence.

Needless to say as the product was introduced with its original and poor marketing strategy it was not a success, and its problems were exacerbated by the launch of a competitive product. The forecasts produced by SPRINTER were extremely accurate, and over 100 per cent closer to the actual share than the company's existing forecasting procedures. Urban concludes:

> After testing on the basis of national data, the model served to analyse the decision to drop or to continue the brand. It showed that, if the price level was reduced as originally recommended, and if a new, 40 per cent better, advertising campaign could be mounted, the brand would respond, achieve a 19 per cent market share, and return $2,000,000 in cash-flow profit in three years. These are essentially the same changes that the model would have originally required for a GO decision, and it is reasonable to say that the model could have saved the firm a year of painful and highly unprofitable national experience.[17]

In the roles it was designed for SPRINTER appears to yield good results, although at considerable cost in terms of complexity and data collection.[18] In particular the estimation of the parameters required as basic inputs store audit data, consumer panel data, awareness, preference, intent, usage and word-of-mouth surveys, salesmen's reports, media audits and accounting data. The parameter values are then computed by sophisticated statistical procedures. However at various points Urban alludes to the possibility of subjective assignment of values should the requisite data not be available, or to modification of the parameter values in the light of managerial judgements. What may militate against the use of SPRINTER prior to a test market is that there are a considerable number of these parameters, and some of them are by nature remote from the usual experience of managers. The subjective *a priori* assignment task might therefore impose excessive strains on the organisation and executives concerned. It would appear that it would only be possible to use SPRINTER in this vital role where the management concerned was reasonably sophisticated, and where this model had been used on a reasonable number of previous new product introductions, thereby providing the requisite fund of experience. It could well be that Urban's SPRINTER is the type of model for the situation where the company has already developed a set of operational new product procedures and wishes gradually to upgrade and sophisticate these. However before it is possible to make such a recommendation in a definitive manner it is also necessary that

SPRINTER be tested on a much wider basis, and a far greater number of new product introductions.[19]

What can be concluded with greater certainty is that there is a need for models which are as well, if not better, grounded in the theory of innovative behaviour but which are less complex and can be related to pre-test market data in a more immediate manner.

Recently Assmus (1975) has presented a model which goes some way to overcoming the last two of these problems, that is complexity and the nature of the parameters. Assmus argues that if a model is to be accepted by industrial organisations then it must possess four qualities, three of which have much in common with those advocated here. The model must be capable of yielding forecasts before the test market, it must include marketing decision variables and the parameter definitions must coincide with the concepts and terminology of the managers concerned. The fourth characteristic is that the model must be one which the manager can trust, that is it bears a close resemblance to his own implicit decision making model.[20]

With these desirable qualities in mind Assmus produced the model displayed in Figure 9.3, and called NEWPROD. Again this model is one of the flows between the various categories or states defined in the figure, and one in which these flows are represented by simple equations determining the fraction leaving a state during one time period. Assmus's model has something in common with NEWS and also, although this is not immediately apparent, with the general theory of innovative behaviour. We shall return to this point shortly.

NEWPROD is reported as being highly successful both in forecasting national sales from test market results and, more importantly, in predicting market response from information available prior to these tests. Figure 9.4 presents five such predictions of market share made on the basis of pre-test market data. The dynamic performance of the model can be seen to be satisfactory. These analyses were based on historical data; Assmus also reports that similar results have been obtained in on-going new product development situations.

If this model is applied during or after a test market then estimation of the parameter values is a fairly easy task. They may be obtained from an analysis of consumer panel data and awareness studies. However if it is desired to make forecasts prior to this then two methods may be used, either independently or in combination with each other.

Firstly it is possible for the manager to make a subjective assignment of these values. The three critical factors are the rates at which individuals enter the advertising-aware category, the purchase-trier

Fig. 9.3: The NEWPROD Model

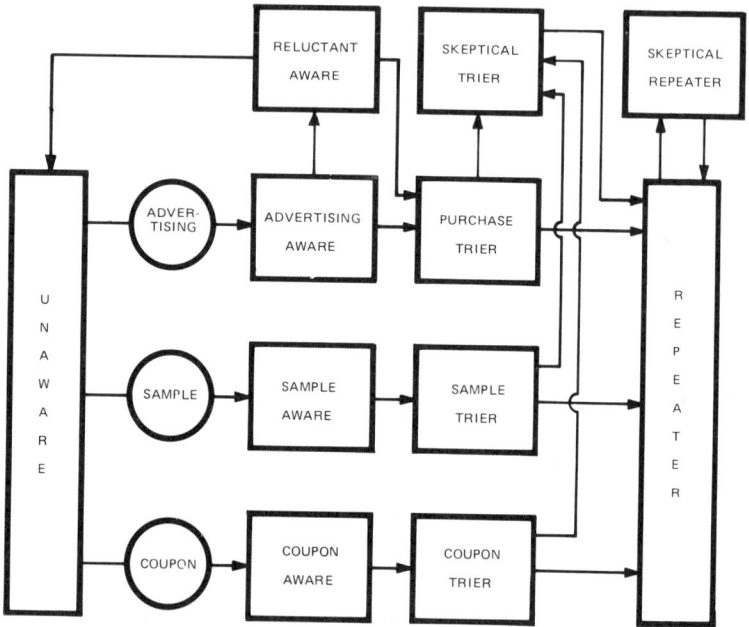

Source: Assmus (1975), p.18, and used by permission of the American
Marketing Association.

category and the repeater category.[21] These quantities are sufficiently
close in conception to the ideas of awareness level, trial level and
repeat purchase level which are familiar to most consumer goods
managers. A reliable subjective estimation scheme can therefore easily
be devised.[22] Furthermore the likely awareness, trial and repeat levels
are all quantities for which some surrogate measure or another will have
been made during product and advertising tests and experiments. This

Fig. 9.4: Comparison of Actual Market Share with Predictions Based on Pre-Test
Market Measurements

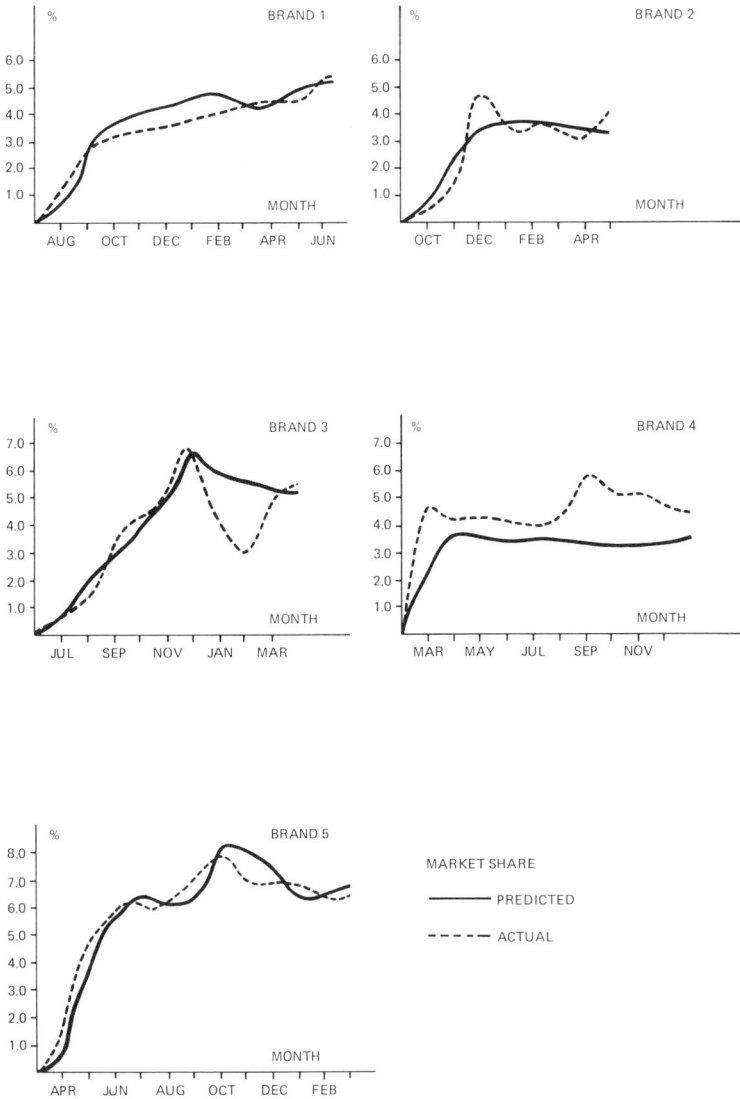

Source: Assmus (1975), p.22, and used by permission of the American
Marketing Association.

procedure is therefore not simply guessing but a valid technique.

Secondly if the company has kept detailed records of all the surrogate measures made of previous new products then an appropriate modification of the technique suggested by Claycamp and Liddy (1969) can be used. Indeed as such records existed in his case Assmus employed this method. Effectively a series of regression analyses were run seeking to explain the relationship between the awareness, trial and repeat rates observed in previous product launches, and the numerous surveys and experiments that had been conducted prior to these product introductions. For the particular company it was found that unaided recall from advertising copy tests best predicted the awareness rate, buying intention from an in-home experiment predicted the trial rate, and a combination of advertising and product ratings best predicted the repeat rate.

Thus we have a clear indication that surrogate measurements can be related to the parameters of a predictive model, and hence to a forecast of market response. In this case the forecasts proved reasonably accurate but Assmus does not go on to show how a comparison between forecast and actual sales may be used to improve future predictions. Given that it may be necessary subjectively to modify estimates arrived at in this manner (this product may be different from the earlier ones), then this comparison system can become a vital part of the on-going development of new product procedures. We will discuss this in the following section.

It is apparent that NEWPROD is not explicitly based on the theories of innovative behaviour, and for this it must be criticised. In some ways it is more sophisticated than the majority of the models discussed here, and has a few ideas in common with the general theory of innovative behaviour. For instance by defining categories of 'reluctant awares', 'sceptical triers' and 'sceptical repeaters' Assmus does acknowledge that not every individual will find the product satisfactory. However at this point the similarity ends as there is no mechanism by which these individuals may express their opinion, just as there is no role provided for interpersonal communication in the rest of the model.

Now in some circumstances and for predictive purposes this may not be of great importance. As with earlier models (NEWS, AYER) the way NEWPROD's structure and parameters are defined takes implicit account of interpersonal communication, and this is why it can generate reasonable predictions whilst at the same time being theoretically suspect. This needs to be expanded a little.

The three critical parameters, that is awareness, trial (adoption) and repeat rates, are all determined either empirically or by subjective judgement. As the latter is formed from previous experiences, in the context here these methods are equivalent. Essentially the awareness and trial rates represent the end result of various communication processes which we know from Chapters 4 and 5 to be both interpersonal and mass media in nature. However as these end results (which are effectively communication effectiveness measures) have been determined empirically then it may be possible to generate an accurate prediction whilst wrongly ascribing the cause of these effects solely to advertising. In a similar manner the repeat purchase rate is a measure both of satisfaction with the product and interpersonal communications about other individuals' experience of it. Put simply the component parameters of this, and the other similar models, are summary statistics for the complex communication and psychological processes involved in the diffusion of an innovation. There is therefore no paradox in the fact that we may obtain a good prediction with such a theoretically incorrect model.

The major difficulty arises when we wish to explain the prediction (why are we likely to get such a low market share?) or to use the model for the purpose of devising the best marketing strategy (what will happen if we decrease advertising 10 per cent?). NEWPROD, NEWS, AYER and models of similar ilk incorrectly assume advertising and promotion are the sole cause of effects. We are therefore likely to obtain misleading advice from these models, as they ignore the fact that a major source of effects is outside the control of the decision maker, that source being interpersonal communication. Put another way, all of these models create the impression that correct manipulation of the marketing mix variables will invariably yield the desired result, whereas in fact the perceived characteristics of the product create considerable inertia in the system, either for or against the product, and hence manipulation of the media will never be as effective as the model leads one to believe. In certain circumstances such models might lead the decision maker to increase advertising when a more realistic model — by projecting unfavourable communications — would force him to re-examine the product's performance to the customer.[23]

The value of the results obtained with the NEWS, AYER and NEWPROD models is that these prove conclusively that it is possible to predict market response prior to the test market, and from the surrogate measures available at that point in time. The only other conclusion possible is that if we wish to move a stage beyond prediction and seek the explanation for the forecast response, which will enable us to improve both product and strategy and to make more realistic evaluations of the product, then we need models based on the general theory of innovative behaviour. Or at the very least models which recognise the power of interpersonal communication.

Since the models discussed here represent the limits of current knowledge it seems appropriate to conclude this section by making some suggestions as to the possible courses of action open to a company wishing to develop a predictive and diagnostic model. In other words how it may proceed to implement more realistic and powerful forecasting tools than the above, and in the context of the organisation's specific marketing problems. There would appear to be two such courses of action.

Firstly it should be possible to modify one of these existing models to take explicit account of communicated experience. In this respect the NEWPROD model would seem to be particularly appropriate for most consumer product companies,[24] with the simplest modification being to separate the trial rate (between 'advertising aware' and 'purchase trier'), into that due to advertising and that due to interpersonal communication. During the early stages of implementation, estimation of these two parameters could be achieved by subjective interpretations of the product tests, and as experience was built up these assessments would be complemented with the results of regression analyses. When used in a diagnostic capacity the modified model would provide for a more realistic appraisal of advertising strategies, the adoption rate due to interpersonal communication being relatively 'fixed' by the product's perceived performance, and only the adoption rate due to advertising under the control of the organisation. It is possible to envisage more sophisticated modifications, and similar models for other situations (consumer durables, industrial products, etc.). Nor should we exclude the possibility that one of the other models discussed might be of greater relevance to a specific situation.

The second course of action would be to employ the general theory of innovative behaviour, or rather as was suggested in Chapter 5 a special theory derived from the general theory for a particular type of market. While it could be argued that this course might well result in a more realistic model, capable of yielding predictions which are at once both accurate and informative in a diagnostic sense, it must be admitted that there are one or two obstacles to be overcome.

Until the various lines of research suggested in Section 5.6 have been followed up and brought to a successful conclusion, then there are no empirically defined links between the parameters of the special theory and marketing variables and/or surrogate measures. In itself this is not a problem; an organisation could develop its own links by regression just as was done for the AYER and NEWPROD models. The problem is that some of the parameters are defined in ways likely to be unfamiliar to managers, and subjective assignment may therefore prove difficult during the first few applications of the special theory.

To use the special theory developed and tested for low risk products as an example, then it is probable that these difficulties would be encountered with the constants or parameters associated with state transfers between the three adopter states (favourables, passives, rejectors), as executives are not accustomed to thinking in terms of the consumers (and non-consumers) of their product constantly changing attitudes and opinions. The remaining parameters are much easier to assign as they all relate either to the probability that advertising will cause an individual to adopt (j_1, j_2, j_3), or that favourable communicated experience will result in a trial (k_1, k_2, k_3)[25]. The personnel concerned would obviously have to allocate these probabilities between the three states, but provided the requisite data was collected at the product test stage this would present no difficulties. To digress, this has added advantages in that it forces the venture team to consider what proportion of the population is likely to find the product unsatisfactory, and having made such an assessment a means is provided of incorporating the information into a forecast, the theory or model itself generating an indication of the possible net effect of an initial segment of rejectors.[26]

The solution to these and other problems would appear to lie in the organisation collecting the necessary information, and conducting several dummy runs with a special model, carrying out curve fitting and regression exercises with the main objective of learning what the parameter values were, and how these values related to the surrogate measures and controllable marketing mix variables. As with SPRINTER a special theory or model of innovative behaviour requires an initial investment of time and resources before it can be used in the desired manner. It could be that a combination of both courses of action might well prove effective, by initiating the new product procedures with a model of the NEWPROD type while developing a more sophisticated and theoretically sounder model.[27] There is in any event a strong argument for using more than one model at a time; the comparisons obtained are often extremely interesting and capable of yielding considerable insight into the new product development problem.

Finally, whatever the course of action chosen a predictive model is a central and vital component in any established procedure. For this reason any reliable model, even one not grounded on a sound theoretical basis, is preferable to no model at all. The predictive model provides a way of integrating all the relevant objective and subjective information, and a means of projecting the probable return on investment, the end result being a valid assessment of the product's worth to the company. If the model also integrates the effects of communicated experience, then it may be used in a diagnostic fashion, to suggest how the product and/or the marketing strategies may or may not be improved.

9.3 The Role of Predictive Models in New Product Development

In order to establish less subjective and more empirically derived relationships between the parameters of the chosen predictive model and the surrogate measures obtained from concept tests, product tests, copy tests and the like, it will be necessary for the company to maintain accurate records over several new product introductions.[28] Records of the values of the surrogate measures, the values assigned to the parameters, the predictions made at various stages in the development process, and the actual market response in both the test and national markets. Details should also be kept of the reasons behind the assignment of parameters, and the numerous decisions made about the product concept. In this way, the organisation can build up a fund of experience and knowledge, and learn how to make improved predictions and decisions in the future. Should it later wish to implement a more sophisticated model, then it will have the necessary data bank on tap, and much of the lengthy developmental phase of model building may be eliminated. This model development and improvement process can be systematised, and one possible system is displayed in Figure 9.5.

In the figure, it can be seen that a series of predictions are made during the development of the product and before test marketing, the parameter values being assigned according to the postulated relationship between them and the various surrogate measures taken. Naturally these relationships are specified in a fairly loose and subjective fashion for the initial series of new product programmes. Assuming the product is test marketed and then launched nationally, the various predictions can be compared with actual market response and a post mortem held on the differences between predicted and actual sales, resulting in an adjustment and respecification of the postulated

Fig. 9.5: An Adaptive New Product Forecasting System

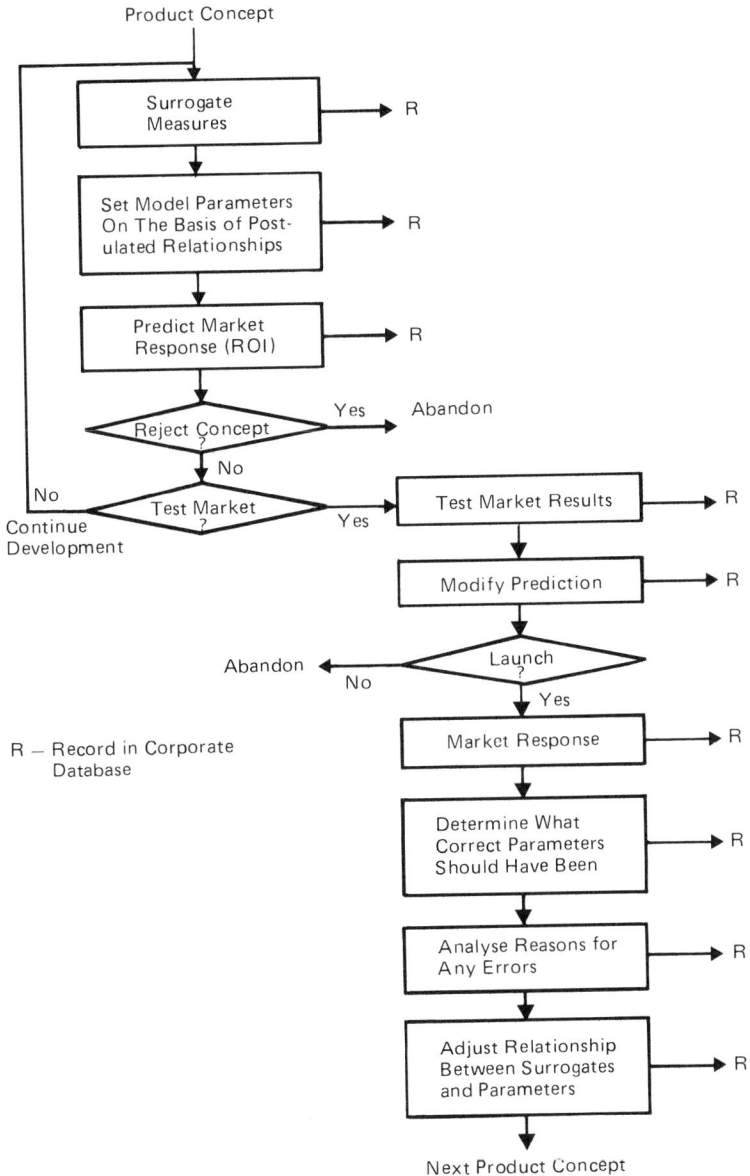

R — Record in Corporate
Database

relationships, made on the basis of the experience gained. Over a series of new product introductions the subjective element in the assignment of parameter values will be gradually replaced by empirically based procedures.[29]

One additional point here is that it will be necessary to collect sufficient information to generate these post mortem analyses, which requires a commitment to continue to conduct the types of research previously suggested for a test market well into the early phase of national introduction (see p.238).

Given that the organisation has developed and implemented a suitable predictive model in this manner, then a few concluding comments should be made on the uses of this model within the various stages of the new product development process. For the purposes of discussion, it is assumed that relationships between surrogate measures and model parameters have been determined to at least some degree, and that the model has been extended to compute a forecasted return of investment as well as predictions of the adoption and repeat purchase levels.

It appears likely that the first use of the model would be made in the business analysis stage. However at that point in time there would be few or no surrogate measures, so the venture team would primarily base their forecasts on previous experience and applications of the model. While this could only provide a rough estimate, the figure obtained would indicate the relative impact the product might have on the company's returns, and would enable the potential winners to be sorted out from those products which were unlikely ever to make a significant contribution. Furthermore, by interacting with the model the executives concerned might assess how alterations and modifications to the concept would affect the forecast return, and thus guide further development of the product. This is not an insignificant role because it suggests what the limits of any particular concept are.

Once we move into the concept testing and development states, then the venture team may utilise the established relationships between surrogates and parameters, and begin to make more accurate and informative forecasts. They will also begin to investigate the consequences of different marketing strategies, with the objective of determining the best mix of advertising, promotion and price. As the product takes on a definite form, the combination of tests and model will enable possible problems to be detected and overcome, or if these are assessed as insurmountable, then the product will be abandoned. However, making the assumption that the company has a potential market leader, then this refinement and development process will proceed, with the forecasts becoming increasingly more accurate.

Eventually a test market/pilot launch will be conducted, and on the basis of this, the parameters of the model can be empirically determined. Adjustments to these estimates may be necessary if the test area is thought to be markedly different to the national market, but the next step is a prediction of the results of a national launch. If this forecast seems satisfactory, the company will, either sequentially or in one step, introduce the product nationally. While this is happening the model will be used to monitor market response, detect problems before they become disasters, and finally to assess what there is to learn from this launch that may be useful for future new product development programmes.

9.4 Summary

The first models discussed were those of the growth curve type, that is simple forecasting models with a few macro-parameters. It was observed that there were two basic approaches to assigning values to the parameters of any model, either directly or by *a priori* assignment. The direct approach requires data on the results of an actual diffusion process and therefore cannot be used prior to a test market exercise. The *a priori* assignment approach requires that it be feasible to assess the parameter values on the basis of product and advertising tests, that is by use of the various surrogate measures. As the simple growth curve models have parameters which are by definition highly abstracted and divorced from the normal experience of managers, then it is virtually impossible to assign values to them subjectively. Since forecasts are required before the test market stage, this type of model is of little use to the new product manager. Nevertheless, an examination of some growth curve models (Gompertz, Bass, Parfitt and Collins), served to deduce what the attributes of a more useful model would be. It was concluded that a realistic predictive model should be: (i) based on a theory of innovative behaviour; (ii) have parameters whose values could be assigned from product tests, and assigned *before* a test market; and (iii) allow the executive to experiment with different marketing strategies. At that point, various models which possessed some of these three qualities were examined, the first being DEMON.

As was noted, DEMON is a network model and only really qualified for inclusion because it represents a similar point of view on new product development to that expressed here. The originators of DEMON also recognise that all the various product and advertising tests provide surrogate measures of likely national demand. Unfortunately, they do not provide any useful suggestions as to how these measures may be turned into forecasts. Therefore DEMON demonstrates what could be achieved once the company had evolved a reliable predictive model.

The next model discussed was NEWS, a relatively simple model, but one which is reported as having produced good forecasts of test market results. This model was seen to be based on the sequence awareness, adoption, repeat purchase, and the number of individuals in each of these states was generated from a set of simple equations. The model's parameters are all quantities defined in terms familiar to most managers, and it is therefore a straightforward matter to assign values on the basis of pre-launch information. Marketing variables were also incorporated assisting the manager to assess the consequences of different advertising levels, and so on.

The discussion of NEWS led naturally to an examination of the work of Claycamp and Liddy, for whereas NEWS was designed first to predict national results from a test market, and only subsequently applied to the pre-test market situation, the AYER model was specifically formulated for this latter role. The AYER model was seen to comprise two interconnected equations, one predicting advertising awareness and the other adoption, both of which represented weighted indices of the relevant parameters and marketing variables, the weights being determined from an empirical analysis of past product histories. Having thus established an empirically based method for relating the surrogate measures to market response, Claycamp and Liddy obtained accurate forecasts for eight test market exercises, using a combination of empirical and subjective pre-test market information. The diffficulties noted with the AYER model were that it did not have any theoretical basis and it only provided a static picture of the future.

The most ambitious model discussed in the chapter was SPRINTER, the only model mentioned which was explicitly based on a theory of innovative behaviour. SPRINTER focused on the overall states of awareness, intent, search, choice and post purchase behaviour and utilised over five hundred equations to describe the movement of individuals between these states. Various response functions being specified for advertising, interpersonal communication, price, etc. SPRINTER computes not only the expected rate of return on investment, but also the probability of exceeding the organisation's rejection level. Another advantage of this model was that it was possible for the manager to determine interactively the best marketing strategy.

While SPRINTER was seen as an immensely powerful tool, it was noted that it was only designed to predict national sales from test market results, and that there were some difficulties in employing it any earlier in the development process. It was concluded that it might be possible to overcome these difficulties by developing expertise and experience with the model, and therefore that for most companies models of this type were more appropriate to the situation where it was required to upgrade an already established set of new product procedures.

The last model discussed was NEWPROD, a model specifically designed to resolve some of the problems encountered previously. Again, the theme of the model was the allocation of individuals to a series of states, and on the basis of relatively simple mathematical expressions. However, unlike the AYER model, NEWPROD presents a dynamic picture of adoption and sales, and has parameters defined at a low level of abstraction. Values can therefore be assigned to these parameters either by the subjective judgement of the manager, or by the regression methods used by Claycamp and Liddy. By using a combination of both these techniques, the originator of the NEWPROD model was able to predict the results of several test markets with a high degree of accuracy.

While the results obtained with all these models were encouraging, it was noted that, with the exception of SPRINTER, none of them were explicitly based on the theory of innovative behaviour. However, it was observed that they all incorporated the effects of interpersonal communication into their parameters since the values assigned to these parameters were deduced (empirically or subjectively) from the end results of actual diffusion processes. This it was argued that in most situations they would be capable of generating accurate predictions. On the other hand, it was concluded that models of this type could not explain these predictions as they wrongly ascribed the observed phenomena to be due to advertising, promotion and other marketing variables. When used in a diagnostic role, or to determine the best marketing strategy, such models might well be misleading, ignoring as they do the key role of communicated experience.

It was concluded that there were two courses of action an organisation might take in order to overcome the above problem and develop a more realistic predictive and diagnostic model. One course is to modify an existing model and the other to devise a special theory of innovative behaviour. It was stressed that the latter would result in the more powerful and informative management tool, but that it would also necessitate a considerable developmental effort.

Finally, some comments were made on the topic of evolving empirical relationships between surrogate measures and model parameters. In particular it was argued that the only way this might be achieved was by the systematic collection and recording of sufficient information, and some suggestions were made as to what should be recorded. A system of this nature allows the organisation to build up a bank of experience and data which will be invaluable in evolving more sophisticated and successful new product development procedures.

Notes

1. In any event the use of a model constrains the manager to providing specific detailed estimates, rather than intuitive global ones, and thus inherently produces more realistic projections.
2. See Hendry (1972), p.43.
3. N.V. Philips, Eindhoven. Private communications.
4. Bass (1968) p.216.
5. Mansfield (1961) presents a similarly sophisticated growth model for industrial products. It should be pointed out that only some of the many simple forecasting models are discussed in this section.
6. Nakanishi (1973), p.242. This author also presents a stochastic forecasting model which incorporates the effects of advertising and promotion. Regrettably it too requires actual sales data for forecasting purposes.
7. This is an important point. It would be possible, for instance, to use the results of past curve fitting exercises (with similar products) as a basis for assigning values to the parameters of a simple model. Indeed this course of action is often advocated. However unless these estimates can be revised in the light of product test results for the particular new product in question, then there is little point to the exercise.
8. Among which are the STEAM model due to Massey (1969) and Amstutz's simulation of new product diffusion in the drug industry (1967). The former is not based on a theory of innovative behaviour, requires panel data from a test market, and has highly abstracted parameters. While suggestions have been made on the incorporation of marketing variables (Massey, 1967), at the time of writing this does not appear to have been achieved. Amstutz's model is omitted because even though it is based on diffusion theory it is too complex and resource-consuming to be a useful practical tool.
9. Batten, Barton, Durstine and Osborn, Inc. who were also responsible for DEMON. Some aspects of NEWS are described in Light and Pringle (1970).
10. Because the type of word-in-mouth communication indicates whether or not the product is satisfactory (to the consumer).
11. In the context of Claycamp and Liddy's study the marketing variables were in fact taken as fixed parameters since the marketing strategies were assumed to be predetermined and unalterable. The distinction between parameter and variable is therefore somewhat blurred. However it can be noted that the values of the marketing variables can be changed comparatively easily, while

to change the other quantities requires alterations to the product or advertising copy.
12. Claycamp and Liddy (1969), p.419.
13. The only other of note being Amstutz (1967).
14. A microanalytic simulation being one in which hypothetical individual consumers and their behaviour are modelled in detail, and then aggregated to form a picture of market behaviour.
15. This being achieved by a costly Monte Carlo simulation, and therefore only recommended once a definite strategy has been decided on.
16. Which supports comments made in Chapter 9 concerning how a predictive model can overcome such problems.
17. Urban (1970), p.8.
18. In 1970 Urban estimated the costs at $US200,000 for the development of the model, and $US25,000 for each complete application of it plus a 30-50 per cent increase in survey costs.
19. It is also necessary that the proponents of this type of approach justify the complexity in cost benefit terms, and in comparison with simpler models.
20. This should, perhaps, not be taken to extremes; managers often have the wrong implicit model. There is a need for educating managers as well as utilising their present fund of experience.
21. The coupon and sample categories being determined from the known promotional plan.
22. By asking the executives questions couched in their existing terminology and subsequently relating the answers to the model.
23. It is interesting to note that most of these models usually result in recommendations to increase advertising or to make it more effective. An objective observer of the same forecasted market share might equally well conclude that there was room for improvement in the product itself.
24. It is also possible to envisage similar models for industrial products.
25. For the purposes of this discussion promotions and samples are ignored; the effects of these could easily be incorporated if necessary.
26. In order to use the special theory in this manner it is also necessary to include a repeat purchase expression. Suggestions on this aspect were made in Chapters 5 and 9.
27. Which could be of the type discussed here, or of the SPRINTER type, or indeed specially devised by the company for its own needs.
28. This process may be accelerated by collecting data on other companies' new product introductions and using these as case histories.
29. Although it is never likely to be completely eliminated.

10 CONCLUSIONS

To assure its short-term future in any market a company must pioneer, and to ensure itself of longer-term profitability it must pioneer on a continual and regular basis. At any point in time its existing products have a strictly limited life span. Pioneering cannot be achieved by trivial product modification. Each new product must be an innovation, perceived by the consumers as a distinct improvement over existing solutions to their problems, and as performing according to their expectations of it. The only way for the organisation to meet such objectives is by assigning new product development a central role in the company, and one supported by adequate and totally committed resources. Furthermore the approach cannot be piecemeal, according to the exigencies of the day, but must be continuous, co-ordinated and systematised. The organisation needs to evolve a well-defined new product development system, supported and maintained by specialists, but involving all departments of the company and organising the application of explicit tested procedures to every aspect of the development process.

Moreover it is vitally necessary that this system be designed around a theoretical framework, that is in order that the day-to-day activities have relevance to the end objective — a successful innovation. It is hoped that this book has provided one such framework in the theory of innovative behaviour put forward, a theory which suggests both how these procedures should be applied and, more importantly, what the component elements of the new product development system should be. The author has deliberately not gone into any greater detail on aspects of this sytem as it is obviously necessary for each organisation to work out such details according to its needs and resources. What has been indicated is what the major components of the system should be. Effectively, these components can be grouped into three sub-systems, which may be termed:

- . the corporate sub-system
- . the procedural technology sub-system
- . the specific programme sub-system

The corporate sub-system is responsible for broad strategic aspects, on

278

an on-going basis. Its component tasks are:

- looking for new markets
- monitoring the life cycles of existing products
- monitoring the activities of competitors
- organising the new product development function
- reviewing specific new product development programmes

Under the last heading, those responsible at the corporate level will delegate to the staff specialist(s) the responsibility for the procedural technology sub-system. The components of this are:

- developing, testing and improving new product procedures
- developing, testing and improving a predictive/diagnostic model
- evolving empirical relationships between surrogate measures and model parameters
- maintaining and incrementing a data base
- generating and maintaining a bank of new product ideas
- educating other members of the organisation

The output of the corporate sub-system is the need for a new product in a certain market, and as a consequence of this need the specific programme sub-system is established, designed to develop a successful innovation in the particular market, and operated by a venture team who apply the various procedures in the predetermined manner, advancing the various ideas through a sequence of stages, namely:

- concept screening
- concept testing
- business analysis
- development
- product testing
- pilot launch
- national launch
- market success

at which point the process may begin again.

Above all else the organisation must cultivate a sound understanding of the phenomenon — the diffusion of innovations — and express this as a conceptual framework, a theory of innovative behaviour. Not only will this theory guide each and every one of the numerous activities involved in developing a new product but, when represented as a predictive/diagnostic model, it will enable the organisation to forecast the consequences of its actions, and thus subject every potential product to a rigorous scrutiny. By these means the company will raise its success rate, to the benefit of itself and to society as a whole.

All of this will only be attained gradually, as it requires the systematic collection and collation of data and experiences over many new product introductions. The proposed system of procedures is unlikely to be completely effective the first, second, third, or perhaps even the tenth time it is applied. But in the long run it will enable the company to reach a level of overall efficiency far above that reached by current management practices. The way to greater success with new products lies in the painstaking and methodical accumulation of scientific knowledge, which will only come about if the company is willing to invest in its future.

BIBLIOGRAPHY

Amstutz, A.E., *Computer Simulations of Competitive Market Response,*
MIT Press, Cambridge, Mass., 1967.

Arndt, J. 'The Role of Product-Related Conversations in the Diffusion
of a New Product', *Journal of Marketing Research,* IV (August
1967 a), p.291.

——, *Word of Mouth Advertising: A Review of the Literature,*
Advertising Research Foundation Monograph, New York, 1967 b.

Assmus, G., 'NEWPROD: The Design and Implementation of a New
Product Model', *Journal of Marketing,* 39 (January 1975), pp.16-23.

Bailey, N.T.J., *The Mathematical Theory of Epidemics,* Charles
Griffin, London, 1957.

Bass, F.M., 'A New Product Growth Model for Consumer Durables',
Management Science, 15 (January 1969), pp.215-227.

——, 'The Theory of Stochastic Preference and Brand Switching',
Journal of Marketing Research, XI (February 1974), pp.1-20.

Baumgarten, S.A., 'The Diffusion of Fashion Innovations Among U.S.
College Students'. In *Proceedings of the XXXI ESOMAR Seminar*
'Fashion, Research and Marketing' ESOMAR, Amsterdam,
December 1974.

Beattie, D.W., 'Marketing a New Product', *Operational Research
Quarterly,* 20 (December 1969), pp.429-436.

Becker, S.W. and Whisler, T.L., 'The Innovative Organisation:
A Selective View of Current Theory and Research', *Journal of
Business,* 40, (October 1967), pp.462-469.

Belk, R.W., 'An Exploratory Assessment of Situational Effects in Buyer
Behaviour', *Journal of Marketing Research,* XI (May 1974),
pp.156-163.

Bell, W.E., 'Consumer Innovators: A Unique Market for Newness'. In
Proceedings of the American Marketing Association, Greyser, S.,
(ed.), American Marketing Association, Chicago, 1963.

Bellas, C.J. and Samli, A.C., 'Improving New Product Planning with
GERT Simulation', *California Management Review,* XV (Summer
1973), pp.14-21.

Berlo, D.K., *The Process of Communication,* Holt, Rinehart and
Winston, New York, 1960.

Berning, C.A.K. and Jacoby, J., 'Patterns of Information Acquisition in

New Product Purchases', *Journal of Consumer Research*, 1 (September 1974), pp.18-22.

Booz, Allen and Hamilton, Inc., *The Management of New Products*, 1965 and 1968.

Brockhoff, K., 'A Test of the Product Life Cycle', *Econometrica*, 35 (July 1967), pp.472-484.

Bunge, M., *Scientific Research I and II,* Springer-Verlag, Berlin, 1967. .

Buzzell, R.D. and Nourse, R.E., 'The Product Life Cycle'. In *Grocery Manufacturing in the United States,* Marple, G.A. and Wissman, H.B., (eds.) Praeger, New York, 1968, pp.39-83.

——, Gale, B.T. and Sultan, R.G.M., 'Market Share — a key to profitability', *Harvard Business Review*, 53 (January 1975), pp.97-106.

Cardozo, R.N., Ross, I. and Rudelius, W., 'New Product Decisions by Marketing Executives: A Computer-Controlled Experiment', *Journal of Marketing*, 36 (January 1972), pp.10-16.

Cerha, J., 'Bringing opinion leadership back to realities', *Admap.* (April, May, July and September 1967), pp.131-135, 193-194, 304-306, 354-392.

Charnes, A., Cooper, W.W., DeVoe, J.K. and Learner, D.B., 'Demon: Decision Mapping via Optimum Go-No Networks — a Model for Marketing New Products', *Management Science*, 12 (July 1966), pp.865-887.

——, ——, ——, and ——, 'Demon, Mark II: An Extremal Equation Approach to New Product Marketing', *Management Science*, 14 (May 1968 a), pp.513-524.

——. ——, ——, and ——. 'Demon, Mark II: Extremal Equations Solutions and Approximation, *Management Science*, 14 (July 1968 b), pp.682-691.

Christopher, M.C., 'Venture Analysis'. In *Creating and Marketing New Products,* Hayhurst, R., Midgley, D.F. and Wills, G.S.C. (eds.), Crosby Lockwood Staples, London, 1973.

Claycamp, H.J. and Liddy, L.E., 'Prediction of New Product Performance: An Analytical Approach', *Journal of Marketing Research*, VI (November 1969), 414-420.

Clemens, J. and Thornton, C., 'Evaluating Non-Existent Products', *Admap* (May 1968).

Coleman, J., Katz, E. and Menzel, H., 'The Diffusion of an Innovation among Physicians', *Sociometry*, 20 (1957), 253-270.

Coleman, J., *Mathematical Sociology*, Free Press, Glencoe, 1964.

Control Data Corporation, *PERT/TIME Reference Manual*, Control

Data Corporation, Minneapolis, 1974.

Corkindale, D., Kennedy, S.H., Henry, H. and Wills, G.S.C., *Advertising Resource Allocation,* Research Papers in Marketing and Logistics, Cranfield, 1974.

Cox, W.E., 'Product Life Cycles as Marketing Models', *Journal of Business,* 40 (October 1967), pp.375-384.

Crawford, C.M., 'The Trajectory Theory of Goal Setting for New Products', *Journal of Marketing Research,* III (May 1966), pp.117-125.

Czepiel, J.A., 'Word of Mouth Processes in the Diffusion of a Major Technological Innovation', *Journal of Marketing Research,* XI (May 1974), pp.172-180.

Darden, W.R., and Reynolds, F.D., 'Predicting Opinion Leadership for Men's Apparel Fashions', *Journal of Marketing Research,* IX (August 1972), pp.324-328.

——, and ——, 'Backward Profiling of Male Innovators', *Journal of Marketing Research,* XI (February 1974), pp.78-85

Davis, E.J., *Experimental Marketing,* Nelson, London, 1970.

——, 'Testing Marketing: An Examination of Sales Patterns', In *Creating and Marketing New Products,* Hayhurst, R., Midgley, D.F. and Wills, G.S.C., (eds.), Crosby Lockwood Staples, London, 1973.

de Bono, E., *The Use of Lateral Thinking,* Cape, London, 1967.

Dixon, L.C.W., *Nonlinear Optimisation,* English Universities Press, London, 1972.

Donnelly, J.H., 'Social Character and Acceptance of New Products', *Journal of Marketing Research,* VII (February 1970), pp.111-113.

—— and Etzel, M.J., 'Degrees of Product Newness and Early Trial', *Journal of Marketing Research,* X (August 1973), pp.295-300.

—— and Ivancevich, J.M., 'A Methodology for Identifying Innovator Characteristics of New Brand Purchasers', *Journal of Marketing Research,* XI (August 1974), pp.331-334.

Durbin, J. and Watson, G.S., 'Testing for Serial Correlation in Least Squares Regression: II,' *Biometrika,* 38 (June 1951), pp.159-178.

Ehrenberg, A.S.C., *Repeat Purchasing,* North Holland, Amsterdam, 1972.

Engel, J.F., Blackwell, R.D. and Kegerreis, 'How Information is Used to Adopt an Innovation', *Journal of Marketing,* 33 (July 1969), pp.15-19.

——, ——, and Kollat, D.T., *Consumer Behaviour,* Holt, Rinehart and Winston, New York, 1973.

Eskin, G.J., 'Dynamic Forecasts of New Product Demand Using a Depth of Repeat Model', *Journal of Marketing Research,* X (May 1973), pp.115-129.

Festinger, L., *A Theory of Cognitive Dissonance,* Row, Peterson, Evanston, Ill., 1957.

Freimer, M. and Simon, L.S., 'The Evaluation of Potential New Product Alternatives', *Management Science,* 13 (February 1967), pp.279-292.

Gabor, A. and Granger, C., 'The Pricing of New Products', *Scientific Business,* 3 (August 1965).

Gaikward, V.R., cited in Rogers, E.M. and Shoemaker, F.F., *The Communication of Innovations,* Free Press, Glencoe, 1971.

Gisser, P., *Launching the New Industrial Product,* American Management Association, New York, 1972.

——, 'New Products are a Gamble, but the Risk can be Reduced', *Industrial Marketing,* 58 (May 1973), pp.28-32.

Glaister, S., 'Advertising Policy and Returns to Scale in Markets where Information is Passed Between Individuals', *Economics,* 41 (May 1974), pp.139-156.

Gold, J.A., 'Testing Test Market Predictions', *Journal of Marketing Research,* 1 (August 1964), pp.8-16.

Gordon, W.J.J., *Synectics: The development of creative capacity,* Harper and Row, New York, 1961.

Green, P.E. and Tull, D.S., *Research for Marketing Decisions,* Prentice-Hall, Englewood Cliffs, 1970.

Gruber, H.E., Terrell, G. and Wertheimer, M. eds., *Contemporary Approaches to Creative Thinking,* Atherton, New York, 1963.

Haines, G.H., 'A Study of Why People Purchase New Products'. In *Proceedings of the American Marketing Association,* Haas, R.M., (ed.) American Marketing Association, Chicago, 1966.

Hansen, F., *Consumer Choice Behaviour: A Cognitive Theory,* Free Press, New York, 1972.

Hayhurst, R., 'Control and Self-Control in Test Marketing'. In *Exploration in Marketing Thought,* Wills G.S.C., (ed.), Crosby Lockwood London, 1971.

——, Midgley, D.F. and Wills, GSC., (eds.), *Creating and Marketing New Products,* Crosby Lockwood Staples, London, 1973.

Hayward, G., 'Diffusion of Innovation in the Flour Milling Industry', *European Journal of Marketing,* 6 (August 1972), pp.195-202.

Hendry, I., 'The Three-Parameter Approach to Long Range Forecasting', *Long Range Planning,* 5 (March 1972), pp.40-45.

Herniter, J.D., 'An Entropy Model of Brand Purchase Behaviour',

Journal of Marketing Research, X (November 1973), pp.361-375.

Hlavacek, J.D. and Thompson, V.A., 'Bureaucracy and New Product Innovation', *Academy of Management Journal,* 11 (September 1973), pp.361-372.

——, 'Toward More Successful Venture Management', *Journal of Marketing,* 38 (October 1974), pp.56-60.

Hovland, C.I. and others, *Communication and Persuasion,* Yale University Press, New Haven, 1953.

Howard, J.A. and Sheth, J.N., *The Theory of Buyer Behaviour,* Wiley, New York, 1969.

Ingman, D., *Colour Television,* Young and Rubicam, London, 1968.

Iuso, B., 'Concept Testing: An Appropriate Approach', *Journal of Marketing Research,* XII (May 1975), pp.228-231.

Johnston, R.D., 'Project Selection and Evaluation', *Long Range Planning,* 5 (September 1972), pp.40-45.

Karlins, M. and Abelson, H.I., *Persuasion,* Springer, New York, 1970.

Katz, E. and Lazarsfeld, P.F., *Personal Influence,* Free Press, New York, 1955.

Kelly, W.T., *Marketing Intelligence,* Crosby Lockwood Staples, London, 1968.

King, C.W., 'Fashion Adoption: A Rebuttal to the 'Trickle Down' Theory'. In *Proceedings of the American Marketing Association,* Greyser, S., (ed.), American Marketing Association, Chicago, 1963.

—— and Summers, J.O., 'Overlap of Opinion Leadership Across Consumer Product Categories', *Journal of Marketing Research,* VII (February 1970), pp.43-50.

King, S.H.M., 'Identifying Market Opportunities', In *Proceedings of the National Conference on Long Range Planning for Marketing and Diversification,* University of Bradford Management Centre and the British Institute of Management, June 1969.

——, *Developing New Brands,* Pitman, London, 1973.

Kirk, D.E., *Optimal Control Theory,* Prentice-Hall, Englewood Cliffs, 1970.

Klapper, J.T., *The Effects of Mass Communication,* Free Press, New York, 1960.

Knight, K.E., 'A Descriptive Model of the Intra-firm Innovation Process', *Journal of Business,* 40 (October 1967), pp.478-496.

—— and Wind, Y., 'Innovation in Marketing: An Organisational Behaviour Perspective', *California Management Review,* 11 (Fall 1968).

Kotler, P., *Marketing Decision Making: A Model Building Approach,* Holt, Rinehart and Winston, New York, 1971.

Lazarsfeld, P.F., Berelson, B. and Gaudet, H., *The People's Choice,* Columbia University Press, New York, 1948.

Lazer, W. and Bell, W.E., 'The Communication Process and Innovation', *Journal of Advertising Research,* 6 (September 1966), pp.2-7.

Lehmann, D.R., O'Brien, T.V., Farley, J.U. and Howard, J.A., 'Some Empirical Contributions to Buyer Behaviour Theory', *Journal of Consumer Research,* 1 (December 1974), pp.43-55.

Light, L., and Pringle, L., 'New Product Forecasting Using Recursive Regression'. In *Research in Consumer Behaviour,* Kollat, D.T., Blackwell R.D., and Engel, J.F., (eds.), Holt, Rinehart and Winston, New York, 197

Light, L., 'Light says problem research will give more benefits than benefit research', *Marketing News,* IX (September 26th, 1975), p.12.

Lockyer, K.G., *An introduction to critical path analysis,* Pitman, London, 19(

Mansfield, E., 'Technical Change and the Rate of Imitation', *Econometrica,* 29 (October 1961), pp.741-766.

Martilla, J.A., and Carvey, D.W., 'Four Subtle Sins in Marketing Research', *Journal of Marketing,* 39 (January 1975), pp.8-15.

Massey, F.J., 'The Kolmogorov — Smirnov Test for Goodness of Fit', *Journa of the American Statistical Association,* 46 (March 1951), pp.68-78.

Massy, W.F., 'Extensions to STEAM', Working Paper No.4, Graduate School of Industrial Administration, Carnegie Institute of Technology, January 1967.

———, 'Forecasting the Demand for New Convenience Products', *Journal of Marketing Research,* VI (November 1969), pp.405-412.

Mcguire, W.J., 'The Nature of Attitudes and Attitude Change', In *The Handbook of Social Psychology* (2nd ed.), Lindzey, G. and Aronson, E., (eds.), Addison-Wesley, Boston, 1969.

Mendez, A., 'Social Structure and the Diffusion of Innovation', *Human Organisation,* 27 (Fall 1968), pp.241-249.

Midgley, D.F., 'Innovation in the Male Fashion Market: The Parallel Diffusion Hypothesis'. In *Proceedings of the XXXI ESOMAR Seminar* 'Fashion, Research and Marketing', ESOMAR, Amsterdam, December 1974.

———, and Wills, G.S.C., 'Management Information Systems for the Retail Menswear Industry'. In *Proceedings of the XXXI ESOMAR Seminar* 'Fashion, Research and Marketing', ESOMAR, Amsterdam, December 1974.

———, 'A Quantitative Theory of Innovative Behaviour', unpublished doctoral thesis, University of Bradford Management Centre, 1974.

———, *Managing New Products,* Cranfield: Research Papers in Marketing and Logistics, 1975.

———, 'A Simple Mathematical Theory of Innovative Behaviour', *Journal of Consumer Research,* 3 (June 1976).

Montgomery, D.B., and Silk, A.J., 'Clusters of Consumer Interests and Opinion Leaders Spheres of Influence', *Journal of Marketing Research,* VIII (August 1971), pp.317-321.

———, 'New Product Distribution – an Analysis of Supermarket Buyer Decision', *Journal of Marketing Research,* XII (August 1975), pp.255-264.

Nakanishi, M., 'Advertising and Promotion Effects on Consumer Response to New Products', *Journal of Marketing Research,* X (August 1973), pp.242-249.

Nicosia, F.M., 'Opinion Leadership and the Flow of Communications: Some Problems and Prospects'. In *Proceedings of the American Marketing Association,* Smith, G., (ed.), American Marketing Association, Chicago, 1964.

Nielsen Ltd., 'Out of Stock – Who Loses?', *Nielsen Researcher* (U.K.), 16 (No.3 1975).

O'Meara, J.T., 'Selecting Profitable Products', *Harvard Business Review,* 39 (January 1961), pp.83-89.

Ostlund, L.E., 'Perceived Innovation Attributes as Predictors of Innovativeness', *Journal of Consumer Research,* 1 (September 1974), pp.23-29.

Parfitt, J.H., 'Market Predictions and the Computer'. In 'The Role of the Computer in Marketing', Seminar, University of Bradford Management Centre, March 1968.

———, and Collins, B.J.K., 'Use of Consumer Panels for Brand-Share Prediction', *Journal of Marketing Research,* 5 (May 1968), pp.131-145.

Parnes, S.J. and Harding, H.F., (eds.), *A Source Book for Creative Thinking,* Charles Scribner's Sons, New York, 1962.

Parsons, L.J., 'An Econometric Analysis of Advertising, Retail Availability, and the Sales of a New Brand', *Management Science,* 20 (February 1974), pp.938-947.

Pessemier, E.A., *New Product Decisions: An Analytical Approach,* McGraw-Hill, New York, 1966.

Peters, M.P. and Venkatesan, M., 'Exploration of Variables Inherent in Adopting an Industrial Product, *Journal of Marketing Research,* X (August 1973), pp.312-315.

Peterson, R.A., 'A Note on Optimal Adopter Category Determination', *Journal of Marketing Research,* X (August 1973), pp.325-329.

Pizam, A., 'Psychological Characteristics of Innovators', *European*

Journal of Marketing, 6 (Autumn 1972), pp.203-210.

Polli, R. and Cook, V., 'Validity of the Product Life Cycle', *Journal of Business,* 42 (October 1969), pp.385-400.

Prince, G.M., *The Practice of Creativity,* Harper & Row, New York, 1970.

Riesman, D., Glazer, N. and Denny, R., *The Lonely Crowd,* Yale University Press, New Haven, 1950.

Roberto, E., and Pinson, C., 'Compatibility Analysis for the Screening of New Products', *European Journal of Marketing,* 6 (Autumn 1972), pp.182-189.

Robertson, T.S., 'Determinants of Innovative Behaviour'. In *Proceedings of the American Marketing Association,* Moyer, R., (ed.), Chicago: American Marketing Association 1967.

—— and Kennedy, J.N., 'Prediction of Consumer Innovators: Application of Multiple Discriminant Analysis', *Journal of Marketing Research,* 5 (February 1968), pp.64-69.

—— and Myers, J.H., 'Personality Correlates of Opinion Leadership and Innovative Buying Behaviour', *Journal of Marketing Research,* 6 (May 1969), pp.164-168.

——, *Innovative Behaviour and Communication,* Holt, Rinehart and Winston, New York, 1971.

Rogers, E.M., *Diffusion of Innovations,* Free Press, New York, 1962.

—— and Cartano, D.G., 'Methods of Measuring Opinion Leadership', *Public Opinion Quarterly,* 26 (Fall 1962), 435-441.

—— and Shoemaker, F.F., *Communication of Innovations,* Free Press, New York, 1971.

Ryan, B. and Gross, N.C., 'The Diffusion of Hybrid Seed Corn in Two Iowa Communities', *Rural Sociology,* 8 (March 1943), pp.15-24.

Sampson, P., 'Can Consumers Create New Products', *Journal of the Market Research Society,* 12 (January 1970), pp.40-52.

Shannon, C.E. and Weaver, W., *The Mathematical Theory of Communication,* Illinois University Press, Urbana, 1949.

Shepard, R.N., Romney, A.K. and Nerlove, S.B., (eds.), *Multi-dimensional Scaling: Theory and Applications in the Behavioural Sciences,* Seminar Press, New York, 1972.

Sheth, J.N., 'Word of Mouth in Low-Risk Innovations', *Journal of Advertising Research,* 11 (June 1971), pp.15-18.

Shocker, A.D. and Srinivasan, V., 'A Consumer-Based Methodology for the Identification of New Product Ideas', *Management Science,* 20 (February 1974), pp.921-937.

Siegel, S., *Nonparametric Statistics for the Behavioural Sciences,*

McGraw-Hill, New York, 1956.

Silk, A., 'Overlap Among Self-Designated Opinion Leaders: A Study of Selected Dental Products', *Journal of Marketing Research,* 3 (August 1966), pp.255-260.

Slocum, D.H., *New Venture Methodology,* American Management Association, New York, 1972.

Smirnov, N., 'Table for Estimating the Goodness of Fit of Empirical Distributions', *Annals of Mathematical Statistics,* 18 (1948), pp.279-281.

Stefflre, V.J., 'Market Structure Studies: New Products for Old Markets and New Markets (Foreign) for Old Products'. In Bass F.M., King, C.W., and Pessemier, E.A., (eds.), *Application of the Sciences in Marketing,* Wiley, New York, 1969.

Stein, M.I. and Heinze, S.J., *Creativity and the Individual,* Free Press, Glencoe, 1960.

Summers, J.O., 'The Identity of Women's Clothing Fashion Opinion Leaders', *Journal of Marketing Research,* VII (May 1970), pp.178-185.

——, 'Generalised Change Agents and Innovativeness', *Journal of Marketing Research,* VIII (August 1971), pp.313-316.

——, 'Media Exposure Patterns of Consumer Innovators', *Journal of Marketing,* 36 (January 1972), pp.43-49.

Tarde, G., trs Parsons, E.C., *The Laws of Imitation,* Henry Holt, New York, 1903.

Tauber, E.M., 'HIT: Heuristic Ideation Technique', *Journal of Marketing,* 36 (January 1972), pp.58-61.

——, 'Reduce New Product Failures: Measure Needs as well as Purchase Interest', *Journal of Marketing,* 37 (July 1973), pp.61-64.

——, 'How Market Research Discourages Major Innovation', *Business Horizons,* 17 (June 1974), pp.22-26.

——, 'Discovering New Product Opportunities with Problem Inventory Analysis', *Journal of Marketing,* 39 (January 1975), pp.67-70.

——, 'Why Concept Tests and Product Tests Fail to Predict New Product Results', *Journal of Marketing,* 39 (October 1975b), pp.69-71.

Taylor, C.W., (ed.), *Creativity: Progress and Potential,* McGraw-Hill, New York, 1964.

Uhl, K., Andrus, R., and Poulsen, L., 'How Are Laggards Different? An Empirical Inquiry', *Journal of Marketing Research,* VII (February 1970), pp.51-54.

Urban, G.L., 'SPRINTER Mod 111: A Model for the Analysis of New

Frequently Purchased Consumer Products', *Operations Research,* 18 (September 1970), pp.805-855.

Webster, F.E., 'Informal Communication in Industrial Markets', *Journal of Marketing Research,* VII (May 1970), pp.186-189.

Whyte, W.H., 'The Web of Word-of-Mouth', *Fortune,* (November 1954), p.140.

Wills, G.S.C., (ed.) *Exploration in Marketing Thought,* Crosby Lockwood, London, 1971.

———, *Technological Forecasting,* Penguin, London, 1972.

Wind, Y., 'A New Procedure for Concept Evaluation', *Journal of Marketing,* 37 (October 1973), pp.2-11.

Zaltman, G., Pinson, C.R.A., and Angelmar, R., *Metatheory and Consumer Research,* Holt Rinehart and Winston, New York, 1973.

AUTHOR INDEX

SUBJECT INDEX

)